The Complete Guide
to Java Database
Programming

The Complete Guide
to Java Database
Programming

Matthew D. Siple

McGraw-Hill

New York   San Francisco   Washington, D.C.
Auckland   Bogota   Caracas   Lisbon   London
Madrid   Mexico City   Milan   Montreal   New Delhi
San Juan   Singapore   Sydney   Tokyo   Toronto

Library of Congress Cataloging-in-Publication Data

Siple, Matthew D.
    The complete guide to Java database programming with JDBC /
Matthew D. Siple.
       p.   cm. — (Java masters series)
    Includes index.
    ISBN 0-07-913286-3
    1. Internet programming.   2. Database management.   3. Java
(Computer program language) I. Title. II. Series.
QA76.625.S557   1998
005.75'6—dc21   97-41802
                                  CIP

McGraw-Hill

A Division of The McGraw-Hill Companies

The views expressed in this book are solely those of the author, and do not
represent the views of any other party or parties.

   234567890 DOC/DOC   902019

P/N 048787-1
PART OF
ISBN 0-07-913286-3

*The sponsoring editor for this book was Judy Brief. It was set in New Caledonia by
Patricia Wallenburg, freelance designer for McGraw-Hill's Professional Book Group
Composition unit. The Chapter opener art and icons were created by William Aquart, Jr.,
freelance illustrator for McGraw-Hill's Professional Book Group Composition unit.*

Printed and bound by R.R. Donnelley & Sons Company.

*McGraw-Hill books are available at special quantity discounts to use as premiums and
sales promotions or for use in corporate training programs. For more information, please
write to the Director of Special Sales, McGraw-Hill, 11 West 19th Street, New York, NY
10011. Or contact your local bookstore.*

*Product or brand names used in this book may be trade names or trademarks. Where we believe that
there may be proprietary claims in such trade names or trademarks, the name has been used with an
initial capital or it has been capitalized in the style used by the name claimant. Regardless of the
capitalization used, all such names have been used in an editorial manner without any intent to convey
endorsement of or other affiliation with the name claimant. Neither the author nor the publisher
intends to express any judgement as to the validity or legal status of any such proprietary claims.*

 This book is printed on recycled, acid-free paper containing
a minimum of 50% recycled de-inked fiber.

Dedication

*For my wife Kathryn,
for my son Damon,
and for my mentor and friend Fr. Damien*

ACKNOWLEDGMENTS

I would like to take this opportunity to say thank you to the many people who have helped make this book a reality. First and foremost I would like to thank Irving Salisbury III for being the one to put the bug in my ear about writing a book on JDBC in the first place. Without his encouragement I am sure the idea would not have taken hold. Next in line would be my technical editor Jeff Rice. Jeff provided invaluable insight and helped me stay focused on the task at hand. From the initial proposal to the final chapter he was there with a helping hand and keen eye. A special thanks to my Chief Editor at McGraw–Hill, Judy Brief for her patience and understanding throughout the last several months.

As with any book there are always a whole host of other people that indirectly contribute to the endeavor. I would like to thank Mike Shon, Greg Waffen, Bernie Dumka and Mike Peck for all there support and encouragement on a daily basis. And of course all the other folks at the Sun office who always seemed to smile as I gave them yet another update on the status of the book whether they wanted to listen or not.

I would also like to thank those people who have helped me get to the point in my life where writing a book was even possible. Nearly 8 years ago Dr. Owen Hill and Dr. Stacie Nunes took a chance and gave me an opportunity to prove myself. I can attribute many aspects of this book directly back to the day they gave me that opportunity.

Finally I would like to thank my wife for all her support over the several few months. From proof reading every page to giving my the quiet space I needed to get the job done, she has always been there for me. Thanks also for taking care of all the little things, like paying the electric bill and changing the oil in the car, not to mention the big things like not throwing me out of the house for ignoring her.

Contents

Introduction

Who Should Read this Book xvi
How this Book is Organized xvi
Conventions Used in this Book xvii
What's on the CD-ROM xvii

PART 1

Chapter 1

Overview of the JDBC API 3

What is the JDBC API? 3
Where Did the JDBC API Come From?: The ODBC Connection 4
JDBC Drivers 6
Relational Database Management Systems and SQL 8
Security Issues 10
JDBC Products 11
    The java.sql Package 11
    JDBC Driver Test Suite 13
    JDBC-ODBC Bridge 13
    Documentation 14
Getting Started 14

Chapter 2

JDBC Application Design Considerations. 17

Design Considerations 17
Drivers Revisited 18
    Type I: JDBC-ODBC Bridge 18
    Type II: Native-API-Partly-Java Driver 20
    Type III: JDBC-Net-All-Java Driver 21
    Type IV: Native-Protocol-All-Java Driver 23
Two-Tier Client-Server Model 24
Three-Tier Client/Server Model 27
JDBC and RMI 29
    RMI 29
Chapter Summary 30

Chapter 3

JDBC Fundamentals **31**
   The Seven Basic Steps to JDBC 32
      Step 1: Import the java.sql Package 34
      Step 2: Load and Register the Driver 34
      Step 3: Establishing the Connection 35
      Step 4: Create a Statement 36
      Step 5: Execute the Statement 36
      Step 6: Retrieve the Results 36
      Step 7: Close the Connection and Statement. 37
   Finishing Up 37
      Exception Handling 37
   Adding More Building Blocks 38
      Meta Data 38
   Chapter Summary 42

PART 2
Chapter 4

Getting Connected **45**
   The Driver Interface 45
   The DriverManager Class 46
   Loading and Registering the JDBC Driver 46
      Loading Multiple Drivers 48
      Establishing a Connection 49
      More about Matching URLs and Drivers 49
      Connecting to a Database Using Connect 51
      Connecting to a Database Using getConnection 53
      Internet URLs 54
      JDBC URLs 56
   More Driver Methods 59
      The getMajorVersion and getMinorVersion Methods 59
      The getPropertiesInfo Method 60
      The jdbcCompliant Method 62
   More DriverManager Interface Methods 62
      The deregisterDriver and registerDriver Methods 63
      The getDriver Method 63
      The getDrivers Method 64
      The getLoginTimeout/setLoginTimeout Methods 65
      The getLogStream/setLogStream Methods 66

      The println Method 66
   Chapter Summary 67
   What's Next 67

Chapter 5
Working with Connections: The Connection Interface **69**

   Creating a Connection Object 69
   Making a Statement 70
      The Statement Object 70
      The PreparedStatement Object 70
      The CallableStatement Object 72
   Managing Transactions 72
      Getting Committed 73
      Transaction Isolation 76
      Session Management 81
      The getCatalog/setCatalog methods 83
      The isReadOnly/setReadOnly Methods 83
      The nativeSQL Method 84
      The getMetaData Method 84
   Chapter Summary 85
   What's Next 85

Chapter 6
Working with Statements: The Statement, PreparedStatement and Callable Statement Interfaces **87**

      Setting IN Parameters 88
      Setting Stream IN Variables 90
      Using OUT Parameters 90
   The Execution Methods 93
      The executeQuery Method 94
      The executeUpdate Method 94
      The execute Method 95
   Managing Statement Objects 100
      The cancel Method 100
      The getMaxFieldSize/setMaxFieldSize Methods 102
      The getMaxRows/setMaxRows Methods 103
      The getQueryTimeout/setQueryTimout Methods 104
      The clearParameters Method (Prepared Statement Only) 105
   Chapter Summary 105
   What's Next 106

Chapter 7
Creating and Executing SQL Statements **107**

SQL Basics in JDBC 107
   Simple Queries 108
   Simple Updates 109
   Simple DDL Statements 110
Complex SQL Statements 110
   Handling Double Quotes in a SQL Statement 110
   SQL Statements Containing the LIKE Operator 111
JDBC Escape Syntax 113
   Calling Stored Procedures and Functions 114
   Escape Characters 114
   Time and Date Literals 115
   Scalar Functions 116
   Outer Joins 118
Chapter Summary 121
What's Next 121

Chapter 8
Working with Results: The ResultSet Object **123**

Getting the ResultSet 124
Processing ResultSets 124
   Determining the Row 125
   Determining the Column 126
   Using the "get" Methods 128
The getMetaData Method 131
ResultSet Management 131
Chapter Summary 132
What's Next 132

Chapter 9
Using Result Set Meta Data: The ResultSetMetaData Interface **133**

The getColumnCount Method 134
Determining Column Titles 135
Sizing Up a Column 136
   Columns with Text Values 136
   Columns with Numeric Values 137
Working with Numeric Results 137
   Signed and Unsigned Numbers 137

Working with Currency 139
Discovering SQL Data Types 139
    The getColumnType Method 140
    The getColumnTypeName Method 142
Determining a Columns Source 143
Column Properties 143
    The isAutoIncrement Method 144
    The isNullable Method 144
    The isReadOnly Method 144
    The isSearchable Method 144
    The isWritable and isDefinitelyWritable Methods 145
Chapter Summary 145
What's Next 145

Chapter 10
Working with Database Meta Data The DatabaseMetaData Interface . . 147

Product Identification Methods 148
Discovering Database Objects 149
Working with Catalog Objects 150
    The getCatalogTerm Method 150
    The getCatalogSeperator and isCatalogAtStart Methods 150
    The getCatalogs Method 151
    Catalog Name Support 152
Working with Schema Objects 153
    The getSchemaTerm Method 153
    Getting Schema Names 153
    Determining the Current Schema Name 154
    Schema Name Support 155
Working with Table Objects 155
    Getting a List of Table Types 156
    Getting a List of Tables 156
    Getting Table Privileges 157
A Dynamic Table Tree Example 158
    Getting More Table Information 161
Stored Procedures 161
Supported Features 162
    Supported Syntax 162
Database Limitations 163
Chapter Summary 163

Chapter 11
Odds and Ends **165**
The Time Class 165
    Time Class Methods 166
    The TimeStamp Class 166
    TimeStamp Class Methods 167
The Types Class 169
The DriverPropertiesInfo Class 169
Error Handling 170
    The SQLException Class 170
    The SQLWarning Class 171
    The DataTruncation Class 172
    Handling DataTruncation Objects 173
Chapter Summary 174

PART 3
Chapter 12
Building Reusable Database Objects **177**
The DataBeans Objects 177
    JDBC and JavaBeans 178
    The DataBeans Goals 178
    The DriverListManager Class 179
        The DBAccess Class 184
    Chapter Summary 197

Chapter 13
Buiding Data Handling Components **199**
The DataBeans Package: DataTable Class 199
    The DataTable Class 200
    Chapter Summary 212

Chapter 14
RMI and JDBC **213**
Building Remote Database Access Components 213
    Overview of RMI Framework 214
    The Remote Interface 214
    The Remote Interface Implementation 214
    The RMI Server 215
    The Client Applet 215

The DataBeans Remote Interfaces 216
The Remote Interface Implementation 218
    The RMI Server Object 225
Chapter Summary 226

Chapter 15
Building the Database Browser Client **227**

The DBClient Application 228
A Word about Java Fondation Classes 228
The DBClient Source Code 229
Chapter Summary 244
What's Next 244

Appendix A
ODBC Call to JDBC Method Mappings **245**

The Driver Interface Table 1 245
The DriverManager Interface Table 2 246
The Connection Interface Table 3 246
The Statement Interface Table 4 247
The Prepared Statement Interface Table 5 247
The CallableStatement Interface Table 6 248
The ResultSet Interface Table 7 248
ResultSetMetaData Interface Table 8 249
The DatabaseMetaData Interface Table 9 250

Appendix B
Data Type Mappings **257**

Java Primitive Data Types Mapped to SQL Data Types Table 1 257
SQL Data Types Mapped to Java Types Table 2 258
Java Object Types Mapped to SQL Data Types Table 3 258
SQL Data Types Mapped to Java Object Types Table 4 259
ResultSet "get" Methods Table 5 260
Prepared and Callable Statement setObject Mappings Table 6 261

Appendix C
java.sql Package Class Reference **263**

The Date Class Methods 263
The DriverManager Class Methods 264
The DriverPropertyInfo Class Variables 267
The Time Class Methods 268

The Timestamp Class Methods 268
The Types Class Variables 269

Appendix D
java.sql Package Interface Reference 271
The CallableStatement Interface Methods 271
The Connection Interface Variables 275
The Connection Interface Method Index 276
The DatabaseMetaData Interface Methods 281
    Category I – Methods that Return a Boolean 281
    Catagory II – Methods that Return a Integer Representing a Maximum Value . . 283
    Catagory III – DatabaseMetaData Methods not
              Returning a Boolean or Maximum Integer Value 284
The Driver Interface Method Index 299
The PreparedStatement Interface Method Index 301
The ResultSet Interface Methods 307
ResultSetMetaData Interface Variables 314
 ResultSetMetaData Interface Methods 315
The Statement Interface Method Index 320

Appendix E
java.sql Package Exception Reference 325
The DataTruncation Class Methods 325
The SQLException Class Methods 327
The SQLWarnings Class Methods 328

Index 329

INTRODUCTION

In January of 1996, Sun Microsystems officially released Java 1.0. The network-centric nature and ease of use and portability of Java class files positioned Java as the ideal candidate for Internet/Intranet "Webcentric" applications. Increasingly however, "Web" applications rely on dynamic data sources created on the fly rather than static data stored in *Hyper Text Markup Language* (HTML) documents. As the complexity and dynamic nature of Web pages increases, it is no longer feasible to maintain individual HTML documents and keep them current. Instead, many of today's Web documents are simply templates filled in with data supplied by databases. Until recently, this meant Web administrators had to create complex *Common Gateway Interface* (CGI) scripts which first obtain the data, then format the data into HTML documents. This process of retrieving and converting data is often very slow and difficult to manage, especially when data sources are scattered among multiple machines with any number of *Relational Database Management Systems* (RDBMS). To address the need for fast, efficient extraction of dynamic data, the *Java Database Connectivity Application Programming Interface* (JDBC API) was developed.

This book is designed to provide you with an in-depth understanding of the JDBC API and how to design and build real-world database access and management applications. By the time you have completed this book, you will have an in-depth understanding of the API's design, and will have mastered it's methods to access a database.

Who Should Read this Book

This book is for developers and programmers interested in exploiting the power of Java to build applications that interact with a SQL database server. The focus of this book is on using the JDBC API to build applications. As such, this book will appeal to any programmer interested in creating client/server database applications. These applications could be stand-alone applications or Web-based applets.

This book assumes you are familiar with relational database concepts such as joining tables, selective queries, and schemas. Similarly, it assumes you are comfortable with object-oriented programming and the Java programming language.

How this Book is Organized

The book is divided into three parts. Part One will present an overview of the JDBC API. This section concentrates on aspects of application design and developing a thorough understanding of the two- and three-tier client/server models. Part One also demonstrates the seven key steps in developing a JDBC application, taking you through each step and showing you how to apply each step in writing a simple application that connects to a database, makes queries, and retrieves data. By the end of Part One, you will have a solid foundation on which to build JDBC.

Part Two details all of the JDBC classes, interfaces, methods, and variables. It provides explanations for all of the methods and gives clear examples of the key components. It also provides example solutions to some of the more complex tasks required of today's client/server database applications. Among the many topics covered in Part 2 are:

- How to execute stored procedures.
- How to utilize transaction locking.
- Work with multiple results.
- Details of database and result set meta data.
- How to handle errors and warnings.
- Create database independent SQL statements.

After completing this section, you will be well versed in the constructs and methods of the JDBC API.

Part Three of the book leads you through the development of a dynamic and extensible database browser. The browser will allow a user to connect to any SQL92 compliant server and query the server for all user available objects in the database, as well as information about the database (database meta data). The application is built in stages, using well-planned, object-oriented, and reusable code. Each stage builds on the previous one, starting with a reusable set of foundation classes for the browser application. To provide maximum reusability of the database access objects, all server side classes are written to the Java Beans specifications. This will have the added benefit of allowing you to use these objects in any Java Beans visual development environment.

Conventions Used in this Book

Text: *Italicized* text is used to call attention to definitions.
          MONOTYPE is used to for Java Classes, Methods, and Variable names.

Notes are used to explain or further define a particular concept or term.

Warnings are used to call attention to a potential problem or a known common error.

Web is used to denote a paragraph containing a World Wide Web site that contains additional information about the subject.

What's on the CD-ROM

- The accompanying CD-ROM contains:
- The Java Development Kit 1.1 for Solaris
- The Java Development Kit 1.1 for Windows95/NT

- A complete set of Type II and Type III JDBC Drivers from Weblogic
- Source Code for the Database Browser application including the RMI server application in both standard Windows/DOS format and UNIX format.
- Installation and setup instructions.
- To use the CD-ROM simply insert it into your driver, and point your favorite browser to the index.html file located at the root directory of the CD-ROM. From there you can read the installation instructions for the components you want to load. If you want to run the example programs, copy the appropriate version for your platform to your hard drive and re-compile the java files.

PART
1

CHAPTER 1

Overview of the JDBC API

What is the JDBC API ?

Though not actually an acronym, JDBC API stands for *Java Database Connectivity Application Programming Interface*. As its name implies, the JDBC API is a set of specifications that defines how a program written in Java can communicate and interact with a database. It defines how the communication is to be carried out and how the application and database interact with each other. More specifically, the JDBC API defines how an application opens a connection, communicates with a database, executes SQL statements, and retrieves query results. JDBC provides a vehicle for the exchange of SQL between Java applications and databases. Figure 1.1 illustrates the role of the JDBC API.

Throughout this book, the term **application** refers to both stand-alone Java applications and Java applets, since most of the concepts apply to both. In cases where there are differences, I will explicitly state the type to which I am referring.

Figure 1.1
Data Flow Model.

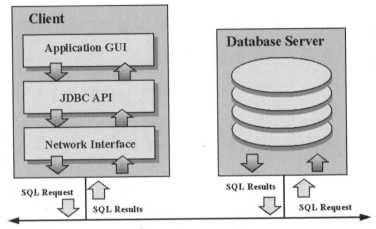

You should note that the acronym "GUI" does not appear in JDBC API. There are no *Graphical User Interface* components in the JDBC API. All interaction with the database is done via raw SQL statements, therefore all GUI elements must be imported from other packages. All user interface components used in this book are contained in the Java *Abstract Windowing Toolkit* (AWT) or in the *Java Foundation Classes* (JFC). Later, in Part 3, we will use some of the new JFC components to build a GUI for our database browser application.

Where Did the JDBC API Come From?: The ODBC Connection

Being a great supporter of Java (some might use the term *zealot*) I would love to say that the JDBC API is a completely fresh and new idea, designed entirely by the brilliant folks at JavaSoft. But, as you probably suspect, this is not entirely true. Like many other aspects of the Java programming language, much of the JDBC API concepts are borrowed from other sources, in particular, Microsoft's *Open Database Connectivity* (ODBC).

Both ODBC and JDBC are based on the X/OPEN call level interface for SQL. Since ODBC is well established and one of the most widely accepted database interface currently available, it only makes sense to use it as a starting point. While JDBC is certainly not a derivative of ODBC, they both share the same parent and can be thought of as "siblings." JDBC, of course, is the younger child who has learned important lessons from the older sibling's experience and mistakes.

A common misconception is that JDBC is simply a port of ODBC to the Java programming language. However, if you examine both ODBC and JDBC, you will see that while both provide similar functionality, they are very different in their implementation. The most obvious difference is that ODBC is written in "C" and makes extensive use of pointers. Since Java does not have pointers, porting would be extremely difficult and labor intensive. However, even more important than this technical issue are the design goals of ODBC and JDBC. JDBC was designed to be a very compact, simple interface focusing on the execution of raw SQL statements and retrieving the results. ODBC is much larger in scope and attempts to pack as many features as possible in each driver. ODBC often provides multiple mechanisms for performing a single task and adds additional data handling capabilities. While these added functionalities of ODBC are sometimes useful, they can make even simple tasks difficult and complex to perform.

In an effort to keep the JDBC API as simple as possible, JDBC only incorporates those tasks that are considered essential. The goal is to create an interface that keeps simple tasks simple, while ensuring the more difficult and uncommon tasks are at least possible. It is assumed that developers and vendors will use the basic building blocks provided by JDBC to build any higher level interfaces desired. This means that the JDBC API is much smaller and easier to implement than ODBC.

If you have ODBC programming experience and are familiar with the ODBC programming interface, Appendix A contains a table of all the JDBC methods, and how they map to ODBC calls.

There is one final point to be made regarding the origin of the JDBC API. To ensure that JDBC fulfilled the needs of the database community, many database vendors and third party developers were solicited by JavaSoft for design input into the JDBC API. By including industry experts, JavaSoft had hoped to ensure that the JDBC standard would gain the wide acceptance. This strategy seems to have worked well. JDBC has been endorsed by many major vendors. Included are industry leaders such as:

- Borland
- IBM
- Informix
- Intersoft

- Intersolve
- Oracle
- Sybase
- Symantic
- SCO
- WebLogic

A complete list of vendors currently supporting the JDBC API can be found at: **http://splash.javasoft.com/jdbc/jdbc.drivers.html**.

JDBC Drivers

As with any interface, the JDBC API actually defines two things. On one side, the JDBC API specifies how information is to be presented to your application. It tells your application what it can expect from the database. Conversely, the JDBC API also defines what the database can expect from your application. Essentially, it defines the common ground between the database and the application. It defines what commands can be executed, how to execute them, and how data will be formatted. The JDBC API ensures that your application can interact with all databases in a standard and uniform way. At the heart of all this is the JDBC driver.

The JDBC driver is responsible for ensuring that an application has consistent and uniform access to any database. It is also responsible for ensuring that any requests made by the application are presented to the database in a way that is meaningful to the database. Figure 1.2 shows how a driver works.

The first thing you notice in Figure 1.2 is that the driver is in the middle and has two sets of arrows representing the communications between the database and the application. One set of arrows is the Java methods that the application developer sees and writes applications to use. The other set of arrows represents the database access requests made by the JDBC driver using the database native protocol. As you can see, the JDBC driver in the center acts as a translator. It receives the client applications request, translates it into a format that the database can understand, and then presents the request to the database. The response is received by the JDBC driver, translated back into Java data format, and presented to the client application. In order for this all to occur, the JDBC driver must speak both Java to the application and the native language of the database.

It would seem to follow that, since all databases speak SQL, there only needs to be one JDBC driver: a Java to SQL translator. However, although

Figure 1.2
The JDBC Driver.

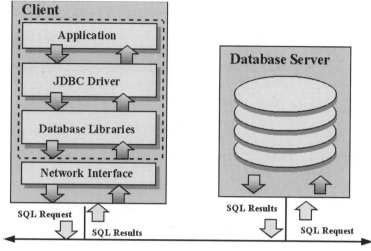

SQL is the spoken language of all databases, each vendor has its own interface, semantics, and syntax for data access. For example, lets say that you want to know all the table names in your current schema.

In Oracle, the SQL statement to perform this function is:

```
SELECT table_name FROM user_table;
```

In Sybase, the same results are yielded by executing a stored procedure:

```
EXECUTE sp__helptable;
```

As you can see, each is a valid SQL statement and retrieves the desired data, but the implementation is very different. As a result of the different implementations, a monolithic all-in-one type JDBC driver would need to know the specific SQL statement used by every database for every JDBC function, otherwise it could not provide a uniform method for accessing the data. This would mean hundreds of functions implemented and any number of variations. The size of such a driver would be very large and would be impractical in many instances where applets are involved.

Applets are designed to be downloaded over the Internet and must be fast, efficient, and highly optimized code, so as not to overburden networks. In most instances, a JDBC driver will be used to access one or two different databases. This would mean that only a fraction of the driver code would be used. More importantly however, it would mean that most of the time used to download the driver was unnecessary. I certainly would not call this practice very efficient nor highly optimized.

The net result of having each database vendor with their own implementation is that a separate driver for each different database vendor is needed. Fortunately, there are drivers for nearly every major database vendor currently available. Even for those that do not have native JDBC drivers available, there are alternatives that can be used. For more details on this alternative driver and other driver topics, please refer to Chapter 2, *JDBC Application Design Considerations*.

Relational Database Management Systems and SQL

A *Relational Database Management System* (RDBMS) is a computer program designed to perform the storage, update, and retrieval of data. SQL is a specialized language used for the access and management of the RDBMS. Although the SQL language has been standardized, it can be found in many varieties and forms. Therefore, in order to ensure access to the widest range of databases possible, JDBC was designed to support the most common form of SQL among them: ANSI SQL92 Entry Level standard.

SQL was originally an acronym for **Structured Query Language**. However, as the SQL standard evolved the definition no longer accurately described the language. Currently, SQL92 is simply the name of the standard that defines the language and is not an acronym or an abbreviation.

What is SQL92 Entry Level and why is it used ? To answer this, we have to look at a bit of SQL history. SQL has been around since the mid-seventies and was first standardized in 1989. This standard is known as SQL89. Later, in 1992, the standard was revised and a new functionality added. The SQL92 standard incorporated several key features lacking in the earlier version. One of the most important additions to the SQL92 standard was the addition and standardization of the information schema. The information schema is a table containing information about the database itself. This information is known as *database meta data* in JDBC. The database meta data tells you who owns a table, where it is located, and what types of data are stored in it. Before the SQL92 standard, each vendor kept track of this information in a different way and made uniform access of this information extremely difficult if not impossible.

SQL92 also standardized the procedures for database structure definition and manipulation. Before the standard, procedures for altering tables, deleting tables, or even adding a column were vendor specific. With SQL92, these procedures are common among all major databases, making the transfer of data among them much easier.

SQL statements that alter the database's structure are known as **data definition language** (DDL) statements. SQL statements that alter the contents of the database are **data manipulation language** (DML) statements.

As a result of all the improvements and additions to the language, the SQL92 standard is much larger (nearly 5 times) than its predecessor SQL89. It also specifies standards for some features that not all vendors may want to implement. These could be features deemed particularly difficult to implement or are of only small relative importance to the majority of users. As a result of the large size and scope of its changes, SQL92 is broken into three levels: SQL92 Entry Level, SQL92 Intermediate Level, and Full SQL92. The SQL92 Entry Level standard primarily includes features that are either fixes for, deprecated from, or incompatible with, the SQL89 standard. It also includes new features deemed of major importance to a large number of users, such as the addition of the information schema and DDL statements.

So why does JDBC only support SQL92 Entry Level and not Full SQL92? As mentioned above, the Full SQL92 standard specifies many features that may be of limited use to many users or may be very complex to implement. Even today, only a few databases are Full SQL92 databases. By supporting the SQL92 Entry Level standard, JDBC application programmers can be sure that the SQL will be uniform across all RDBMS and that their application will be portable to any database.

In addition to the SQL Entry Level Standard, JDBC has included support for certain features of FULL SQL92. The reason for this is tht while few databases support all of the full SQL92 standard, nearly all support a small subset of featrues found in the full standard. In particular, JDBC supports the use of a vendor-independent syntax (escape syntax) for using stored procedures, scalar functions, and outer joins. These are discussed in greater detail in Chapter 7.

Since no syntax check is performed by JDBC, you can execute any SQL statements, including those defined in the Full SQL92 standard or even SQL89. There is no guarantee that these statements will execute on all databases. If your application does not require that it remain vendor neutral, you are free to use any functions or extensions provided by the database.

SQL92 Entry Level is the minimum a JDBC driver is required to support. Driver developers are free to add any functionality they see fit. If your application depends on any vendor extensions, your application will not remain driver independent.

Security Issues

If you have ever done any client/server application development before, you already know how important security is. This is especially true when remote access is given to your database via the Internet. In Java there are two categories of applications that need to be considered: *trusted* and *untrusted*.

A trusted application is essentially any stand-alone application that is stored on a local drive and has access to local resources. Trusted applications can read and write to files, open network connections, and modify memory content. Essentially, trusted applications have free reign of your entire system. It is assumed you are completely confident of the source of the application and believe it to be genuine.

You do not want complete control of your system given to an untrusted application or applet. Normally applets are downloaded from a Web server as part of an HTML document. They may be coming from questionable sources and can be loaded without your explicit permission. In other words, they are untrustworthy. Downloaded applets therefore have permissions severely limited access to local resources. Untrusted applets cannot write to local files, open arbitrary network connections, or even read environment variables. The reasons for this should be obvious.

Does this mean that you cannot create applets that are trusted? No, in fact, you can build trusted applets. Using code signing, you can convince the Java virtual machine that your applet can be trusted. However, while security is an important aspect of any application, this book is focused on JDBC application development. All stand-alone applications in this book are considered trusted and all applets are considered untrusted.

There is one further point to be made regarding security. JDBC applets are restricted from opening network connections to any host other than the one in which it was downloaded. This would imply that the database needs to reside on your Web server. For most environments putting a database on a server directly accessible to the Internet is unrealistic. In Chapter 2, I will discuss techniques that allow databases on remote systems to be accessed without compromising data security. In general, the following guidelines should be followed:

- Never allow untrusted applets direct access to your database. They are called untrusted applets for a reason.
- Users should be required to provide credentials for every connection made. This will ensure that a connection is not made by unauthorized personnel.

- User credentials should not come from a local source such as a current login ID. Local resources cannot be verified and therefore should be considered untrustworthy sources.
- All drivers should be tested and approved as JDBC COMPLIANT™ (discussed later in this chapter) to ensure the proper registration with DriverManager. Drivers that do not register themselves properly (discussed in Chapter 3) could be manipulated into providing unauthorized access.

For more information on how to create trusted applets please refer to the Java Security API. You can download a copy of the Security API at **http://java.sun.com/products/jdk/1.1/docs/guide/security/index.html**.

JDBC Products

The JDBC API is only part of the entire JDBC product line. Currently there are three components to the JDBC:

- The java.sql package
- The Test suite
- The JDBC-ODBC bridge

The java.sql Package

As discussed in this chapter, the JDBC API defines a set of interfaces and classes to be used for communicating with a database. This set of interfaces and classes are all contained in the java.sql package. In version 1.0 of the Java Development Kit (JDK), the java.sql package was separate from the Java core classes. In version 1.1 of the JDK, however, the entire java.sql package is included in the Java core just as the java.awt or java.lang packages are. Here is a quick overview of the interfaces:

Interfaces

Callable Statement   Methods provided are for the execution of SQL stored procedures. Both IN and OUT parameters are supported.

Connection   The **Connection** interface is used for the
                          maintenance and status monitoring of a data-
                          base sessions. It also provides data access con-
                          trol through the use of transaction locking.

DatabaseMetaData   The **DatabaseMetaData** interface provides
                          information regarding the database itself, such
                          as version information, table names, and sup-
                          ported functions. It also has methods for dis-
                          covering database information specific to the
                          current connection, such as available tables,
                          schemas, and catalogs.

Driver   The primary use of the **Driver** interface is to
                          create **Connection** objects. It can also be used
                          for the collection of JDBC driver meta data
                          and JDBC driver status checking.

PreparedStatement   The **PreparedStatement** interface is used to
                          execute pre-compile SQL statements. Pre-
                          compilation allows for faster and more effi-
                          cient statement execution.

ResultSet   The **ResultSet** interface provides methods for
                          the retrieval of data returned by a SQL state-
                          ment execution. It also contains methods for
                          SQL data type and JDBC data type conversion.

ResultSetMetaData   **ResultSetMetaData** interface are used for
                          the collection of meta data information associ-
                          ated with the last **ResultSet** object.

Statement   The **Statement** methods are used to execute
                          SQL statements and retrieve data into the
                          ResultSet.

Only those portions of the API that are not database dependent are included
as fully implemented classes in java.sql package rather than an interface.

The following is a list and brief description of the classes included in JDK 1.1:

Classes

Date   The **Date** class contains methods to perform
                          conversion of SQL date formats and Java **Date**
                          objects.

DriverManager   The primary use of the **DriverManager** class
                          is to handle the loading and unloading of drivers
                          and establish the connection with the database.

DriverPropertyInfo	Methods in the **DriverPropertyInfo** class are for the retrieval or insertion of driver properties. The properties can then used by the **Connection** object to connect to the database.
Time	The **Time** object methods are used to perform SQL time and Java **Time** object conversions. This class is similar to **Date** class.
TimeStamp	**TimeStamp** provides additional precision to the Java **Date** object by adding a nanosecond field.
Type	There are no methods in the **Type** class. The **Type** class simply defines the constants used to identify SQL types.

The java.sql package also defines the following **Exceptions**:

Exceptions

- DataTruncation
- SQLException
- SQLWarning

Figure 1.3 shows an interface hierarchy of the java.sql package and is followed by Figure 1.4 , the class hierarchy.

JDBC Driver Test Suite

The JDBC test suite is used to test the functionality of a JDBC driver. The test suite exercises the driver to ensure that all of the classes and methods defined in the JDBC API are implemented and that it supports the SQL92 Entry Level standard. Once a driver has passed all the tests in the test suite it can be designated as JDBC COMPLIANT™.

JDBC-ODBC Bridge

The JDBC-ODBC bridge is a JDBC driver designed to let Java applications communicate with a database via an underlying ODBC driver. The primary purpose of this driver is to provide a way for developers to begin writing JDBC applications without having to wait for a native driver for their database. The bridge is freely available from JavaSoft and is part of the JDBC package.

Figure 1.3
JDBC Interfaces.

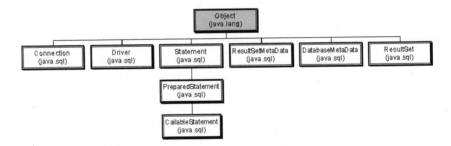

Figure 1.4
JDBC Classes.

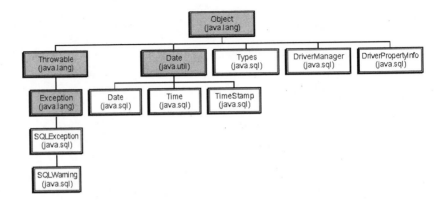

Documentation

As with most of the packages in the JDK, documentation for all the classes, methods, and exceptions in java.sql package are provided in HTML format. However, most vendors also provide documentation for the java.sql package with their JDBC driver. The documentation provided from the vendor is usually more current than the ones shipped with the JDK and will also include documentation on any special features the driver may support. When available, the vendor documentation should be consulted.

Getting Started

In order to start programming using the JDBC API, you will need:

1. A SQL92 compliant database.
2. A JDBC driver for your database.
3. The Java Development Toolkit version 1.1 (JDK 1.1).

For most of the applications in this book, you will need JDK 1.1. The JDK 1.02 can, however, be used for the short example programs where no GUI interface is used, such as those found in Part 2. Some GUI components and event handling used in the database browser are not compatible with the older version of the JDK.

If JDK 1.02 is to be used, you will also need to get the separate JDBC API package from JavaSoft at **http://splash.javasoft.com/jdbc**.

You can download JDK 1.1 directly from JavaSoft at **http://www.javasoft.com** or you can install it from the accompanying CD-ROM.

Drivers can be obtained from several vendors. A partial list of vendors that currently have drivers available can be found at: **http://splash.javasoft.com/jdbc/jdbc.html**.

The CDROM also contains JDBC drivers from WebLogic. You will need to obtain and install a license from WebLogic before you can use the driver. To obtain a license, follow the instructions found at their web site at **http://www.weblogic.com**.

CHAPTER 2

JDBC Application Design Considerations

Design Considerations

In Chapter 1, we discussed in general terms what a JDBC driver is and what its role is in JDBC applications. We said the driver can be thought of as a translator between the Java application and the native language of a database. This chapter will discuss the various client/server models and how the JDBC driver fits into each architecture. Both of these subjects are closely related and will determine the application framework that is best suited for your applications and environment. We will begin with an in-depth look at the various driver types. Later in the chapter, we will look at multi-tiered client/server models to illustrate how to build applications for use on the Internet and intranets.

Drivers Revisited

Currently, all drivers fit into four distinct categories. Each type has specific properties that make it more or less useful for a particular environment or purpose. It will be up to you to decide which environment is best for your application. The four types of drivers and a brief description of their unique properties are listen in Table 2.1.

Table 2.1
JDBC Driver Types.

Driver Type	Description
I. ODBC–JDBC Bridge	Maps JDBC calls to ODBC driver calls on the client.
II. Native API–Java	Maps JDBC calls to native calls on the client.
III. JDBC Network–All Java	Maps JDBC calls to "network" protocol, which calls native methods on server.
IV. Native Protocol–All Java	Directly calls RDBMS from the client machine.

Many vendors and developers refer to the JDBC drivers by their type number rather than thier name. Throughout this book I will do the same.

Type I: JDBC-ODBC Bridge

The JDBC - ODBC bridge driver is the only driver currently supplied by JavaSoft. The reason for this is simple. The ODBC bridge is the only driver that can be used with multiple databases and is vendor independent. ODBC, like JDBC, defines an interface. The ODBC interface remains constant no matter which database is used. This means that this type of JDBC driver only needs to speak one language: *ODBC*. Once JDBC passes the request off to the ODBC driver, it is the responsibility of the ODBC driver to communicate with the database. The JDBC driver, therefore, has no knowledge of the actual database it is communicating with.

One drawback of the JDBC-ODBC bridge driver is that it adds another layer of complexity to our program and can make software bugs more difficult to isolate. The obvious benefit to this is that any database that has an ODBC driver can be used with Java, even if a native JDBC driver does not exist. Figure 2.1 shows how the JDBC-ODBC bridge is implemented.

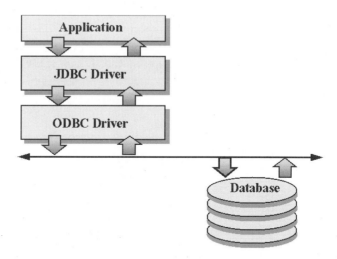

Figure 2.1
JDBC-ODBC Bridge.

As you can see from the diagram, the Java application submits an SQL statement through the JDBC driver. The JDBC driver translates the request to an ODBC call. The ODBC driver then converts the request again and presents it to the database interface. The results of the request are then fed back through the same channels but in reverse. As you can see, the JDBC-ODBC bridge ends up making two translations for each request and for each result returned. One side effect of the double translation is that the JDBC-ODBC bridge driver can be a bit slower than other JDBC drivers.

At this point you may be wondering why anyone would even consider the JDBC-ODBC bridge driver in instances where native drivers exist. The answer to this is quite simple: the JDBC-ODBC bridge is very inexpensive. In fact, it's free (provided you have an ODBC driver for your database already). The JDBC-ODBC bridge driver comes bundled as part of the JDK 1.1 package. So, for someone who is not overly concerned about performance, and has already invested in an ODBC driver, the bridge makes sense.

Using the JDBC-ODBC Bridge

Now that we know what the JDBC-ODBC bridge is and how it works, let's see how it can be used in an application. To do this, we need to take a closer look at the client/server environment. Figure 2.2 shows a typical scenario of how an ODBC client accesses a database server.

If you plan to write a stand-alone application, the configuration shown in Figure 2.2 will work fine. You can simply load the JDBC-ODBC bridge software and the ODBC driver on the client machine and you are on you way. However, there is one problem with this implementation if you are building applets. If the driver is downloaded as an applet, the standard security manager will not allow access to local files. This means that the downloaded driver will not be able to access the locally installed native libraries needed to complete the database connection. For these situations where the driver is to be downloaded as an applet, the JDBC-ODBC bridge is not a viable solution.

Figure 2.2
The JDBC-ODBC
Bridge Driver
Implementation.

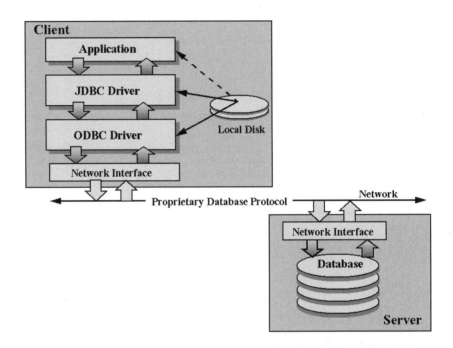

The primary role of the bridge is to provide an interim solution. That is, a quick fix so that developers could begin writing JDBC applications without having to wait for a driver to be written first. As other types of drivers become more readily available, use of the JDBC-ODBC bridge should be phased out.

Type II: Native-API-Partly-Java Driver

The Native-API-Partly-Java driver makes use of local native libraries to communicate with the database. The driver does this by making calls to the locally installed native (vendor specific) *call level interface* (CLI). The CLI libraries are typically written in "C" but can be in any one of many programming languages. The CLI libraries are responsible for the actual communications with the database server. When a client application makes a request, the driver translates the JDBC request to the native method call and passes the request to the native CLI. After the database services the request, results are then translated from their native format back to JDBC and presented to the client application. Figure 2.3 shows how a Type II driver is implemented.

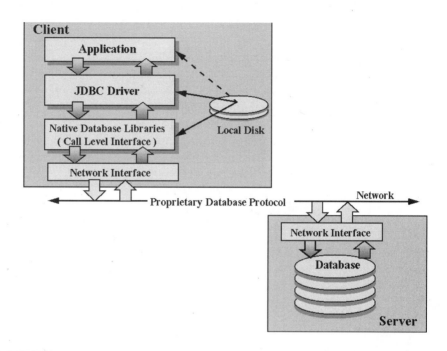

Each RDBMS uses its own vendor-specific CLI libraries. This means that for each different RDBMS you connect to, you must have a separate driver.

As we saw with the JDBC-ODBC bridge, this type of driver cannot be used as part of a downloaded applet because it cannot gain access to local files on the client. One advantage over the JDBC-ODBC bridge, however, is that since the driver is making requests to the database through the databases own library routines, there is no double translation. This makes Type II drivers somewhat faster than the JDBC-ODBC bridge driver. Currently, there are Type II drivers for nearly all major database vendors. When available, Type II drivers are recommended over Type I drivers.

Type III: JDBC-Net-All-Java Driver

Although Type III JDBC-Net-All-Java drivers sound different from the previous two, they actually offer little that is new. The only difference between Type

I, Type II, and Type III drivers is the placement of the native database access libraries. With Type I drivers, it was necessary to have the ODBC driver loaded locally on the client. Similarly, with Type II drivers, all native CLI libraries are located on the client. All communications between the server processes and the JDBC driver have been through native program interfaces. The main difference when using a Type III driver is that the native CLI libraries are placed on a remote server and the driver uses a network protocol to facilitate communications between the application and the driver. This splits the driver into two parts: an all-Java portion that can be downloaded to the client and a server portion containing both Java and native methods. All communications between the application and the database server are 100% Java to Java. However, the communications between the database itself and the server process is still done via a native database CLI. Figure 2.4 shows how this would look.

Figure 2.4
Type III Driver
Implementation.

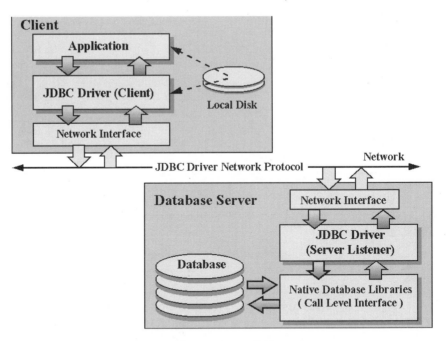

The Type III drivers still implement the same type of Java-to-native call translation we saw in Type II drivers. Instead of the Java-to-native CLI translation occurring on the client, it is done on a remote server. When using Type III drivers, the client side of the driver translates the client request into a driver-specific network protocol. It then sends the request to a listener process on the server. It is the responsibility of the remote process to present the client request to the database. The remote server process is a proxy for the client.

By using Type III drivers, the client is freed from the database-specific protocol translation. The client piece of a Type III driver only translates requests into the network protocol that the proxy-server process understands.

It is also important to note that with Type III drivers, you do not download the portion of the driver that communicates with the database-native libraries to the client. As a result of this, Type III drivers are not subject to the same security restrictions found with Types I and II and do not have the same size constraints. Since all of the database-specific code resides on the server, you can create one large driver capable of connecting to many different databases.

One way of creating such a driver is simply to use existing Type II drivers and link them all together via a single listener process on the server.

One drawback to Type III drivers, however, is that the network protocol is not standardized. The vendor's driver decides how the network protocol is designed and implemented. This means that you cannot use one vendor's driver on the client and another vendor's driver on the server. Even in cases where both client and server use the same vendor's driver, strict version control may be required to ensure complete compatibility between them.

The benefit of Type III drivers is that they can be used over the Internet. Since all of the native library calls are made on the remote server, the client does not need to access any local native libraries. Currently, this is the preferred method of access for applets. In Part 3 of this book, we will write an application that uses a Type II driver to build our own pseudo Type III driver.

Often this type of driver is referred to as a three-tier driver because it involves a third server that acts as the "middle-man" between the client and the database server. Later in this chapter, we will discuss in more detail how this is done and why you would want to use a three-tier configuration.

Type IV: Native-Protocol-All-Java Driver

Type IV drivers are unlike any of the drivers we have discussed so far. These types of drivers are 100% Java and use no CLI native libraries. A Type IV driver is capable of communicating directly with the database without the need for any type of translation as we have seen in the previous driver types. Implementing a Type IV driver is very straightforward. Figure 2.5 shows a Type IV implementation.

Figure 2.5
Type IV Driver
Implementation.

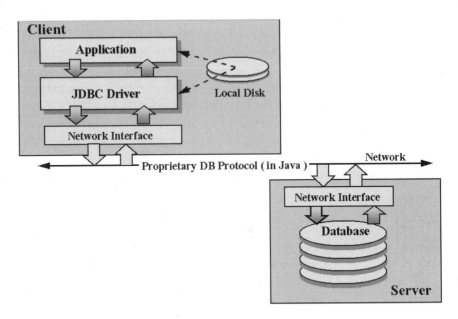

Since Type IV drivers require that the native database protocol be rewritten, they are taking a bit longer to develop than the other types of drivers. At the time this book was written, only beta versions of this type were available from a few vendors but not fully released. When they are available, Type IV drivers will greatly simplify database access for applets by eliminating the need for native CLI libraries. This will allow applets containing the driver to be downloaded over the network, thereby eliminating one of the hurdles found with Types I and II. It would also eliminate the need for Type III drivers, since the applet could communicate directly with the database.

Two-Tier Client-Server Model

The architecture of any client/server environment is by definition at least a two-tier system, the client being the first tier and the server being the second. Similarly, in a two-tier JDBC environment, the database application is the client and the DBMS is the server. In this configuration, the client communicates directly with the database server without the help of another server or server process. Figure 2.6 illustrates a two-tier client/server model.

In a typical two-tier implementation, SQL statements are issued by the application and then handed off by the driver to the database for execution. The results are then sent back via the same mechanism, but in reverse. It is the responsibility of the JDBC driver (or ODBC in the case of Type I drivers) to present the SQL statement to the database in a form that the database understands. This can be done by translating the Java call into a native CLI library or ODBC call and handing the request off to the next layer as in driver Types I and II, or by contacting the database directly as in Type IV drivers.

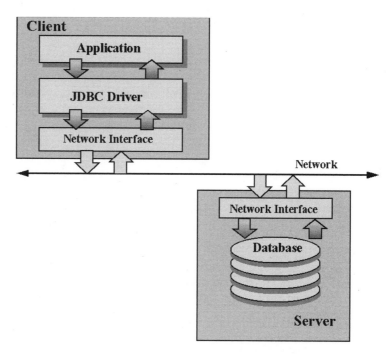

There are several advantages to a two-tier database access system:

- A two-tier access system is the least complicated to implement.
- The two-tier architecture maintains a persistent connection between the client and the database, thereby eliminating overhead associated with opening and closing connections.
- A two-tier system is usually faster than a three-tier implementation.

Conversely, a two-tier architecture has some disadvantages:

- Most currently available drivers require that native libraries be loaded on a client machine.
- Local configurations must be maintained for native code if required by the driver.

- Applets can only open up connections to the server from which they were downloaded.

Looking back at the JDBC driver section, you can see how Types I, II, and IV are implemented in a two-tier environment. In each case, the Java application passes off the SQL request to the driver and the driver in turn makes the connection to the database either directly or indirectly through native libraries. As we saw in Figure 2.2, the client side driver is also responsible for making all database requests to the database either directly or via the underlying CLI library or ODBC driver. The database server listens for requests made by the client and, when one is received, services the request. To the database server, requests from Java applications are indistinguishable from requests that originate from applications implemented in C, C++, or any other language.

It is easy to see that a Type IV would be the best solution for a two-tier configuration. A Type IV driver would provide the benefits of a direct access to the database, and eliminate complications associated with maintaining native code on each client.

While the two-tier model offers a great deal of flexibility and simplicity in management, it does have a few problems when used on the Internet. As I discussed earlier, drivers that are downloaded as part of an applet cannot access local files. This means that only Type IV drivers could be used in downloaded applets.

Even when Type IV drivers are used, however, we still have the restriction of only being able to open a connection back to the server from which the applet was downloaded. That would mean that you need to have your database running on the same server as your Web server. This is usually not a good idea for several reasons, one of which is that Web servers are the most prone to attacks from outside and are most vulnerable to hackers because they are directly visible to the Internet. Not too many corporations would be willing to put their corporate repository or general ledger on a server directly visible to the entire Internet community. Additionally, both RDBMS and Web servers can be very resource-intensive applications. Some platforms (and budgets) may not be able to scale to the size necessary to run both applications simultaneously on the same server.

As we have just seen, when deciding on which model to adopt for your application, you will need to consider several factors:

- Is your application stand-alone or to be downloaded as an applet?
- If applets are used, can the database and Web server be located on the same server?
- If applets are used, will the database/Web server scale be large enough to allow for both applications on a single server?

- Should the data be on a server accessible to the Internet?

If you do intend to use applets your decision is a bit more difficult. If you do not want your database visible to the Internet, cannot scale your server to the needed size, or just simply wish to keep your database server separate from your Web server, you will need to consider the three-tier client/server model.

Three-Tier Client/Server Model

In a three-tier model, a third server is employed to handle requests from the client and then pass them off to the database server. The third server acts as a proxy for all client requests. The three-tier model has the benefit of allowing you to separate your database server from your Web server. All client requests for the database are routed through the proxy server, thereby creating a more secure environment for your database.

In a two-tier environment, we saw that the client used a driver to translate the client's request into a database native library call. In a three-tier environment, the driver translates the request into a "network" protocol and then makes a request via the proxy server. As we saw earlier, Type III drivers use a three-tier model. Figure 2.7 shows how a typical three-tier environment might look.

Figure 2.7
Type II Driver,
Three-Tier Model.

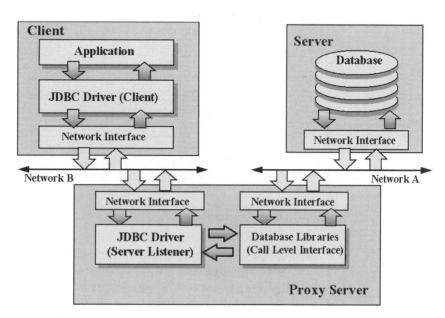

In Figure 2.7, the client application does not use the JDBC driver directly but rather communicates with a database server via a proxy server. The proxy server makes database requests on behalf of the client and then passes the results back after they have been serviced by the database. This approach eliminates the need for the RDBMS to be located on the same server as the Web server. It also eliminates the need for applets to download the driver to the client, thus freeing us from the native library security access issue.

There are a couple of drawbacks to this method however. One is that it requires that a small server process (or listener) be set up on the middle server. Secondly, it requires all your client requests be translated into a "network" protocol. As we saw with Type III drivers, the network protocol can be proprietary and therefore not vendor independent. Fortunately, however, Java provides a network protocol that is well suited to this task: *RMI* (remote method invocation).

In Part 3, we'll build a three-tier database application that uses RMI in conjunction with a Type I or II. Figure 2.8 demonstrates how this is done.

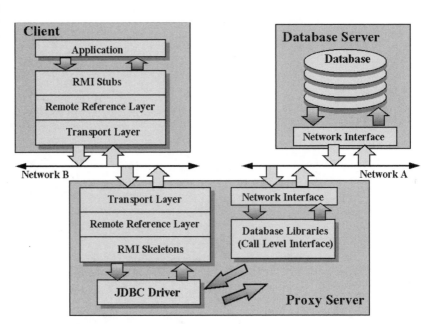

Another option for creating a three-tier application is to use a Type III driver. In the earlier section on Type III drivers, we saw that Type III of drivers are only slightly different from driver Type I and II. Type III drivers use a "network" protocol to communicate with a proxy server which listens for database requests. When the listener receives a request, the listener passes the request to a JDBC driver. By definition, Type III drivers are a three-tier solution. Type III drivers take much of the work out of creating a three-tier environment by implementing their own network protocol. Another benefit of using type three drivers is that they are often bundled with several different database drivers so that you can purchase a single solution, even if you have multiple vendors databases. This allows for easier management of heterogeneous database environments. Some of the advantages of using a three-tier model include:

- Clients do not need to have native libraries loaded locally.
- Drivers can be managed centrally.
- Your database server does not have to be directly visible to the Internet.

Some disadvantages are:

- The client does not maintain a persistent database connection.
- A separate proxy server may be required.
- The network protocol used by the driver may be proprietary (Type III).
- If a Type I, II, or IV driver is used, added development time may be required to incorporate the network protocol.
- You may see increased network traffic if a separate proxy server is used.

JDBC and RMI

Implementing a three-tier client/server architecture can solve many of the difficulties that arise from using applets to access database servers. It can also create a few of its own. One issue that often creates some difficulties is the network protocol to be used to communicate with the middle tier. The role of the middle tier is to listen for client requests, receive the request, convert them to the proper format, and pass them on to the JDBC driver for further execution.

RMI

In a three-tier JDBC application, most difficulties arise in developing a robust and efficient network protocol that can be used to pass data back and forth between the proxy server and the client. These difficulties can be avoided by the use of RMI. RMI can be used to transparently transmit objects from one server to another. RMI can easily be programmed to act as a proxy service to a database by setting up a listener process to handle access requests from clients. When access requests are received, RMI can invoke a set of methods that make the request to the database on behalf of the client.

The advantage of using RMI to do this is that RMI is part of Java, not a vendor-specific implementation.

In Part 3, I will demonstrate how to build a JDBC application using RMI. For now, I will just list some of the advantages and disadvantages of using RMI. Some of the advantages of using RMI are:

- It has all the advantages of a three-tier architecture described previously.
- It is an all-Java solution, making it ideal for applets.
- It is a non-proprietary solution. (Type III drivers are proprietary.)
- It maintains a persistent connection with the database.

A few disadvantages of an RMI based solution are:

- An RMI application can require more time and expertise to implement.
- Object serialization can require significant server resources for large objects.

Chapter Summary

In this chapter, I have given a general overview of some of the considerations to take into account when designing and modeling your JDBC application. We have seen how your current environment, computing resources, and type of applications can impact your decision on what JDBC driver and client/server architecture to choose. At this point, you should have a thorough understanding of the different types of JDBC drivers and the various client/server models. The rest of the book concentrates on the details of implementing client/server database applications using JDBC.

CHAPTER 3

JDBC Fundamentals

In previous chapters, much time was spent discussing the JDBC API in general terms and exploring various design considerations. This chapter, however, shifts gears and gets to the nuts and bolts of how to use the JDBC to do some real work. This section will introduce the JDBC objects and interfaces used to connect to and retrieve data from a database. The examples in this chapter concentrate on the JDBC *essentials*, that is, those objects and methods that are required for nearly every application and form the foundation for larger and more complex applications.

The first example in this chapter is the JDBC equivalent of the famous "Hello World" program every programmer is familiar with. It simply connects you to a database, retrieves some data, and prints it to the screen. By the end of the chapter, you should have a thorough understanding of the key steps involved in database application programming.

All of the examples in this book are available on the CD-ROM for you to try. I highly recommend that you run the examples as you read the book and modify them to experiment. Additionally, sample database tables are also supplied on the CD-ROM. The database creation SQL scripts can be found on the CD-ROM.

The Seven Basic Steps to JDBC

There are seven basic steps to using JDBC to access a database. Each step has a distinct purpose, and is necessary to complete a database transaction. As with any computer program, there is an infinite number of ways that these steps can be implemented. However, the first example concentrates on the most common methods for performing each task. No matter how you implement the seven steps or what JDBC driver and RDBMS you are using, the same basic principals apply. Here is a list of the seven steps to database programming with JDBC:

1. Import the *java.sql* package.
2. Load and register the driver.
3. Establish a connection to the database server.
4. Create a statement.
5. Execute the statement.
6. Retrieve the results.
7. Close the statement and connection.

While each of the first six steps are absolutely necessary to get data out of a database, it is not actually required that you close the connection after each execution. In my opinion, this is akin to stating it is not absolutely necessary to ever change the oil in your car. Eventually your car is going to seize up, as will your database. Simply put, connections that are not closed can wreak havoc on the database server. I can almost guarantee that the connection to be refused by the server will be yours the day you try to demonstrate your application to your supervisor. With that in mind, it is highly recommended that you close your connections when you are done using them. It just makes good sense.

Figure 3.1 is a flow diagram for the example application 3.1. The diagram shows clearly the seven required steps and the `while` loop used to process each of the rows in the result set.

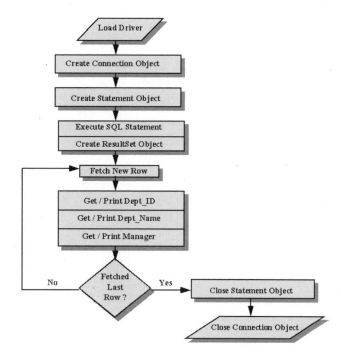

Now it is time to jump in and start writing some code. Example 3.1 is a short
Java application that will connect to an Oracle database named *fool* as user
jdbcuser and select all of the data in the *department* table. If you don't understand what is going on in the application just yet, don't worry. I will explain
each line in the discussion following the example.

Example 3.1: A SQL "Select" JDBC Application

```
import java.sql.*;

public class sqlselect {

public static void main(String args[]) {
Statement stmt1;
ResultSet rs1;
try {
  try {
    Class.forName("weblogic.jdbc.oci.Driver");
     }
    catch (Exception e)
      {
      System.out.println ("\n Class not found exception");
      }
    Connection conn1 = DriverManager.getConnection
               ("jdbc:weblogic:oracle:fool:",
                    "jdbcuser","jdbcisfun");
```

```
        stmt1 = conn1.createStatemtent();
        rs1 = stmt1.executeQuery("select * from department");
        while (rs1.next())
          {
            System.out.println (rs1.getInt ("department_id") + ",");
            System.out.println (rs1.getString ("dept_name") + "," );
            System.out.println (rs1.getString("manager") );
          }
        }
        catch (SQLException exception)
          {
            System.out.println ("\n SQL Exception "
                            + exception.getMessage() + "\n" );
          }
    stmt1.close();
    conn1.close();
  }
}
```

Let's go back now and take a look at the example code and see how it relates to the seven steps outlined above.

Step 1: Import the java.sql Package

The JDBC API is a set of classes and interfaces. The package name for these classes and interfaces is *java.sql* and is imported in the first line of the example:

```
import java.sql.*;
```

Any application you intend to use the JDBC API in must import the `java.sql` package.

For Java 1.0x, this actually poses a significant problem. Java has a built-in security feature for untrusted applets that prevents the loading of any package that begins with the word "Java" from anywhere but the Java core. This is to prevent someone from writing an applet that pretends to be a core function and gaining access to your local machine. Imagine what someone could do if they were able to write a package called **java.SecurityManager** and you downloaded it to your machine. Under JDK 1.0x you cannot write an applet that uses the *java.sql* package directly.

Step 2: Load and Register the Driver

Step two actually involves two steps in and of itself. The first is to load the driver, the second is to register the driver. However, although they are two very distinct processes, only one method call is needed to perform both steps.

Loading the Driver

The driver can be loaded in any one of several different ways. The most common and easiest method to load the driver using the `Class.forName()` method is used in Example 3.1 .

```
Class.forName("weblogic.jdbc.oci.Driver");  \
```

The `Class.forName()` method takes the complete package name of the driver as its argument. In this example, I am using the Oracle driver from WebLogic found in the *weblogic.jdbc.oci.Driver* package. Your driver package name may be different. Please refer to your vendor documentation for the actual name of your driver package. For more information on loading drivers, see Chapter 4.

Registering the Driver

If you have examined the example code closely you may have noticed that there does not appear to be any "driverRegister method()" in the example code, although it is called out as part of Step 2. The reason for this is very simple. All drivers are required to register themselves at load time. The driver itself calls the `DriverManager.registerDriver()` method at load time to ensure that the driver is properly registered. The `DriverManager.registerDriver()` method should never have to be called explicitly by an application. A complete discussion of the `DriverManager` class is in Chapter 4.

Step 3: Establishing the Connection

Once a driver is loaded , the standard method of establishing a connection to the database is to call `DriverManager.getConnection()` method. The `getConnection()` method takes at least two arguments. The first is a string representing the URL of the database followed by a set of login properties, such as the user name and password. In Example 3.1, we established our connection using:

```
Connection conn1 = DriverManager.getConnection
                ("jdbc:weblogic:oracle:fool:",
                 "jdbcuser","jdbcisfun");
```

Here, the URL used is "jdbc:weblogic:oracle:fool." The next string is the user name "jdbcuser" and finally the password for the "jdbcuser." Chapter 4 contains a complete discussion on URLs and connection properties.

Step 4: Create a Statement

Once you have established a connection to the database, you need to create a statement object from which to execute your query. This is done in Example 3.1 using the `Connection.createStatement()`.

```
Statement stmt1 = conn1.createStatement();
```

Note that to create a `Statement` object, you must use the `Connection.createStatement()` method. As with nearly all class objects in the JDBC, `Statements` cannot be instantiated using the new keyword.

It should also be mentioned that the `Statement` created in this example is only one of three types of statement objects. The other two types of statement classes, `PreparedStatement` and `CallableStatement`, are subclasses of the `Statement` class. All three types of statement types are discussed in greater detail in Chapter 5.

Step 5: Execute the Statement

Finally, after all the preparations, we are ready to actually execute an SQL statement. The method used to execute a simple query is `Statement.executeQuery()`. Here is the code used in the example:

```
ResultSet rs = stmt1.executeQuery ("select * from department");
```

The code for a simple SQL query is fairly straight forward. The `executeQuery()` method takes an SQL query string as an argument and returns the results of the query as a `ResultSet` object. The `ResultSet` object contains both the data returned by the query and methods for retrieving the data.

There are several variations on execution methods. The `executeUpdate()` method is used to update the database (write to) results and the `execute()` method is used for SQL statements that return multiple. For further information on the execute methods, please refer to Chapters 6 and 7.

Step 6: Retrieve the Results

After you have executed your SQL statement, your next task is to retrieve the results. Results are stored in a `ResultSet` object. Unlike the rest of the seven steps, retrieval of the data takes more than one line of code.

To retrieve the data out of the `ResultSet` and into a Java variable, you need to use one of the `ResultSet` "get" methods. The "get" method retrieves the data from the `ResultSet` and converts it to a Java type. Each "get" method is used to retrieve a different Java type. For instance, in Example 3.1, I used the `getInt()` method to retrieve an integer value from a particular column. I also used the `getString()` to retrieve a string value. In all, there are 17 "get" methods that can be used to retrieve SQL data into usable Java types.

The "get" methods all take the column index as an argument and return the value found in the current row of that column. By placing the "get" method in a loop and incrementing the row pointer using the `Result-Set.next()` each time, you can step through the entire result set. In our example, we used the following code to accomplish this.

```
while (rs1.next()) {

        System.out.println (rs1.getInt ("department_id") + ",",
        System.out.println (rs1.getString ("dept_name") + ",",
        System.out.println (rs1.getString("manager") );
            }
```

For more information on `ResultSets` and retrieving other types of results, please refer to Chapter 8.

Step 7: Close the Connection and Statement.

The final steps in any database application should be to close the connection and any open statements. As noted earlier, open connections can often cause trouble for databases and can also cause security problems. While it is not absolutely necessary that you close every connection and its statement object, it is highly recommended. Simply add the lines as in the following example:

```
stmt1.close();
conn1.close();
```

Finishing Up

Now that we have our core building blocks, i.e., seven steps of JDBC, the last thing we need to do is put a big wrapper around them to keep them tidy.

Exception Handling

The only two lines of code not discussed so far are the `try` and `catch` statements. Since nearly all of the methods used in the example have the potential to throw SQLException, we must either catch them or allow them to propagate up to the next level. In the following example, I chose to catch them and handle them locally by simply printing out the error message:

```
catch (SQLException exception) {

        Sytem.out.println ("\n SQL Exception " + exception.
                            getMessage() + "\n" );
                    }
```

We also could have added a `throws` clause to the main clause if we wanted to. Line three of Example 3.1 would have the looked like this:

```
public static void main(String args[]) throws Exception
```

While this is perfectly acceptable, I prefer to handle exceptions at the lowest level possible rather than allow them to propagate up. You can choose whatever method you prefer.

Adding More Building Blocks

Now that you have had a chance to get your feet wet with JDBC, it is time to look at some of the other basic building blocks provided by the API. So far, we have looked at only those classes that are absolutely necessary to build a minimal database access application. To build applications that are really useful, however, we will need to add a few more objects and methods to our tool chest.

Meta Data

JDBC provides many methods to access meta data objects. What is *meta data*? Quite simply, meta data is information that describes the structure and properties of your data. For instance, when you build a table you specify each column's name, what type of data it holds, restrictions on values, and who owns it. In JDBC, this "description" is known as *meta data*.

In JDBC, there are two flavors of meta data. The first type, `ResultSet` meta data, is information about data contained in a `ResultSet`. `Result-Set` meta data is stored in a `ResultSetMetaData` object and describes properties such as column names, number of columns and column data types. However, it is important to remember that methods in the `ResultSet-MetaData` class are only relative to the `ResultSet` that it was created from.

The second type of meta data is database meta data. *Database meta data* is information about the database itself and is stored in a `DatabaseMetaData` object. The methods in the `DatabaseMetaData` class return information such as supported functions, SQL92 conformance, user names and current transaction isolation level. Of course one of the most interesting things about modern databases is that they manage all of this information in tables. Essentially, they use themselves to manage themselves. For JDBC users, this is relative because you can query those tables to and then use the ResultSet to create ResultSetMetaData. This means that you can get meta data that describes how your meta data is stored. In some dynamic applications, this can be very important information. Here is example 3.1 again, with a few meta data methods added to it.

Example 3.2: A SQL "Select" with Meta Data JDBC Application

```java
import java.sql.*;

public class sqlselect {

public static void main(String args[]) {
Statement stmt1;
ResultSet rs1;
DataBaseMetaData dbmd1;
try {
  try {
    Class.forName("weblogic.jdbc.oci.Driver");
      }
    catch (Exception e)
      {
      System.out.println ("\n Class not found exception");
      }
    Connection conn1 = DriverManager.getConnection
                ("jdbc:weblogic:oracle:fool:",
                "jdbcuser","jdbcisfun");

        stmt1 = conn1.createStatemtent();
        rs1 = stmt1.executeQuery ("select * from department");
        while (rs1.next())
          {
          System.out.println (rs1.getInt ("department_id") + ",");
          System.out.println (rs1.getString ("dept_name") + "," );
          System.out.println (rs1.getString("manager") );
          }
        dbmd1 = conn1.getMetaData();
        System.out.println ("You are connected to:"
                        + dbmd1.getDatabaseProductName());

        System.out.println ("The database version number is: "
                        + dbmd1.getDatabaseProductVersion());

        System.out.println ("Your currently logged in as: "
                        + dbmd1.getUserName ());

        ResultSetMetaData rsmd1 = rs1.getMetaData();

        for ( int i = 1; i <= rsmd1.getColumnCount(); i ++)
          {
            System.out.println ("Column " + i + " Name is:    "
```

```
                                    + rsmd1.getColumnName(i));

            System.out.println ("Column " + i + "Size is:       "
                                    + rsmd1.getColumnSize(i));

            System.out.println ("Column " + i + " SQL Type is:  "
                                    + rsmd1.getColumnType(i));
        }
        }
        catch (SQLException exception)
        {
          System.out.println ("\n SQL Exception "
                                    + exception.getMessage() + "\n" );
        }
      stmt1.close();
      conn1.close();
    }
}
```

In this example, we have added a few more lines. In addition to getting the data ResultSet for the SQL statement, the example also demonstrates how to retrieve meta data about the table and database itself.

Database Meta Data

Information about the database is stored in the DatabaseMetaData object. To create a DatabaseMetaData object you create a new instance of the DatabaseMetaData object and assign the results of the Connection object method getMetaData().

```
DataBaseMetaData dbmd1 = conn1.getMetaData ();
```

After you have created the DatabaseMetaData object you can use one of its methods to display the information about the database that you would like to see. In this example, I have used the getDatabaseProductName, getDatabaseProductVersion, and getUserName methods to get information about the database and the current connection.

```
System.out.println (" You are connected to:" +
                        dbmd1.getDatabaseProductName() );

System.out.println (" The database version number is: " +
                        dbmd1.getDatabaseProductVersion());

System.out.println (" Your currently logged in as: " +
                        dbmd1.getUserName ());
```

Each method returns a string object that can be easily printed out. A more complete example and detailed discussion of DatabaseMetaData is in Chapter 10.

Result Set Meta Data

Once you have retrieved your data from the database, it is often helpful, if not necessary, to know more about the data itself. To get this information, you can create a `ResultSetMetaData` object and assign the results of the `ResultSet.getMetaData()` method to it.

```
ResultSetMetaData rsmd1 = rs1.getMetaData();
```

WARNING!

Note that this is the `ResultSet.getMetaData()` method and not the `Connection.getMetaData()` method. The `ResultSet` meta data is only valid and meaningful for a table, while database meta data is valid for an entire connection or session. If you try to assign database meta data to the `ResultSet-MetaData` object you will get an error.

After you have the `ResultSetMetaData` object you can call any number of its methods to get table and column information. In Example 3.2, the first method used is buried in the `for` loop.

```
for ( int i = 1; i <= rsmd1.getColumnCount(); i ++) {
```

Here we call the `getColumnCount()` method to determine the number of columns in the table just retrieved. Next, we use the number returned to set the number of iterations of the loop. For each iteration of the loop, we will print information on each of the columns. The information to be retrieved is: the name (column heading), the maximum data size, and the SQL data type for each column.

```
System.out.println (" Column " + I + " Name is:   " +
                    rsmd1.getColumnName(i));

System.out.println (" Column " + I + "Size is:   " +
                    rsmd1.getColumnSize(i));

System.out.println (" Column " + I + " SQL Type is:   " +
                    rsmd1.getColumnType(i));
```

We will revisit `ResultSetMetaData` again later in Chapter 9. For now, it is important that you understand the concepts of result set meta data and database meta data and how each differs from the other.

Chapter Summary

In this chapter, we covered a lot of ground and introduced a great deal of new material. If this chapter has raised as many questions as it has answered, however, then it has done what I hoped it would: giving you a feel for the power and flexibility that the JDBC API can deliver. You should also have gained a solid understanding of the minimum requirements (the seven steps) for any database access application and how meta data can be used to gain useful information about the database and tables it contains.

PART
2

Getting Connected

Earlier in Chapters 1 and 3, I introduced some of the fundamental components to building a JDBC application. In this chapter, we will take a closer look at the operations of the JDBC driver, focusing on `Driver` and `DriverManager` interfaces. These interfaces provide the foundation from which all SQL statements are executed and a thorough understanding of them is important to the success of any JDBC application.

The Driver Interface

At the heart of all database access is the *JDBC driver*. The JDBC driver implements the `Driver` interface and provides the means to interact with the database. With only six methods, the `Driver` class is the smallest, but inarguably the most important. The `Driver` is essential to all database interaction.

One of the most important methods in the `Driver` class is the `connect()` method. The `connect()` method is used to make the connection to the database. Upon a successful connection, the `connect()` method returns a `Connection` object through which all SQL statements are executed. However, as important as the `connect` method is, that in most instances, you will never call any `Driver` method directly. Instead, the `Driver` methods are called via the `DriverManager` class methods.

The DriverManager Class

The `DriverManager` class, unlike any other interface or class in JDBC, does not simply provide basic functionality, but rather provides a higher-level interface to the `Driver` methods. Essentially, the `DriverManager` class is a set of utility functions that interact with the `Driver` methods and manages multiple JDBC drivers automatically for you.

One of the main functions of the `DriverManager` interface is to maintain a list of drivers currently loaded. Using the list, the `DriverManager` can test each `Driver` for the ability to connect to an arbitrary URL. Without the `DriverManager` class, you would have to test each driver yourself. However, you could do it. That is what makes the `DriverManager` class unique: it provides a higher-level interface to `Driver` methods.

Additionally, the `DriverManager` class is responsible for tracking which class loader provided the driver. The `DriverManager` uses this information to ensure that drivers only open up connections back to the server from which they came. This would all have to be done manually without the class. The `DriverManager` class also provides methods for setting database login time-outs, deregistering drivers, and determining which drivers are loaded.

Loading and Registering the JDBC Driver

The first step in using any JDBC driver is to load the driver into the Java interpreter. In Example 3.1, I showed you how to do this using the `Class.forName()` method.

```
Class.forName("weblogic.jdbc.oci.Driver");
```

When loaded, the driver will call the `DriverManager.register-Driver()` method to register itself. Registering simply means that the driver name is added to a list of available `Driver` objects kept by the `DriverManager`. The driver manager will then use the list of available objects to service requests from applications for connections and other activity.

The `DriverManager` itself is loaded and initialized when the first method call to the `DriverManager` class is made. In this case, it is initialized when the driver attempts to register itself using the `register-Driver()` method.

 You cannot create a new instance of the `DriverManager` class by using the new keyword. Each application should have only one `DriverManager` class loaded at a time.

Although the method outlined above is considered the preferred method for loading a driver, it certainly is not the only one. In some instances, you may not want to just simply load the driver into the Java virtual machine, but to actually create an instance of the `Driver` class. This is normally only done when you wish to access one of the `Driver` methods directly rather than through the `DriverManager` class. At other times, you may want to specify the driver name at run time rather than at compile time and therefore using the `Class.forName()` method is inappropriate. In these instances, you can use one of the alternative methods shown below. Depending on your needs, you may choose to actually create an instance of the `Driver` class or use a command line option at run time.

One alternative method of loading a driver is to create a new instance of the `Driver` using the new keyword:

```
Driver ocidriver = new weblogic.jdbc.oci.Driver;
```

Another option for creating a new instance is to use the `Class` method `newInstance`:

```
Driver ocidriver =
     Class.forName(weblogic.jdbc.oci.Driver).newInstance();
```

One benefit to these two techniques for `Driver` creation is that you have a `Driver` object that you can easily reference, thereby allowing direct access to the `Driver` methods. However, in all but one case (the `getProper-tiesInfo` method), all of the Driver methods can be accessed through alternative methods and, therefore, direct access is not normally required.

A fourth method of loading the driver is to add it to the system property *jdbc.drivers*. This property can be set at the command line by using the -D option as shown:

```
java -Djdbc.drivers=weblogic.jdbc.oci.Driver sqlselect
```

Keep in mind that no matter which method you choose to load your driver, all JDBC COMPLIANT drivers call the `DriverManager registerDriver()`

command to automatically register themselves. The `registerDriver()` method should never need to be called explicitly by any application.

Also note, that if you specify a driver at the command line with the -D option, the `Driver` does not load until the `DriverManager` initializes. This would mean that the `Driver` would get loaded when it calls the `DriverManager.registerDriver()` method. However, as you can see this creates a bit of a conundrum because you cannot load the `Driver` until the `DriverManager` initializes, but the `DriverManager` won't initialize until `Driver` tries to register itself. So when does the driver get loaded? It would seem that neither the driver nor the `DriverManager` would ever get loaded. However, if you recall, I said the `DriverManager` will initialize itself when any of its methods are called, not just the `registerDriver()` method. Therefore, the `DriverManager` will initialize and consequently load the driver which will register itself when you attempt to create your first connection, i.e.:

```
Connection conn1 = DriverManager.getConnection
                   ("jdbc:weblogic:oracle:fool:",
                   "jdbcuser","jdbcisfun");
```

Once you call the `DriverManager.getConnection()` method, the `DriverManager` will initialize itself. After the `DriverManager` initializes, the `Driver` will be loaded and register itself.

In the examples above, I assume you are using the driver supplied on the CD-ROM from WebLogic. To use a different driver, simply replace the `Driver` package name with the package name that corresponds to your vendor. For example, a driver package to be loaded for Sybase might have the following syntax:

```
Class.forName("jdbc.sybase.SybDriver")
```

Vendors are free to choose any package name they like so the package name and number of subcategories can vary. If you are unsure of the correct package name to use, please see your vendor documentation.

Loading Multiple Drivers

As discussed earlier, the `DriverManager` class is responsible for maintaining a list of loaded drivers. To load multiple drivers, you need only load the second (or twentieth) `Driver` using the same methods outlined above. Once loaded, the `DriverManager` will handle all the details involved in determining the appropriate driver to use for any connection requests or other `Driver` services.

Establishing a Connection

As demonstrated in Chapter 3, the standard method of establishing a connection to the database is to call `DriverManager.getConnection()` method. While this seems very straightforward, there are many things happening in the background you should be aware of.

When called, the `getConnection()` method does not immediately attempt a connection to the database, but rather employs a two-step process. The `getConnection()` method first checks the URL syntax and current driver for a match. If a match is made, only then does the `getConnection` make an attempt to connect to the database.

In the first step, matching the `Driver` and URL, the `DriverManager` calls the `acceptURL()` method for the first `Driver` in the list. If the return value is `false`, then the next driver in the list is tested by calling the `acceptURL()` method again. This process continues until each driver is tested or until a `Driver` capable of making a connection to the URL is found. If a suitable `Driver` is found, then an actual connection is attempted using the `Driver.connect()` method. If no driver is able to make a connection, then an `SQLException` is raised.

While this may be a somewhat inefficient way to implement this process, it is unlikely that it will pose a significant barrier to many applications. In most applications, only one or two JDBC drivers will ever be loaded simultaneously and the time required to do the URL match will be insignificant.

You should also note that `Driver` objects are listed in the order in which they loaded. This means that if you have more than one `Driver` capable of connection to a single data source, then the first `Driver` in the list will always be used.

More about Matching URLs and Drivers

The `acceptURL()` method is used to determine if the current driver is able to open a connection to the given URL. The method tests whether or not the URL specifies a database of the correct type. This method does not create a connection or test the actual database connection. The `acceptURL()` method merely examines the sub-protocol of the URL and determines if it understands its syntax. If it does understand the sub-protocol syntax then the method returns `true`; if not, `false` is returned. Here is an example of how you could use the `acceptURL()` method to write your own implementation to test for a valid driver. The diagram in Figure 4.1 is a flow diagram for the `validateURL` application.

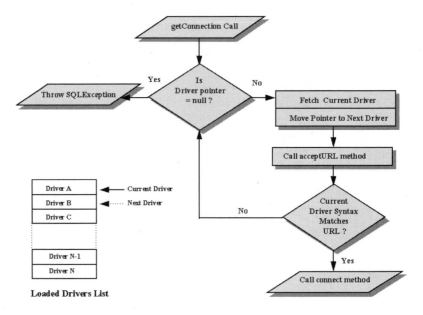

Example 4.1

```
import java.sql.*;

public class validateURL {

public boolean validateURL (String DriverName, String URL) {

    try {
        Driver drv1 = new DriverName;

        if ( drv1.acceptURL (URL)) {
            return true;
         } else
            return false;
    }
        catch (SQLException exception) {
        System.out.println ("\n SQL Exception " +
                            exception.getMessage() +"\n");
    }
}
}
```

To call the method in your application you could use the following code fragment:

Example 4.2

```
.
.
.

String[] driverNames = { "weblogic.jdbc.oci.Driver",
                          "jdbc.sybase.SybDriver"}

String url = "jdbc:weblogic:sybase"
for (int i =0; i <driverNames.length; i++)
  {
   if (validURL (driverNames[i],URL) )
     {
      System.out.println ( "The " + driverNames[i]
                           + " is the correct driver for the "
                           + url + " .");
     } else
        System.out.println ( "The " + driverNames[i]
                             + " is invalid for the"
                             + url + "." );
  }

.
.
.
```

The validateURL() method takes two strings as its arguments. The first
string is the Driver name to be loaded, the second is the URL of the database to be tested. After loading the Driver, the acceptURL() method
will examine the URL sub-protocol and determine if the URL is valid for the
particular driver. The code fragment 4.2 shows how you could use this
method to determine which Driver is the correct one for a particular database URL. This information could be very helpful if you are unsure of what
type of database you are connecting to, or to determine which drivers are
unnecessary and therefore can be unloaded. This allows for a great deal of
flexibility and essentially lets you load drivers dynamically.

Connecting to a Database Using Connect

The Driver.connect() method enables you to create a physical connection to the database and returns an associated Connection object. This
method accepts the database URL string and a Properties object as its
arguments. A URL specifies the protocol and location of a resource while the
properties object normally contains the user login and password. However, as
mentioned before, the only time you can use the connect method directly is if
you have created a new instances of the Driver object.

To aid in diagnosing driver difficulties during connection requests, the `connect()` method will return null if an attempt is made to connect to a database of the wrong type and will raise an `SQLException` if it the type is correct, but the connection fails. Common reasons for an `SQLException` to occur are:

- The database server is unreachable (server or service is down).
- TheLocal CLI libraries are missing.
- The URL subname is incorrect.

As discussed earlier, normally the `connect()` method is not called directly, but instead is called by the `DriverManager.getConnection()` method. This is especially true for any application that uses multiple drivers. However, if you are certain that your application is only going to use a single driver to connect to one type of database you could use the following method for creating the connection to your database.

Example 4.3

```java
import java.sql.*;

public class sqlConnect{

public static void main (String args[] ) {

    try {
        Driver drv1 = new weblogic.jdbc.oci.Driver;
        Properties props = new Properties ();
        props.put ("user", "jdbcuser");
        props.put ("passwd", "jdbcisfun");
        Connection conn1 = drv1.connect("jdbc:weblogic.
                                        oracle",props);

            .
            .
            .   more code here
            .
            .
            .

    }

    catch (SQLException exception) {
        System.out.println ("\n SQL Exception " +
                            exception.getMessage() +"\n");

    }

}
```

In this example, we call the `Driver.connect()` method directly to make the connection to the database, rather than using the `DriverManager getConnection()` method. Note that the connect method only accepts the URL and a list of properties as its arguments. You cannot specify the user and password as strings, as with the `DriverManager.getConnection()` method.

Connecting to a Database Using getConnection

As discussed earlier in this chapter, the `DriverManager.getConnection()` method simplifies connection requests by automating the process for multiple `Drivers`. This can be a huge time saver since you will not need to manually determine which driver to use for every operation. Another advantage of the `DriverManager.getConnection()` method over the `Driver.connect()` method is that it also softens the restrictions on the types of arguments you can pass to create the connection.

When establishing a connection using the `Driver.connect()` method, you must pass two arguments: the URL as a string and the login properties as a `Properties` object. If you use the `DriverManager.getConnection()` method instead, you can specify login properties as either `Strings`, a `Properties` object, or even as null strings. The `DriverManager` handles converting these arguments to the appropriate `Properties` object that the `Driver.connect()` method requires.

The first form of the `getConnection()` method accepts only a URL and attempts to make the connection to the database without any user name or password. Here is an example:

```
Connection con1 = DriverManager.getConnection("jdbc:weblogic:oracle");
```

The second form is to pass the user name and password as literal strings. An example of this form was used in Example 3.1.

```
Connection con1 = DriverManager.getConnection("jdbc:weblogic:oracle",
                                              "jdbcuser","jdbcisfun");
```

You should note that this form of the `getConnection()` method only allows you to set the user and password and does not allow for any other properties to be set. If you need to set other properties in order to connect to the database, you will need to use the third form of the method. This final form of `getConnection()` takes the same arguments as the `Driver connect` method. It takes a URL string and a `Properties` object. Each required property can be set either at the command line or in the body of the application itself. Here is an example again of how you would set the properties at the command line.

```
javac -Dsqlselect.password = "jdbcisfun" -Dsqlselect.user = "jdbcuser"
```

Setting the properties in the body of the application can be done by creating a `Properties` object and assigning the property names and values. Here is a short code fragment demonstrating how to set the user and password properties and then call the `getConnectio()` method.

```
Driver drv1 = new weblogic.jdbc.oci.Driver;
Properties props = new Properties ();
props.put ("user", "jdbcuser");
props.put ("passwd", "jdbcisfun");
Connection conn1 = drv1.connect("jdbc:weblogic.oracle",props);
```

For most applications, either the second or third form of the `getConnection()` method is preferred since most databases will only require a user name and password. Most of the examples in this book use the second form of the method.

Creating a `Properties` object and setting the property name value pairs can be a lot of overhead and doesn't seem to buy much for the effort. (This of course is only a valid argument when the database you are using does not require any other arguments other than user name and password.) As we just saw, the third form also has a few variations to it, i.e, setting properties in the application or on the command line. My recommendation is to avoid setting the values at the command line, since this would mean that the user would have to logout, shut down the application, and then restart it with new command line arguments each time they need to change a property. Of course, there may be times when this is a good idea (although I can't seem to think of any), so the choice of course is yours.

Internet URLs

Up until now, I have purposely glossed over the URL string passed to both the `connect()` and `getConnection()` method. But now that we have seen how to connect to a database, it is time to take a closer look at the JDBC URL syntax. Perhaps the easiest way to understand how JDBC URLs (Uniform Resource Locators) work however, is to start with URLs in general and see what they are made up of.

The URL provides all the necessary information that a connection request needs to access a particular resource. The resource may be a text file, an executable application, a communications service or any number of other resources.

A URL is a lot like a postal address. In a postal address, you need to know:

1. *What* type of package you are sending (i.e. letter or package)?
2. *Where* you are sending it (i.e. the street and city ?

3. *Where* or *whom* to deliver it to at that address?

Similarly, the standard Internet URL has three parts to it:

1. The *access protocol*: determines *what* type of packet are you sending and how is to be handled when it is received.
2. The *host information*: *where* is the information going.
3. The *path* to the resource: tells *where* to deliver the information to once you get to the address.

Access Protocol

The access protocol is always the first string in any URL. The protocol determines the method used to connect to a given Internet service and how to handle them. In a URL, the access protocol is followed by a colon.

Some of the most common protocols are *http*, *ftp* and *telnet*. Other protocols you may see are *gopher*, *archie*, and *wais*. Each of these protocols has its own unique properties and provides different types of connections. For instance, ftp (file transfer protocol) is used to send and retrieve binary files from one machine to another. FTP does not however, provide any mechanism for you to actually view any of the data that is transferred. Therefore, to transfer text or image data to be viewed on the screen, you need a different protocol, such as http (hyper text transfer protocol). Here are some examples of standard URLs for various protocols:

```
ftp://ftp2.netscape.com/java/jdk1_1.1/myfile
telnet://sundog.ee.sunynp.edu/java/jdk1_1.1/myfile
http://www.javasoft.com/java/jdk1_1.1/myfile
```

Host Information

The host information portion of the URL tells what address to connect to and how to access the desired service. Normally, only the host name is required. The host name can be in the form of an actual name or an IP address. As long as the name can be resolved to an address, it is valid. The host information is always preceeded by a double slash "//" and ends with a "/." Here is an example of host names:

```
ftp://130.60.1.123/java/jdk1_1.1/myfile
http://www.javasoft.com/java/jdk1_1.1/myfile
```

The host information can also contain a particular port number. The port number is used when a service is provided by the server on a port number not known by the client. This can happen when nonstandard protocols are used or when the server administrators have moved a known server to a different port for some other reason. The port number always follows the last portion of the address and is preceded by a colon. Here is an example:

```
http://www.oraserver.com:8888/java/jdk1_1.1/myfile
```

Although not recommended, you can also specify a user name and password in the host information. The user name and password must be quoted and separated by a period. The user name and password follow the host name and are placed after the host name and before the port number. Here is an example:

```
http://www.myhome.com."matthew"."mypass":80/java/jdk1_1.1/myfile
```

The protocol "file" is a special protocol that indicates that the resource to be loaded is located in the local file system. When using the file protocol, selecting a directory causes the directories file names to be displayed. Selecting a file name causes the file to be loaded into the browser for viewing. Unlike most all other protocols, file is not used for network communications. Also, note that since the host information is known to be the local host, no host information is in the URL. A file protocol URL, therefore, does not contain a double slash "//." Here is a file URL:

```
file:/java/jdk1_1.1/myfile
```

Path to the Resource

The final part to a URL is the path to the resource. The path is separated by the single slash "/." For people who are used to DOS path names, the slash is backwards, but other than that, the notation is the same as DOS or UNIX file system notations.

JDBC URLs

Now that we have a full understanding of what makes up a standard URL let's look at how all this applies to JDBC URLs. Remember that the reason for a URL is to provide all the necessary information for the application to access or connect to a particular resource. In this case the resource is a database. Like a standard URL, the JDBC URL has three components to it. The three components are:

1. Protocol name. (*What* is to be delivered.)
2. Sub-protocol. (*Where* it is going.)
3. Subname. (*Where* does it go once it gets to the sub-protocol.)

The syntax for a JDBC URL is:

```
protocol:<subprotocol>:<subname>
```

Protocol Name

Just like the standard URL, the first part of the JDBC URL string is the access protocol. The protocol used to access the database is JDBC. So it only stands to reason that the access method portion of the URL is JDBC. All JDBC URLs have the following form:

```
jdbc:<subprotocol>:<subname>
```

Sub-Protocol

Unlike a standard protocol, a JDBC protocol comes in many different flavors since the underlying database access methods are not all the same. To compensate for this, the JDBC URL also includes a sub-protocol. The sub-protocol is used to identify the underlying database source. The sub-protocol name is separated by a colon from the protocol name "jdbc." The sub-protocol normally identifies the database source type such as Sybase, Oracle, or Informix. A Sybase database URL may start with the following string:

```
jdbc:sybase:......
```

One notable exception to this is ODBC. Since ODBC acts as a middle man, it is technically not the data source, but rather just the "information broker." However, ODBC is used as the sub-protocol for any database to be accessed via a JDBC-ODBC bridge driver. The ODBC sub-protocol syntax has been extended to allow access to ODBC attributes. The syntax for the ODBC sub-protocol is:

```
jdbc:odbc:<data-source-name>[;<attribute-name>=<attribute-value>]
```

Unlike the protocol name "jdbc," sub-protocol names are defined by the vendor. Each vendor is encouraged to register its sub-protocol name with JavaSoft, but is not required to do so. This means that it is possible for two different vendors to have the same sub-protocol name.

Subname

The subname is used to identify a database server or server process. The syntax for a subname is extremely dependent on the sub-protocol since the information required to locate a database may be different for each RDBMS vendor. The subname is very similar to the host information in a standard URL. The subname may contain:

1. Network host name/IP address
2. Database listener port name
3. Database listener port number
4. Database instance name

Each vendor also dictates how each of these items is to be separated. They can use a colon, slash, double slash, or any combination of the three. Let's look at some examples of valid JDBC URLs so that you will get an idea of the variations possible.

For a "Waycool" driver accessing an Oracle database named fool on a local machine:

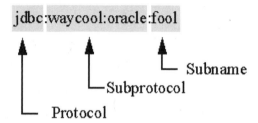

The same example, but assuming the fool database is on a remote server called sundog:

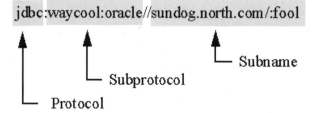

Now let's assume you're using the SQL V1 listener for your Oracle database and a WebLogic driver:

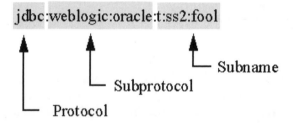

For a Sybase database, using the transfer protocol for SQL on port 3697, database name fool:

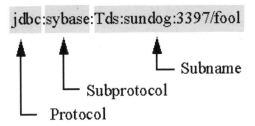

An ODBC URL might look like this with the user and password attributes set:

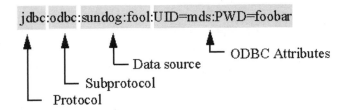

As you can see, there are many variations of URLs, but they all follow the same pattern as standard Internet URLs. If you are still unsure of what your URL syntax should be, consult the vendor documentation.

More Driver Methods

So far, I have only discussed two out of the six methods in the `Driver` interface. That is because they are the two methods that you are most likely to use. However, the remaining four do have very valid purposes and therefore deserve some attention.

The getMajorVersion and getMinorVersion Methods

As you would assume from their names, the `getMajorVersion()` and `getMinorVersion()` methods enable you to determine the version numbers of the current driver. As with all the `Driver` methods, in order to use this method, you must have a Driver object instance variable to reference when using these methods. Both of the methods return an integer representing their respective version numbers. For example, if the current driver version is 2.12, then `getMajorVersion()` will return the integer 2 while `getMinorVersion()` returns 12.

In Chapter 10 you will see how you can get this same information using the `DatabaseMetaData.getDriverMajorVersion()` and `DatabaseMetaData.getDriverMinorVersion()` methods without the need for an instance variable. Using the `DatabaseMetaData` methods is considered the preferred method of getting this information and will be demonstrated.

See related topics `DatabaseMetaData.getDriverMajorVersion()` and `DatabaseMetaData.getDriverMinorVersion()` (Chapter 10).

The getPropertiesInfo Method

The `getPropertiesInfo()` method comes in quite handy when you are unsure of the properties that are required by the database for login and if you need to determine if any of them have been set already. Unlike all the other methods in the `Driver` class, this method is not accessible through the `DriverManager` or any other JDBC class. To use this method therefore, you will need to be able to reference an actual instance of the `Driver` object. To do this, you can either create an instance of the `Driver` using one of the techniques previously discussed, or you can use the `getDriver()` method discussed later in this chapter.

When called, the `getPropertiesInfo` method returns an array of `DriverPropertyInfo` objects. The `DriverPropertiesInfo` object contains four variables. Each variable contains information about a particular property that the database can accept. Table 4.1 lists the variables in the `DriverPropertiesInfo` class.

Table 4.1
DriverProperties
Variables.

Variable Name	Description
choices	An array containing possible choices for this property.
description	A brief description of what the property represents.
name	The name of the property. (eg. userid, password)
required	Boolean value to determine if you must provide a value for this property.
value	Returns the value of the property if the property has been already set.

The getPropertiesInfo() method takes a URL string and a Properties object as its arguments. The following example shows how you can use the getPropertiesInfo() method to determine the required properties (if they are set already), the current value, how to print a brief description of the property, and if the property is to be selected from a preset choice of values.

Example 4.4

```java
import java.sql.*;

public class sqlConnect{

public static void main (String args[] ) {

    try {
        Driver drv1 = new weblogic.jdbc.oci.Driver;
        String url = "jdbc:weblogic:oracle";
        Properties props = new Properties ();
        DriverPropertyInfo propInfo[] =
                        drv1.getPropertyInfo ( url,props));
        for (int i =0; i < propInfo.length; i++ ) {
          System.out.println ("Property Name: " +
                        propInfo[i].name + " \n")

            if ( propInfo[i].required ) {
              System.out.println ( "Is required for
                                Connect: True ");

            } else

              System.out.println ( "Is required for
                                Connect: False ");

            }
            System.out.println ("Current Value is: " +
                        propInfo[i].value + "/n" );

            System.out.println ("Description: " +
                        propInfo[i].description + "/n"
                        );

            String choices[] = propInfo[i].choices;
            System.out.println ("Valid choices are: ")
            for ( k = 0; k < choices.length; k++ ) {
               System.out.println (choices[k] );
            }
            System.out.println ("\n");

        }
     }

    catch (SQLException exception) {
        System.out.println ("\n SQL Exception " +
                        exception.getMessage() +"\n");
    }

  }
```

In this example, the `getDriverPropertyMethod()` is called and returns an array of `DriverPropertyInfo` objects. Next, for each object in the array we retrieve the values in the `DriverPropertyInfo` object. The name of the property is simply a `String` and is printed out directly to the screen.

The next variable is the `required` variable. It is actually a boolean variable, and therefore tested to see if the value is true or not and output the appropriate response. After the `required` variable is checked, I retrieved the `value` and the `description` of the property. Since we did not set any variables in the property list (i.e., props.put ("user", "jdbcuser");), all of the values in this example are null. Again, these are simple strings that are printed out directly.

The last variable to be output is slightly different from the rest however. The `choice` variable contains a predetermined list of values that are available to the user. Each `choice` is a `String` contained in an array. Therefore, to retrieve each of these choices, we must first create an array of `Strings` and then use a `for` loop again to step through each value in the list.

The `getPropertiesInfo()` method is of great use to developers creating applications that are very generic and use a variety of database drivers. This method gives the programmer the flexibility to dynamically determine any required database properties and prompts the user for them.

See related topics: `DriverPropertyInfo` class (Chapter 11) `getDriver()` method (Chapter 4).

The jdbcCompliant Method

The last method in the Driver interface is the `jdbcCompliant` method. The `jdbcCompliant()` method returns true if the driver is a genuine JDBC COMPLIANT driver. In order to be JDBC COMPLIANT, the driver must have passed the JDBC compliance test suite provided by JavaSoft. The test suite ensures that the driver implements all of the classes and methods of the JDBC API and that it fully supports the SQL92 Entry Level standard. If the driver has not been tested or failed any part of the test suite, it should return false.

See related topic: JDBC Compliance testing (Chapter 1).

More DriverManager Interface Methods

As with the `Driver` class, I have limited my discussion of the `DriverManager` class to the most commonly used methods. However, the

`DriverManager` class has many methods that provide valuable information and useful functions to applications. The remaining `DriverManager` methods and their uses are detailed in the following section.

The deregisterDriver and registerDriver Methods

The `registerDriver()`/`deregisterDriver()` methods are used to maintain the list of available drivers. Each method takes a `Driver` as its argument and adds / subtracts the driver from the "available" list. To deregister a driver use:

```
drivername.deregisterDriver();
```

The `registerDriver` method should never need to be called explicitly in any application. The driver should register itself by calling the `registerDriver` method in its constructor method.

The getDriver Method

The `getDriver()` method is used to return a `Driver` object that is valid for the given URL string. Like many other `DriverManager` objects, the `getDriver()` method uses the list of currently loaded drivers to determine which drivers to use. This methods primary use is to create a `Driver` object that can be referenced directly.

The following example improves on the `getPropertiesInfo()` example shown earlier. In this example, I use the `getDriver()` method to dynamically determine the proper `Driver` for the given URL and then use the `getPropertiesInfo()` method to determine the required database properties. Using these two methods in concert will enable you to build very dynamic applications.

Example 4.5

```
import java.sql.*;

    public class sqlConnect{

    public static void main (String args[] ) {

        try {
            class.forName ("weblogic.jdbc.oci.Driver");
            class.forName ("jdbc:sybase:Tds");
            String url = "jdbc:weblogic:oracle";
            Properties props = new Properties ();
```

```
Driver drv1 = DriverManager.getDriver(URL);
DriverPropertyInfo propInfo[] =
                      drv1.getPropertyInfo ( url,props));
for (int i =0; i < propInfo.length; i++ ) {
   System.out.println ("Property Name: " +
                       propInfo[i].name + " \n")

    if ( propInfo[i].required ) {
      System.out.println ( "Is required for
                           Connect: True ");

    } else

      System.out.println ( "Is required for
                           Connect: False ");
    }
    System.out.println ("Current Value is: " +
                        propInfo[i].value + "/n" );

    System.out.println ("Description: " +
                        propInfo[i].description + "/n"
                        );

    String choices[] = propInfo[i].choices;
    System.out.println ("Valid choices are: ")
    for ( k = 0; k < choices.length; k++ ) {
       System.out.println (choices[k] );
    }
    System.out.println ("\n");

   }
  }

catch (SQLException exception) {

   System.out.println ("\n SQL Exception " +
                       exception.getMessage() +"\n");
 }

}
```

See related topic: `DriverManager.getDrivers()` (Chapter 4).

The getDrivers Method

The `getDriver()` method differs slightly from the `getDriver()` method. As we just saw, the `getDriver` method returns a valid `Driver` object for a given URL. In the case of the `getDrivers()` method however, a URL is not specified and rather than return a single `Driver` object, an array of `Driver` objects. Each `Driver` object can then be used as any other `Driver` object would.

See related topic: `DriverManager.getDriver()` (Chapter 4).

The getLoginTimeout/setLoginTimeout Methods

The getLoginTimeout() and setLoginTimeout() methods are used to manage the time a Driver object will wait for a response from a database before it will return an error. As their names would imply, the getLogin-Timeout() method retrieves the current time-out value, while the set-LoginTimeout() method sets the time-out value. The time-out value is reported and set in terms of seconds. Here is a short example that could be used to find out what the minimum time-out value for a particular database should be set at.

Example 4.6

```
import java.sql.*;

    public class getMinLoginTimout{

    public static void main (String args[] ) {

       try {
            Int maxTimout = 300;
            Int minTimout = 1;
            boolean connected = false;
            class.forName ("weblogic.jdbc.oci.Driver");
            DriverManager.setLoginTimeout(1);
            String url = "jdbc:weblogic:oracle";
            while ((i++ < 300) && ( connected == false))
            {
              try {
                 DriverManager.setLoginTimeout(i);
                 Connection conn1 = DriverManager.getConnection
                                           (url,"jdbcuser",
                                            "jdbcisfun");

                 connected = true;
                 minTimout = i;

                 }
              catch {SQLException exception)
                 {
                  connected = false;
                 }
            }
            if (minTimout < 300)
            {

               System.out.println ("The minimum Login Time-out is: "
                                    minTimout );
            } else
               System.out.println ("Connection never established -
                                    maximum time out exceeded !");

            }
       conn1.close();
       }
```

```
catch (SQLException exception) {

    System.out.println ("\n SQL Exception " +
                         exception.getMessage() +"\n");
    }

}
```

In this example, the maximum time-out value is set to 300 seconds. It is assumed that if the connection is not established in this time then there is a real error. Next, we initialize the `minTimout` and `connected` variables. The `while` loop then tests to see if we have either reached the maximum time-out value (300) or if a connection has been established. The `connect` variable is initially set to `false`. Inside the `while` loop the login time-out value is set to i (initially 1) and a connection attempt is made. Next, the value of `connected` is set to `true`. If the connection is established then the exception clause is never executed and the `connected` variable value stays true. If the login time-out value was too low and a connection was not established, then the exception clause is executed, the connected variable set to `false`, the `while` loop counter i is incremented by one, and the process starts over again. The process will repeat until either a connection is made or the maximum value for the login time-out is reached.

The getLogStream/setLogStream Methods

The `getLogStream()` and `setLogStream()` methods work in tandem similar to `getLoginTimeout()`/`setLoginTimeout()` methods do. The `getLogStream()` method reports the current logging stream that the `Driver` object is directing its errors and informational messages to. You can use the `setLogStream()` method to redirect that output to any other stream. The following code fragment shows how you can redirect the output to a log file.

```
PrintStream ps = new PrintStream (new FileOutputStream
                 ("Driver.err"));
DriverManager.setLogStream(ps);
```

The println Method

The `println()` method is used to print a message to the log stream. The input parameter is the message string.

Chapter Summary

In this chapter, we took an in-depth look at the methods available in the
`Driver` and `DriverManager` interfaces. You saw how the `Driver` interface provides the facilities for making connections to databases, while the
`DriverManager` interface helps to manage that connection. You also saw
how most of the `DriverManager` methods use a list of currently loaded
drivers and sequentially tests each one for the ability to make a connection to
the URL given.

I also demonstrated some of the variations that can be used in `Connection`
creation. The URL can be passed as a literal string or as a variable. The user
name and password can also be literals, string variables or set as properties. No
matter what method you use, however, the net result is the same.

What's Next

In the next chapter, we will take a closer look at the `Connection` object.
Until now, we have spent most of the time learning how to connect to the
database. In Chapter 5, we will learn what to do with the `Connection`
object once we have created it.

CHAPTER 5

Working with Connections: The Connection Interface

Creating a Connection Object

In Chapters 3 and 4, I demonstrated how a Connection object can be created by invoking the DriverManager getConnection() method or Driver connect() method. The Connection object represents an SQL session with the database. The Connection object provides methods for the creation of statement objects that in turn execute SQL statements such as queries, stored procedures, and prepared statements. It also contains methods for the management of the session: transaction locking, catalog selection, and error handling. However, it is important to note that the connection does not actually execute the SQL statements, but merely provides a conduit through which other objects can operate. SQL statement execution is the responsibility of the Statement, PreparedStatement, and CallableStatement objects.

Making a Statement

There are three separate statement objects that can be created within a `Connection` object: the `Statement`, the `PreparedStatement`, and the `CallableStatement`. The methods to create these objects are the `createStatement()`, `prepareStatement()`, and `prepareCall()` methods, respectively. Each of these objects has a particular purpose and is used to execute very distinct types of SQL statements.

The Statement Object

The `Statement` object is the most common type of object used. It is used to execute static SQL statements. Static SQL statements are those that do not contain any `IN` or `OUT` parameters. Static SQL statements can be updates, inserts, queries and even DDL SQL statements. As long as no parameters are to be passed to or from the database, a `Statement` object can be used.

Creating the Statement Object

The `Statement` object is created using the `Connection.createStatement()` method. `Statement` objects cannot be created using the new keyword. For example:

```
Connection conn1 = DriverManager.getConnection
                ("jdbc:weblogic:oracle:fool:",
                "jdbcuser","jdbcisfun");

Statement stmt1 = conn1.createStatemtent();
```

As you can see, each `Statement` object is associated with a single `Connection` object. While you are free to have as many `Statement` objects per `Connection` as you want, a single `Statement` object cannot belong to more than one `Connection`.

Also, note that when creating a `Statement` object, you do not specify the SQL statement as an argument to the `createStatement()` method. A `Statement` object can be reused with any number of SQL statements and is not statically associated with any particular type of SQL operation.

The PreparedStatement Object

The `PreparedStatement` is primarily used for the execution of dynamic SQL statements and is created using the `prepareStatement()` method.

More specifically, it is used when the SQL statement to be executed contains IN parameters. What makes `PreparedStatements` unique is that they are pre-parsed and pre-compiled by the database. This results in quicker response times and lower work loads for the database server. For very large statements or statements that are repeated many times, `PreparedStatements` can provide significant improvements.

Therefore, the role of the `PreparedStatement` object is actually two-fold. It provides both the means to execute SQL statements with IN parameters, and allows you to pre-compile statements that are repeated several times to improve performance.

To get a better understanding of how this works, let's take a closer look at how SQL statements are executed by a typical database.

Step 1: The user enters an SQL statement and issues an execute request.
Step 2: The database parses the statement.
Step 3: The database uses the parsing to determine if the syntax is correct.
Step 4: The database compiles the statement.
Step 5: The database executes the statement.

As you would expect, each one of these steps takes time and computer resources. If your application uses the same SQL statement over and over again, it must go through the same 5 steps each time. However, if you use a prepared statement, the database only has to do the first 4 steps one time, essentially cutting your work load to 1/5 the original.

Since compiling a statement is usually expensive, some databases will check for duplicate SQL code after the parse statement. This allows the database to skip the compilation of any SQL statement that has already been compiled. However, this technique is still not as efficient as a prepared statement.

Creating the PreparedStatement Object

The `prepareStatement()` method is used to create a `Prepared-Statement`. Unlike the `Statement` object, the `PreparedStatement` takes the SQL statement to be executed as an argument. Since the `PreparedStatement` is pre-compiled by the database at the time of its creation, the SQL statement must be known.

For dynamic SQL statements (those that contain IN parameters), a place holder is used to tell the database that it can expect a variable in that position. Each variable in the statement is represented by a "?" which holds its place during compilation. When compiled, the place holder is part of the statement and therefore appears static to the compiler. As a result of this, no matter what value is later assigned to the variable, the database does not need to recompile or parse the statement. At run time, you can assign values to the variables by using one of the "set" methods in the `PreparedStatement` object. Here is a short example of a dynamic SQL statement with two variables:

```
String sqlstmt = "SELECT partnum FROM inventory " +
                 " WHERE partnum = ? or partname = ?"
PreparedStatement pstmt = conn.prepareStatement (sqlstmt);
```

See related Topic: Setting IN Parameters (Chapter 6).

The CallableStatement Object

The primary role of the `CallableStatement` is to provide the means for applications to execute stored procedures. Stored procedures, unlike prepared statements, can have both IN and OUT parameters, therefore they require special handling.

Creating the CallableStatement Object

As with the `PreparedStatement` object, `CallableStatement` objects are directly associated with a particular SQL statement. `CallableStatements` are created using the `prepareCall()` method and take the SQL statement to be executed as a parameter. Also, as we saw with `Prepared-Statement` objects, the "?" is used as a place holder for variable parameters. Note that for `CallableStatements`, the "?" can be used for IN, OUT, and IN/OUT parameters, however. The value and type of the parameter is determined after creation time by using either a "set" method for IN parameters or the `registerOutParameter` method for OUT parameters. Here is a short example of how a `CallableStatement` object is created.

```
CallableStatement cs =
            conn.preparCall ("Execute getInventory (?,?,?,?)");
```

Related topics: Setting IN Parameters and Getting OUT Parameters (Chapter 6).

Managing Transactions

The `Connection` class provides several methods to help manage transactions. But before discussing each of these methods, we should come to a common understanding of what a transaction actually is.

For our purposes here, a *transaction* is a measurable unit of work; a business transaction. A transaction can consist of one or more SQL statements and may use multiple tables, schemas, or catalogs. Examples of transactions are:

- An order entry.
- A new user account created.
- The sale of an item.
- An inventory report.

A transaction is explicitly begun when any SQL statement other than a rollback or commit is executed against data in the database. This would include select, update, create statements, or even DDL statements. A transaction is completed when it is either committed or rolled back. The only types of statements that would not begin a transaction are those that do not interact with a database, such as a connect or disconnect statement.

Here is an example of a transaction:

```
SELECT * from user_tables();
INSERT INTO test
    VALUES (1,"abc");
SELECT column1
    FROM test;
COMMIT;
```

A single SQL statement can be a transaction as well:

```
SELECT * from user_tables();
COMMIT()
```

A statement does not necessarily have to end with a commit. A rollback statement would also complete a transaction, as in the following example:

```
SELECT * from user_tables();
INSERT INTO test
    VALUES (1,"abc");
SELECT column1
    FROM test;
ROLLBACK;
```

Getting Committed

One way that JDBC automates transaction management for you is to provide the ability to automatically commit each SQL statement individually. This feature, controlled by the `AutoCommit` switch and enabled by default, ensures that after the execution of any SQL statement completed, a commit command is issued. For some applications, this may be very appropriate and it certainly simplifies the transaction management for the developer. However, in many instances this feature can cause more harm than good. Since each SQL statement is automatically committed, you never have the opportunity to rollback a transaction. If you make a mistake, there is no way to undo it.

Since the commit and the rollback of statements are such an integral part of transaction management, most of the `Connection` object methods in this category are related to these two functions.

The `Connection` class provides methods for setting and discovering the status of the `AutoCommit` switch as well as methods for manually controlling the completion of transactions. Each is discussed in below. Since you cannot use the manual methods for transaction management, we will take a look at the `AutoCommit` related methods first.

The getAutoCommit/setAutoCommit Methods

One of the drawbacks of having `AutoCommit` turned on is that it can often result in very slow performance. As mentioned earlier, `AutoCommit` also prevents a user from rolling back any SQL statements made in error. Therefore, to allow the developer or users manual control over transactions, the `Connection` object provides a means to turn the Automatic Commit feature off. It also provides a method to discover the current status of the `AutoCommit` switch.

The `getAutoCommit()` is used to retrieve the current state of `AutoCommit`. The `getAutoCommit()` method returns true if `AutoCommit` is on. For example:

```
Connection conn1 = DriverManager.getConnection (URL,properties);
boolean autoCommitOn = connection.getAutoCommit();
if (autoCommitOn)
    {
        System.out.println("AutoCommit is turned on");
    }
else
    {
        System.out.println("AutoCommit is turned off");
    }
```

The `setAutoCommit()` method takes a boolean argument and toggles the `AutoCommit` on or off. To disable `AutoCommit`, use the following.

```
Connection conn1 = DriverManager.getConnection (URL,properties);
connection.setAutoCommit(false);
```

It is important to note that a statement that returns a `ResultSet` object is considered complete when the last row in the `ResultSet` has been retrieved or when the `ResultSet` is closed. If the statement returns multiple `ResultSet` objects, then the commit occurs with the last row in the last

ResultSet is read. In cases where an (OUT) parameter is returned, the commit occurs after the parameter has been read. Here is an example that calls a stored procedure called dept_update that updates data in the department table and returns the new results as a ResultSet.

```
import java.sql.*;

public class sqlselect {

     public static void main(String args[]) {

try {
     Class.forName("weblogic.jdbc.oci.Driver");

     Connection conn1 = DriverManager.getConnection
                         ("jdbc:weblogic:oracle:fool:",
                         "jdbcuser","jdbcisfun");

          CallableStatement cstmt =
                         conn1.prepareCall("EXECUTE dept_update");

          ResultSet rs1 = cstmt.getResultSet();

          while (rs1.next()) {

               System.out.println (rs1.getInt ("department_id") + ","
               System.out.println (rs1.getString ("dept_name") + ","
               System.out.println (rs1.getString("manager") );
                    }

     }          // <---------- Commit occurs here, after last row is read

     catch (SQLException exception) {
          Sytem.out.println ("\n SQL Exception "
                              + exception.getMessage() + "\n" );
                    }
     stmt1.close();
     conn1.close();
  }
}
```

See related topics: Connection.commit() and Connection.rollback() (Chapter 5)

The Commit Method

The next() method to be examined is the commit() method. The commit() method is used to issue an explicit SQL commit to the database. Once a commit is issued, all pending transactions are completed and any changes made permanent. This also implies that the next transaction begins at the completion of the commit. Of course, this method is useless unless the AutoCommit switch has been set to false using the setAutoCommit() method discussed above.

See related topics: `Connection.setAutoCommit()`, `Connection.getAutoCommit()`, and `Connection.rollback()` (Chapter 5).

The Rollback Method

Finally, we have the `rollback()` method. As you would expect, the `rollback()` method is used to issue an explicit SQL rollback to the database. Once a rollback is issued, all pending transactions are canceled, and data is reset to its original value. As with the `commit()` statement, the `AutoCommit()` method must be set to false in order for this method to have any meaning.

See related topics: `Connection.commit()` and `Connection.setAutoCommit()` (Chapter 5).

Transaction Isolation

The last set of methods in the transaction management category is not related to transaction commits or rollbacks at all, but rather have to do with how the database ensures data integrity during a transaction. For example, let's say during the course of a single transaction, you read a table into your application, modify some data in it, and then update the table with the new data. What happens if after you read the table someone else updates the same row you need to update? Will your data overwrite the other user's data? To address this type of situation, databases use various forms of transaction isolation. In most cases, the RDBMS will determine the best method for ensuring data integrity for you. However, in some cases, you may need to manually set the level of isolation for a particular transaction. To this end, the `Connection` class provides two methods used to discover and set the transaction isolation levels manually.

Each isolation level exercises control over certain types of transactions and provides a different level of data integrity. At the very lowest level is the TRANSACTION_READ_UNCOMMITED isolation mode. In this mode, dirty reads, non-repeatable reads, and phantom reads are permitted. At the highest level is TRANSACTION_SERIALIZABLE. At this level of isolation, none of these phenomenan are permitted.

As always, there is a trade off. The higher the isolation level, the slower the transaction rate and the more "expensive" each transaction gets. At the low end, you get faster performance and throughput, but you run the risk of data corruption or at least data misinterpretation. As mentioned earlier, most RDBMS's automatically manage data integrity issues based on internal algorithms, however in those cases where you need to manually override the default management you can use the `setTransactionIsolation()` method.

The getTransactionIsolation/setTransactionIsolation Methods

The `setTransactionIsolation`/`getTransactionIsoloation` method pair is used to discover and set the transaction isolation mode of the database. The `getTransactionIsolation()` method takes no argument and returns an integer that corresponds to the current isolation level. The `setTransactionIsolation()` method takes an integer value representing the desired transaction level as a parameter and attempts to change the current value to the new value. The following variables (Table 5.1) are defined in the Connection interface for use with the `getTransactionIsolation()` and `setTransactionIsolation()` methods.

Table 5.1
Connection Interface:
Transaction Isolation
Level Variables.

Transaction Level	Permitted Phenomena		
	Dirty Reads	Nonrepeatable Reads	Phantom Reads
TRANSACTION_NONE	N/A	N/A	N/A
TRANSACTION_READ_UNCOMMITED	Yes	Yes	Yes
TRANSACTION_READ_COMMITTED	No	Yes	Yes
TRANSACTION_PREPEATABLE_READ	No	No	Yes
TRANSACTION_SERIALIZABLE	No	No	No

The following example demonstrates how you would use the `setTransactionIsolation()` level to TRANSACTION_SERIALIZABLE.

```
Connection conn1 = DriverManager.getConnection
                ("jdbc:weblogic:oracle:fool:",
                "jdbcuser","jdbcisfun");
      conn1.setTransactionIsolation(TRANSACTION_SERIALIZABLE);
```

Once set, the isolation level is set for all transactions that are executed within that connection. If you want to simply change the isolation level for one transaction, you will need to call the `getTransactionIsolation()` method before changing the level and then set it back at when the transaction is completed. Here is a short example:

```
Connection conn1 = DriverManager.getConnection
                ("jdbc:weblogic:oracle:fool:",
                "jdbcuser","jdbcisfun");
    int originalTransactLevel = conn1.getTransactionIsolation();
    conn1.setTransactionIsolation(TRANSACTION_SERIALIZABLE);
    .
    .
    . // do some transaction
    .
    . conn1.setTransactionIsolation(originalTransactLevel);
```

> **WARNING!** Changing the isolation level during a transaction will cause a commit to be issued. A rollback to the original start point of the transaction will not be possible. It is highly recommended that you do not change isolation levels during a transaction.

What are Dirty Reads?

Dirty reads occur when a transaction is allowed to read data that has been modified by another transaction but not yet committed. Let's take a look at an example to illustrate this phenomenon.

Table 5.2
Dirty Read Example Timeline.

Time	Transaction	SQL Statement	Data Value
1:00	T1	SELECT qty FROM inventory WHERE partnum = '005273';	13 (qty)
1:10	T1	UPDATE inventory SET qty = 3 WHERE partnum = '005273'	3 (qty)
1:15	T2	SELECT partnum, qty FROM inventory WHERE qty < '5'	005273 (partnum) 3 (qty)
1:20	T1	rollback	13 (qty)

In Table 5.2, there are two users executing two separate transactions. User 1, executing T1, queries the database to see if there are enough parts on hand to fill a user request for 10 of item number "005273." There are 13, so an order entry is made for the 10 items. The number on hand (qty) is decremented by 10 to 3. At 1:15, the manager (User 2, Transaction T2) runs a report to find all parts that he has less than 5 of, to determine what parts he needs to order. The report states that there are 3 of part number "005273" in stock. Based on the data, he orders 2 more of part number "005273" to bring the total up to 5. However, at 1:20, User 1 finds out the customers credit card has been denied, and rolls back the transaction. (More correctly the nontransaction.) Now, when the manager checks the inventory the next day, there are 15 items in stock instead of 5.

As you can see, dirty reads can wreak havoc on your data. This problem can be avoided however, by ensuring that modified data cannot be read until it is committed. This is normally done by either storing the updated data in a temporary location and only letting the user that modified the data access it, or by simply locking the row of data once it has been updated so that no other user has access to it until it is committed.

To eliminate dirty reads in JDBC, set the isolation level to TRANSAC-TION_READ_COMMITTED. By setting this, you are telling the database to not read any data that is uncommitted.

What are Non-Repeatable Reads

A non-repeatable read occurs when a single transaction tries to read a row consecutively and the results are not the same. This can happen when the value of one of the rows originally selected is modified by a second transaction. Here is an example of how this occurs:

Table 5.3
Non-repeatable
Example Timeline.

Time	Transaction	SQL Statement	Data Value
1:00	T1	SELECT qty FROM inventory WHERE partnum = '005273';	13 (qty)
1:10	T2	UPDATE inventory SET qty = 3 WHERE partnum = '005273'	3 (qty)
1:12	T2	COMMIT	
1:15	T1	SELECT partnum, qty FROM inventory WHERE description = LIKE 'CDROM 12X';	005273 (partnum) 3 (qty)

In Table 5.3, User 1 (executing T1) is running a report. The report first generates a list based on part numbers, then it generates a report based on descriptions. In between the reports however, a customer buys 10 of part number "005273." This changes the number on hand to 3. When the manager reviews the report, however, there will be a discrepancy for the part number 005273. In one list, it is reported that there are 13 on hand, while in the other report, there are only 3.

To prevent this discrepancy from occurring, data read integrity must be maintained throughout the entire transaction. To do this, the RDBMS deploys a method of tracking updates and changes to data, and makes a readable "snapshot" of the data for each transaction. That is, the database reads only data that has been committed prior to the start of the transaction and copies it to temporary storage. All subsequent reads for that particular transaction are against the copy of the data.

To prevent both the nonrepeatable and dirty read phenomenons from occurring you need to set the JDBC isolation level to TRANSACTION_REPEATABLE_READ.

What are Phantom Reads?

A transaction exhibits the phantom-read phenomenon when in the course of a transaction, it selects a set of rows based on a search criteria, and when the same criteria is used again, the set of rows returned is not the same as the first. This phenomena is usually a result of a single transaction reading a row of data based on some selection criteria and then having the value of the criteria data for that row changed by another transaction. Here is an example illustrating this (Table 5.4):

Table 5.4
Phantom Read
Example Timeline.

Time	Transaction	SQL Statement	Data Value	
			partnum	qty
1:00	T1	SELECT partnum, qty FROM	004325	12
		inventory WHERE qty > '10';	005273	13
			03416 ...	458 ...
1:10	T2	UPDATE inventory SET qty = 3 '	005273	13
		WHERE partnum = '005273		
1:12	T2	COMMIT	005273	3
1:15	T1	UPDATE inventory SET qty = 10	004325	10
		WHERE qty = (SELECT partnum,	03416 ...	10
		qty FROM inventory WHERE qty > '10')		

* Note that the quantity of 13 is visible to all users in the database except User 2, who sees the updated value of 3.

In Table 5.4, User 1 (executing T1) is the manager. The manager has decided to return to the distributor all of his excess inventory. Any part with more than 10 in stock is considered excess. The manager plans to return all but 10 of each of these items. To do this, he first selects all of the items that have more than 10 items in stock. Since the list is very long, it takes a while to process. One of the items selected is part number 005273. In the meantime, our customer calls back to order 10 of part number 005273. This time his credit card is approved, and the transaction (T2) is completed. After the commit occurs, the database needs to be updated to reflect all of the parts that are going to be returned. However, when (T1) executes another query for all items with more than 10 items in stock, part number 005273 does not appear in the list. The first selection statement had generated a "phantom." This is different from a non-repeatable read because the set of rows selected is not the same, where with non-repeatable reads the data contained in the rows is different.

Eliminating the non-repeatable phenomenon is a bit more tricky than isolating uncommitted transactions. In order to prevent this from occurring, the database must "lock out" every row that is selected by a query until the transaction is committed. That is, if a user selects a particular row, no other user can have any access to that row whatsoever until the first transaction is completed. This is known as *row locking*. Some RDBMS do not support row-level locking, but rather lock pages or sections of tables. This means that if a user selected only one row, the next 100 rows might be blocked too. In instances where a very general selection clause is used, an entire table can be locked out from other users. This is why I had mentioned that as you move up the isolation level, the fixes become more expensive.

If your application needs this level of data consistency, however, you will need to set the isolation level to TRANSACTION_SERIALIZABLE. This, of course, will also prevent dirty and non-repeatable reads from occurring.

Session Management

As discussed earlier in this chapter, a `Connection` object can be thought of as representing a session with the database. Each session has a starting point when the user logs in to the database, and ends when the user logs out. Several methods within the `Connection` class, therefore, pertain to managing the session itself. Session management methods, therefore, pertain to the `Connection` object itself and are not restricted to a particular statement or other objects contained within the session.

The clearWarnings/getWarnings Methods

The `getWarnings()` method retrieves any warnings for the current session and returns a SQLWarning object. The `clearWarnings()` method simply sets the `SQLWarning` object to null. Warnings are generated by the database and normally occur as a result of a database configuration error. These warnings often occur at login time and should be checked for then. Here is an example how to process warnings using the `getWarnings()` method:

```
import java.sql.*;

    public class sqlConnect{

    public static void main (String args[] ) {

        try {
            Driver drv1 = new weblogic.jdbc.oci.Driver;
            Properties props = new Properties ();
```

```
            props.put ("user", "jdbcuser");
            props.put ("passwd", "jdbcisfun");
            Connection conn1 = drv1.connect("jdbc:weblogic.
                                             oracle",props);

            printWarnings (conn1.getWarnings());
        }
    catch (SQLException exception)
    {
            System.out.println ("\n SQL Exception " +
                                exception.getMessage() +"\n");
    }
    conn1.close();
}

public static void printWarnings (SQLWarning warning) {
    while (warning != null ) {
            System.out.println ("Connection Warning: "
                                + ( warning. getErrorCode ) +
                                (warning.getMessage) + "\n" );
            warning = getNextWarning();
            }
    }

}
```

In this example, I call the printWarnings() method after we make our connection, using a newly created SQLWarning object as an argument. In the printWarnings() method, we simply test to see if the SQLWarning object is null, print the error code and error message then get the next warning.

See related topics: SQLWarnings class and SQLException class (Chapter 11).

The close/isClosed Methods

The isClosed() method tests to see if a connection is currently closed. If the connection is open, isClosed() returns false.

The close() method is used to explicitly close a database connection. A connection is automatically closed when the application is exited, but may not terminate the connection properly on the database. It is recommended that you always use the close statement explicitly before exiting the application. As discussed in Chapter 2, improperly terminated connections can cause database server difficulties, and cause connection requests to be denied.

Closing a connection results in disposal all objects within the Connection object. This means all Statements and their associated ResultSets will be closed.

The getCatalog/setCatalog methods

The `getCatalog()` method is used to get the name of the current catalog. As you would expect, the `setCatalog()` method is used to change the current catalog value. Here is a short example:

```
String catalogName = conn1.getCatalog();
conn1.setCatalog("user_tables");
```

As shown, the `getCatalog()` returns a `String` containing the name of the current catalog. The `setCatalog()` method takes a `String` representing the catalog name to select as an argument.

A catalog is a named container object that contains a collection of schemas. A database can have zero or more catalogs and a catalog can contain zero or more schemas.

Not all databases support catalogs. The SQL92 Entry Level standard does not require that catalogs be used. Accordingly, JDBC drivers are not required to support catalog names in order to be JDBC COMPLIANT. It is also important to note that even if a database supports catalogs, they may not use the term "catalog" for them. The `DatabaseMetaData.getCatalogTerm()` can be used to determine the vendor's preferred term. In most cases, a table is uniquely defined by its schema and table name and the catalog can be safely ignored. Applications written for database administration would most likely be the only type of application to need this level of information.

See related topics: `DatabaseMetaData.getCatalogs()` (Chapter 10), `DatabaseMetaData.getCatalogTerm()` (Chapter 10), `DatabaseMetaData.getCatalogSeperator()` (Chapter 10), and `DatabaseMetaData.isCatalogAtStart()` (Chapter 10).

The isReadOnly/setReadOnly Methods

In some instances, a connection may be set to read only. That is, no update, insert, or delete statements can be used with that connection. The `isReadOnly()` method returns `true` if the user does indeed only have read access. If the user does have the ability to update or modify the database, then you can explicitly set the connection to read only by using the `setReadOnly()` method with a true argument.

To set a connection to be read only use:

```
connection.setReadOnly (true);
```

To set a connection to allow data manipulation statements use:

```
connection.setReadOnly (false);
```

Please note that this does not override the permissions granted a user on the database. A user that is granted only read privileges on a table, cannot be given write access to that table by calling `setReadOnly(false)`.

The nativeSQL Method

The `nativeSQL()` method takes a string representing a JDBC SQL statement, and returns the SQL string that the driver presents to the database. This method is normally only useful in conjunction with statements that use escape syntax.

See related topic: Creating and Executing SQL Statements (Chapter 7).

This method would most likely only be used by developers as debugging information. Most application users will not need this level of detail or type of information.

The getMetaData Method

The last method in the session management category is slightly different than the rest. This method does not directly manage the session but rather creates a new object, the `DatabaseMetaData` object. The `DatabaseMetaData` object contains information associated with the current session.

The `DatabaseMetaData` object can be used to determine information about the state of the database, supported features, and an entire litany of other database-specific information. The `DatabaseMetaData` is by far the largest interface and covers a wide range of information. Once a connection is established, you can call the `getDatabaseMetaData()` method as shown here.

```
DatabaseMetaData dbmeta = conn1.getMetaData
```

The inner workings and methods of the `DatabaseMetaData` object are discussed in Chapter 10.

See related topic: `DatabaseMetaData` interface (Chapter 10).

Chapter Summary

In this chapter, we took a close look at the `Connection` interface and its methods. Many of the methods are used to create objects that are then used to execute SQL statements. The only methods that execute SQL statements themselves are the `commit()` and `rollback()` methods. We also saw how you can manually override transaction isolation levels, `AutoCommit`, and other connection defaults.

What's Next

In the next chapter, we will examine how to execute statements including static statements, dynamic prepared statements and stored procedure calls. Chapter 6 will also include a complete discussion on how to execute SQL statements using either a `Statement`, `PreparedStatement`, and `CallableStatement` object.

CHAPTER 6

Working with Statements:
The Statement, PreparedStatement and Callable Statement Interfaces

In the previous chapter we saw how to create `Statement` objects using the `Connection.createStatement()` method. We also saw how to create `PreparedStatement` and `CallableStatement` objects using the `prepareStatement()` and `prepareCall()` methods. Once created, each object is used as the vehicle to channel SQL to the database. Also in Chapter 5, we saw that the `Statement` object is used for static SQL statements, while the `PreparedStatement` and the `CallableStatement` objects are used in conjunction with SQL statements containing IN or OUT parameters. The focus of this chapter will be on how to actually use these newly created objects to execute the SQL and get results from the database.

Preparing for Execution

In the previous chapter, I showed you how to create dynamic SQL statements that contain IN and/or OUT parameters. However, I did not demonstrate how to set the value or retrieve the value of those parameters. The reason for this is that creating the `Statement` object is done using a method from the `Connection` class, while setting or retrieving the value of the parameters is part of the Statement object itself. The following two sections discuss the details of setting IN parameters and getting OUT parameter values.

Setting IN Parameters

Now that you know how to create a `PreparedStatement` with the appropriate number of place holders ("?"), it is time to look at the methods used to set their values. As mentioned in the previous chapter, the `Prepared-Statement` object's main purpose is to execute dynamic SQL statements that contain IN parameters. The value of the IN parameter is assigned using one of the "set" methods. Each "set" method is used to assign a value of particular type to the IN parameter. For example, to set the value of an IN parameter to a `String` you would use the `setString()` method. To set the value to be an integer use the `setInt()` method.

There are three categories of "set" methods: primitive data type methods, object methods, and stream methods. The only difference between primitive data type and object category is the type of value that is used to assign. The syntax is exactly the same. For the stream category, however, both the syntax and the data types are different.

Setting Primitive Data Type and Object IN Values

With only one exception, the `getObject()` method, all of the methods in the primitive data type category and object type category use the same syntax for assigning values to IN parameters.

```
setNNN (Integer,Value);
```

Where: NNN = The Value type.
Integer = The relative position of the IN parameter in the SQL statement, assigned left to right.
Value = The actual value to be assigned to the IN parameter.

For example, let's assume we have the following `PreparedStatement`:

```
String sqlString = "INSERT INTO inventory (qty_on_hand)"
                 + "VALUES(?)"
                 + "WHERE part_number > ?";
```

```
PreparedStatement pstmt = prepareStatement(sqlstring);
```

In this statement, there are two IN variables represented by the placeholder ("?"). The first IN parameter is part of the VALUES assignment clause. For the sake of clarity, lets call this parameter "A." The second IN parameter is part of the selection criteria in the WHERE clause. I will call this parameter "B." Now let's suppose I have sold an item, part number "A111054," and want to set the quantity on hand to 5. I would use the following:

```
pstmt.setInt(1,5);
pstmt.setString(2,"A111054");
```

As you can see, there is no difference in the way you implement the `set` methods in the primitive data type category and the object category. The syntax is the same for the `setInt` and `setString` method.

The following is a list of all the "set" methods in the primitive data type and category:

- setBoolean
- setLong
- setNull

- setByte
- setFloat
- setShort

- setInt
- setDouble

The methods for setting object parameters are:

- setBignum
- setString
- setTimeStamp

- setBytes
- setObject

- setDate
- setTime

The setObject Methods

The `setObject` method has three forms. In its simplest form, `setObject()` takes two parameters. The first, as always, is the position of the variable to be set. The second parameter is an `Object`. Before sending the object to the database, however, the driver converts the `Object` to the standard SQL data type for that `Object`. The SQL type is determined by the data type conversion matrix defined by JDBC. To determine what the standard mapping for a particular object is, refer to the conversion matrix found in Appendix B, Table 3.

The second form of the `setObject()` method adds another input parameter. In this form, the third parameter represents a data type to which explicitly convert the `Object` to. This is analogous to casting the SQL data type on the `Object`. In this form, the DECIMAL and NUMERIC type scale is set to zero resulting in data truncation.

To ensure a certain number of digits is maintained for NUMERIC and DECIMAL types, you must use the third form of the `setObject()` method. The third form adds a fourth integer argument which represents the scale to be used for NUMERIC and DECIMAL types. Here is an example of each form:

```
ps.setObject(1,135);                    // Set the input
                                        object "135" .
ps.setObject(1,135,Type.NUMERIC);       // Force JDBC to con-
                                        vert "135"
                                        // SQL type NUMERIC.
ps.setObject(1,135.11,Type.NUMERIC,2);  // Force type and
                                        scale of number.
```

See related topics: Data Type conversion chart (Appendix B).

Setting Stream IN Variables

In some instances, particularly in applications that retrieve images from databases, the data to be passed as an IN variable is very large. Rather than assign the entire value statically, the methods in the stream category allow you to use an InputStream. The syntax for the methods in this category are as follow:

```
setNNNStream (Integer1, InputStream, Integer2);
```

Where: NNN = The InputStream type: ASCII, Binary or Unicode
        Integer1 = The relative position of the IN parameter in the SQL statement, assigned left to right.
        InputStream = The data stream to be read from.
        Integer2 = The number of bytes to be read from the data stream at a time.

Here is a short example using the `setBinaryStream()` method. It assumes that the data in the file "my_file" is binary data and reads 4k bytes at a time.

```
FileInputStream fileIn = new FileInputStream ("my_file");
String sqlString = "INSERT INTO picture (image)"
                   + "VALUES(?)"
                   + "WHERE pic_number = 100 ";
PreparedStatement pstmt = prepareStatement(sqlstring);
pstmt.setBinaryStream(1,fileIn,4096);
```

Using OUT Parameters

Many of today's RDBMSs use stored procedures to perform complex database functions. An integral part of stored procedures is the OUT parameter.

The OUT parameter can therefor be thought of as simply a variable that the stored procedure returns a value to. In JDBC, the `CallableStatement` object is the only object that provides a mechanism for retrieving the value of OUT parameters. Similar to setting values using "set" methods, the `CallableStatement` class provides several "get" methods for the sole purpose of retrieving the values of OUT parameters. Each "get" method is used to retrieve a specific type of data. However, since OUT values are returned to the application before the "get" method is called, you must first declare what type of data the OUT parameter will return, essentially setting the data type rather than a data value. This is done using the `register-OutParameter()` method.

The registerOutParameter Method

The `registerOutParameter()` method is used to declare what SQL type the OUT parameter will return. This is referred to as *registering the parameter*. Once you have registered a parameter, the parameter is considered an OUT parameter and any parameter that has been set is considered an IN parameter. Therefore, any parameter that has been both set and registered is an IN/OUT parameter. There is no distinction within the `PreparedStatement` between IN, OUT, or IN/OUT parameters. The syntax to register all but NUMERIC and DECIMAL data types is as follows:

```
registerOutParameter (Integer,Type);
```

Where: Integer = The relative position of the OUT parameter in the SQL
statement, assigned left to right.
Type = The SQL data type as found in the java.sql.TYPE class.

For example, assume we have the following CallableStatement:

```
CallableStatement cstmt = conn1.prepareCall
                          ("EXECUTE inv_report(?,?,?");
ResultSet rs = cstmt.executeQuery();
```

Let's assume that the first parameter is an IN, the second parameter is an OUT, and the last parameter is an IN/OUT parameter. Let's further assume we want to set the first parameter to a `String` value, the second to an `Integer`, and the third to a `String`.

```
setString(1,"The input string");
registerOutParameter(2, INTEGER);
setString(3,"The in/out string");
registerOutParameter(3,STRING);
```

The syntax to register NUMERIC and DECIMAL values is only modified slightly to include the scale of the number to be returned.

```
registerOutParameter (Integer1,Type,Integer2);
```

Where: Integer1 = The relative position of the OUT parameter in the SQL statement, assigned left to right.

Type = The SQL data type as found in the java.sql.TYPE class. - NUMERIC or DECIMAL

Integer2 = The scale of the parameter. (Number of digits to the right of the decimal point)

Here is an example of registering a DECIMAL parameter specifying 5 digits to the right of the decimal point:

```
registerOutParameter(2, DECIMAL, 5);
```

Getting OUT Parameters

As mentioned, each of the "get" methods in the `CallableStatement` class are used to retrieve the value in an OUT parameter after the execution of the callable statement. As such, the "get" methods are actually a post execution method.

All of the "get" methods use the same syntax shown below:

```
getNNN(Integer);
```

Where: NNN = The OUT value Java data type.

Integer = The relative position of the OUT parameter in the SQL statement, assigned left to right.

Here is a short example using the `getString()` and `getInt()` methods.

```
CallableStatement cstmt = conn1.prepareCall
                         ("EXECUTE inv_report(?,?,?");
ResultSet rs = cstmt.executeQuery();
setString(1,"The input string");
registerOutParameter(2, INTEGER);
setString(3,"The in/out string");
registerOutParameter(3,STRING);
ResultSet rs = cstmt.executeQuery();
.
. // Process the ResultSet
.
String outparam3 = getString(3);
int outparam2 = getInt(2);
```

In all, there are 13 "get" methods. You should note that JDBC does not support getting OUT parameters as streams.

- getBoolean
- getDate
- getInt (getLong
- getString

- getByte
- getDouble
- getObject
- getTime

- getBytes
- getFloat
- getShort
- getTimeStamp

The getObject Method

The getObject() method is only slightly different from the other "get" methods. Each of the other "get" methods converts the SQL data type into a specific Java type. For example, the getString() method converts the value of the indicated variable to a String and only a String. However, the getObject() method converts the return value to any Java data type specified in the registerOutParameter() method for that variable. The following example demonstrates how to register an OUT parameter as a Date:

```
cs.registerOutParameter(3,Type.Dates);
```

And then to retrieve the data as a String:

```
String today = cs.getString(3);
```

However, if you used the getObject() method, the same code would generate an error without an explicit cast. For example:

```
Date today = cs.getObject(3);          // This is Ok.
String today = cs.getObject(3);        // This will throw an
                                       //   SQLException.
String today = (String)cs.getObject(3);  // This is Ok.
```

The Execution Methods

Each of the three statement objects has a distinct purpose and is used in very specific ways. The type of statement object to be used is determined by the parameters of the SQL statement. It is, therefore, the input that dictates the type of statement object that will be used. Similarly, the execute method to be used is determined by the expected output of the SQL statement.

There are three types of output that can be expected from a SQL statement: a result set containing data in tabular format, an update count indicating the number of rows affected by the SQL statement, or a combination of the two. Each of these output types requires its own special handling. Accordingly, there are three execute methods that can be used for each type of statement object. They are the executeQuery() method, the executeUpdate() method and the execute() method, respectively. Each is discussed in detail on the following pages.

The executeQuery Method

The executeQuery() method is used to execute any SQL statement that returns a data result set. Any SQL statement containing a "select" clause fits into this category. The executeQuery() method can be used with a wide variety of SQL "select" statements, such as those containing database functions, joins, and wild cards.

The executeQuery() method actually comes in two varieties. The first executeQuery() method is used in conjunction with Statement objects. In this form, the executeQuery() method takes the SQL statement string as an input parameter. For example:

```
Statement stmt = conn1.createStatement();
ResultSet rs = stmt.executeQuery("Select * from user_tables");
```

For the PreparedStatement() and Callable() objects, the syntax is only slightly different. For these two methods, a single SQL statement is associated with the Statement object. You do not specify the SQL statement as part of the execute() method. Here is a short example of how to execute a stored procedure called inv_report. To keep the example simple, assume the stored procedure has no input parameters and returns a result set:

```
CallableStatement cstmt = conn1.prepareCall
                          ("EXECUTE inv_report");
ResultSet rs = cstmt.executeQuery();
```

The syntax for SQL statement strings can get rather complicated when using database functions, special quoting, or escape characters. Chapter 7 has a complete discussion on how to handle these special situations.

See related topic: The ResultSet interface (Chapter 8).

The executeUpdate Method

The executeUpdate() method is used for SQL statements that are expected to return a row count rather than an actual result set. A row count is associated with SQL functions, such as update, insert, and delete. Accordingly, the return type of all executeQuery() methods is an integer value representing the number of rows effected by that statement.

As with the executeQuery() method, there are two varieties of the executeUpdate() method. For Statement objects executing static

SQL statements, a string representing the SQL statement is passed as an argument, while the `PreparedStatement` and `CallableStatement` versions do not take any arguments. Here are a couple of short examples:

For a `Statement` object:

```
String sqlString = "INSERT INTO inventory (price)"
                + "VALUES(101)"
                + "WHERE price > 100";
Statement stmt = conn1.createStatement();
int rowcount = stmt.executeUpdate(sqlstring);
```

For a `CallableStatement`:

```
CallableStatement cs = conn1.prepareCall("EXECUTE inv_update");
```

Data Definition Language statements are considered part of this class of SQL statements. DDL statements return a row count of "0" for successful statements and a "–1" for ones that have failed.

See related topic: Creating and Executing SQL Statements (Chapter 7).

The execute Method

The `execute()` method is a highly specialized method that is required only in circumstances where the SQL statement to be executed is not known at compile time or there is a possibility of multiple results being returned by a stored procedure. Unlike the `executeUpdate()` and `executeQuery()` methods, the results of an execute method are not returned as part of the method, but instead must be retrieved using a separate `getResultSet()` or `getUpdateCount()` method. These two methods are part of the `Statement` class and are inherited by the `CallableStatement` and `PreparedStatement`.

Handling an Unknown Result: Single Result Set or Row Count

If your application allows users to enter their own queries, the contents of that query are certainly not known at compile time. The results of such a query could be a `ResultSet` or if the SQL statement contains an UPDATE or an INSERT, the results could be an integer value representing the number of rows effected by the statement. The net effect of this is that we do not know whether or not to use the `executeQuery()` or the `executeUpdate()` statement, nor do we know what data type to expect. The solution to this dilemma is to use the `execute()` method. As noted above, the `execute()`

method does not have a return value. This gives us the ability to first execute the query, then after its completion, determine what data type was returned.

JDBC unfortunately does not provide us with a method that can tell you directly what type of object was returned by the `execute()` method. There is however a fairly simple, albeit roundabout way to do this using either the `getUpdateCount()` method or the `getResultSet()` method. Here is how it works: the `getUpdateCount()` method will return –1 if the results of the `execute()` method are not an integer. Therefore, if we know the results are not an integer, it follows that the results must be a `ResultSet` object. The reverse of this is to use the `getResultSet()` method. The `getResultSet()` method will return null if the results are not a `Result-Set`. Therefore, if you call the `getResultSet()` method and get back a `null` value, then you know that the result is an integer value. The following is a short example of how you could use the `getUpdateCount()` method to determine the return data type:

```
String sqlstring = some_SQL_string
Statement stmt = conn.createStatement();
stmt.execute(sqlstring);
int UpdateCount = stmt.getUpdateCount();
if (UpdateCount == -1)
   {
    ResultSet rs = stmt.getResultSet();
   }
else
   {
    System.out.println (" The update count was" + UpdateCount);
   }
```

Handling Multiple Results

In some instances where stored procedures are called, the results of an `execute` method call can contain `ResultSet()` objects, integers (row counts), or combinations of the two. However, a `Statement` object can only have one active `ResultSet` or row count at a time. Therefore, when multiple results are returned by the database, only the first result can be used until you explicitly get the next result. This means that whenever a stored procedure that returns unknown results is executed, you must access each result sequentially and process them individually.

The `Statement` class provides the `getMoreResults()` method to sequentially access multiple results. When called, the `getMoreResults()` method will replace the current result associated with the `Statement` object with the next result in the result queue. If the result retrieved is a `ResultSet`, then the return value is `true`. If the result retrieved is an integer representing the row count, then the `getMoreResults` method returns `false`. To add a little confusion to this, the `getMoreResults()` method will also return `false` if no results are retrieved. Therefore, in order to determine if you have processed the last result you must use a secondary test: the `getUpdateCount()` method.

If the `getUpdateCount()` method returns –1, it implies that the result is a `ResultSet()` or no result at all. If the `getMoreResults()` method returns `false`, then it implies that the result is either an update count or no result at all. Since in this case, we already know that the `getUpdate-Count()` count has returned –1 indicating that the result is not an update count, we can conclude that there are no more results left. If you are a bit confused still, Table 6.1 should help clarify how all this works together.

Another means of determining that no more results exist, is to use the `getUpdateCount()` and `getResultSet()` method and ignore the `getMoreResults` return value. If the `getUpdateCount` method returns –1, we know the result must be either a `ResultSet` or null. If we then determine that it is not a `ResultSet()` by virtue of the `getResult-Set()` method returning null, then we can also conclude that there are no more results to be processed and the `getResultSet` method returns null, then the `getMoreResults()` method must have returned false. Table 6.2 summarizes how all three of these methods interact with each other and what the various combinations of their results can tell us.

Table 6.1

Using the `getResultSet()` and `getUpdate-Count()` methods to determine result object types.

Testing method name	Return value	What it tells you.
getUpdateCount	> 0	The result is an update count.
getUpdateCount	= –1	The result is not an update count.
getUpdateCount	= 0	Either the update count was zero or a DDL statement was executed.
getResultSet	= null	The result is not a ResultSet.
getResultSet getUpdateCount	= –1 != null	The result is a ResultSet.

Table 6.2
Using
`getMoreResults()`
*to determine when
there are no more
results.*

Testing method name	Return value	What it tells you.
getMoreResults	true	The result contains a ResultSet.
getMoreResults	false	The result could be a update count or there are no more results.
getMoreResults	false	The result is an update count.
getUpdateCount	> 0, = 0	Either the statement was a DDL or the number of rows effected was zero.
getMoreResults getUpdateCount	false −1	There are no more results.
getUpdateCount getResultSet	−1 false	There are no more results.

Example 6.1 shows how to process multiple ResultSets implementing the strategy outlined above.

Example 6.1

```
import java.sql.*;
public class multiResultStatement {

Statement stmt;

public static boolean isResultSet()
 {
  boolean isRS;
  rs = stmt.getResultSet();
  if (rs == null)
     {
       isRS = false;
     }
 else
     {
       isRS = true;
     }
return isRS
}

public static boolean isUpdateCount()
{
  boolean isUC;
  updateCount = stmt.getUpdateCount();
  if (updateCount < 0)
     {
       isUC = false;
     }
```

```
  else
      {
        isUC = true;
        }
  return usUC
}

public static void main (String args[]) {

try {

              Driver drv1 = new weblogic.jdbc.oci.Driver;
              Properties props = new Properties ();
              props.put ("user", "jdbcuser");
              props.put ("passwd", "jdbcisfun");
              conn1 = drv1.connect("jdbc:weblogic.oracle",props);
              stmt= conn1.createStatement();
              stmt.execute( { call mysp() } );
              boolean moreResults = true;
              while (moreResults)
               if (isResultSet())
                   {
                    // process the ResultSet
                    getMoreResults();
                    }
               else
                if (isUpdateCount())
                    {
                     // process the UpdateCount
                      getMoreResults();
                    }
                else
                    {
                     moreResults = false;
                    }
              }
              }


        }
catch (SQLException exception)
        {
              System.out.println ("\n SQL Exception " +
                                     exception.getMessage() +"\n");
        }
    }
}
```

In Example 6.1, I created two new static methods that use a test to determine
what type of result is current. In the main() method, I used a while loop
to iterate through each result. You can see that the while loop will exit when
both the isResultSet() and isUpdateCount() methods return false.
Recall that the getResultSet() method will return null if the result is not
a ResultSet() and that the getUpdateCount() method will return –1
when the result is not an update count. When both of these conditions are
met, then there are no more results to be processed.

Managing Statement Objects

While most of the methods in all three of the statement classes are related to providing the mechanisms necessary to execute SQL statements of one form or another, they are by no means the only methods available. As we have seen with the previous classes, the statement classes provide methods to assist in managing themselves. Most of these methods are concerned with how the statement object interacts with the database and are not specific to a single statement execution. Some of the more useful methods are detailed below.

The cancel Method

The cancel() method is used to halt the execution of a statement once it has been started (I like to think of this method as the "Ctrl-c" of JDBC). This method comes in extremely handy in any application that allows users to input their own SQL statements. At some point in time, it is likely that you will need to cancel an operation. A common error is to create a SQL statement that is a join of two tables without any WHERE clause. This type of statement results in a Cartesian product of the two tables. This can result in an extremely large table since it consists of every row in the first table, joined with every row in the second. Besides being huge, this table is normally useless and simply wastes valuable resources. If not for any other reason, you would always add a cancel() method to your application to allow users to stop this type of error.

The only stipulation to using the cancel() method to stop an errant operation, you must have a multi-threaded application. In a single threaded application you cannot issue the cancel() method until the execution of the statement is complete, which is hardly helpful when you wish to stop the operation in the middle of execution.

Example 6.2 shows how you can create a simple thread to check the elapsed time of the SQL query. If the elapsed time is more than 30 seconds the cancel method is called to kill the request. The time interval can easily be modified to be a user/administrator set variable to tailor it to a particular environment.

Example 6.2

```
import java.sql.*;
    public class cancelTest {

    public static void main (String argv[])

    {

    sqlThread sqlT = new sqlThread();
```

```
            timeThread timeT = new timeThread();
            sqlT.setConnection();
            sqlT.start();
            timeT.start();
            timeT.join();
            if (sqlT.isAlive)
               {
                 sqlThread.cancelQuery();
                 System.out.println ("SQL Query Canceled - 30 second time
                                      limit exceeded");
               }
        }
    }

    public class sqlThread extends Thread {

    Statement stmt;
    Connection conn1;

      public void setConnection ( ) {

         try {
               Driver drv1 = new weblogic.jdbc.oci.Driver;
               Properties props = new Properties ();
               props.put ("user", "jdbcuser");
               props.put ("passwd", "jdbcisfun");

               conn1 = drv1.connect("jdbc:weblogic.oracle",props);


            }

         catch (SQLException exception)

            {

               System.out.println ("\n SQL Exception " +
                                   exception.getMessage() +"\n");
            }


      }


      public void run()
          {
               stmt = conn1.creatStatement();
               ResultSet rs = stmt.executeQuery("select * from
                                                 table1,table2"));
               // This will generate a Cartesian product of the two
                  tables
          }


    public boolean cancelQuery ()
      {
         stmt.cancel();
         conn1.close();
      }
    }
```

```
public class timeThread extends Thread
{
 public void run ()
  {
  try {
     sleep(30000);
     }
  catch (InterrupteException e){}
  }
  }
```

In Example 6.2, I simply encapsulate the `executeQuery()` method inside of a separate thread and then use a second thread to wait a preset amount of time before continuing with the rest of the application. In the `main()` method, you can see tha the `sqlT.start()` method is called to begin the `executeQuery()`. After that thread is started control is returned back to `main()` and the second thread timeT is started. The `timeT.join()` method then tells `main()` to wait until the `timeT` thread has completed. As you can see, `timeT.start()` merely sleeps for 30 seconds and then ends. At the end of the 30 seconds therefore `main()` moves on to the next line of code which in turns determins if the sqlT thread is still running. If it is, then the `sqlThread.cancelQuery()` method is called to cancel the job.

The getMaxFieldSize/setMaxFieldSize Methods

The `getMaxFieldSize()`/`setMaxFieldSize()` methods are used to determine/set the maximum number of bytes that can be returned from a single column of a table. Data that exceeds the set maximum is truncated from the results. These methods only apply to columns containing the following SQL data types:

- CHAR
- VARCHAR
- LONGVARCHAR
- BINARY
- VARBINARY
- LONGVARBINARY

These methods normally would be used in instances where you want to limit the amount of data that is displayed and data truncation does not a pose a problem. It can also be used to ensure that users do not accidentally select erroneous data such as binary images. To do this, you can simply find out what the maximum size of all your "character" fields are and set the maximum limit to that number. In most cases, the maximum column size is at most a few hundred characters; therefore, limiting your column size can ensure that large unreadable binary fields are filtered out.

It is important to note that once a value is set within a `Statement` object, the value applies to all columns. That is to say, you cannot limit the size of one column and not another. Also remember that this value applies to the `Statement` object not the SQL statement. Therefore if you set the value for one SQL statement, all subsequent SQL statements executed within that `Statement` object will also be limited. Once the field size has been limited, all data beyond that limit is truncated.

The following code fragment example shows how to find out what the maximum size is and then increases it by 256 bytes.

```
.
.
.

Statement stmt = conn.createStatement();
int currentMaxFieldSize = stmt.getMaxFieldSize();
if ( currentMaxFieldSize > 0) {
  stmt.setMaxFieldSize(currentMaxFieldSize + 256);
}
.
.
.
```

The default behavior of JDBC is to allow for unlimited column sizes which is indicated by the value zero. In the example above, the `if` statement is used to test for any value greater than zero, to ensure we actually will increase the current value. We would not want to "increase" our size from infinity to 256.

The default value for the maximum field size is zero; infinite. To reset the maximum value back to the default value after it has been changed, simply use zero as the new value, i.e.:

```
stmt.setMaxFieldSize(0);
```

The getMaxRows/setMaxRows Methods

The `getMaxRows()`/`setMaxRows()` method pair is used to determine or set the maximum number of rows that a single `ResultSet` can contain. The default is to allow for an unlimited number of rows indicated by a zero. The syntax for these methods is as follows:

```
.
.
.

Statement stmt = conn.createStatement();
int currentMaxRows = stmt.getMaxRows();
```

```
if ( currentMaxRows > 0 ) {
stmt.setMaxRows(currentMaxRows + 256);
}
  .
  .
  .
```

Similar to the `maxfield()` methods, once the maximum number of rows is set, the limit is applied to all subsequent SQL statements executed within the `Statement` object. It is also important to note that like the "`max()`" field methods, all data that exceed the limit is truncated. Once truncated, the data is lost and cannot be retrieved by any other means.

All data that exceed the limit set by the `setMaxRows()` method is simply dropped. Although its name might imply otherwise, the `getMoreResults()` method cannot be used to retrieve additional rows.

The getQueryTimeout/setQueryTimout Methods

The `getQueryTimeout()` and `setQueryTimeout()` methods are used to determine or set the maximum time (in seconds) the driver should wait for a response from a query. Similar to the other `get/set` pairs in this interface, a zero is the default value and indicates that the driver should wait an infinite amount of time. In some cases, this might be inappropriate and a time-out value should be set.

If the maximum time-out value is exceeded, an `SQLException` is thrown and the `Statement` is closed. As a result of the statement closing, all resources currently used by the `Statement` will be freed up.

The setCursorName Method

The `setCursorName()` method is used to set the name of the cursor to be used by the `Statement` object. If your database supports positional updates/deletes, you can then use the named cursor for these operations. To determine if your database supports positional updates/deletes, you can use the `DatabaseMetaData()`, `supportsPositionedUpdate()`, and `supportsPositionedDelete()` methods. If the database does not support positioned delete or update, the `setCursorName()` method results in a no op (no operation).

See related topics: The `DatabaseMetaData.supportsPositionedUpdate()` method (Chapter 10) and The `DatabaseMetaData.supportsPositionedDelete()` (Chapter 10).

The setEscapeProcessing Method

The `setEscapeProcessing()` method is used to turn on or off escape sequence scanning. In many instances, escape sequences are not used; sequence scanning can be safely turned off. By turning off scanning, the driver will be able to parse your statements faster and you may gain some performance. By default, escape processing is set to true/on.

To turn the scanning off use:

```
stmt.setEscapeProcessing (false);
```

To turn the scanning back on:

```
stmt.setEscapeProcessing (true);
```

The clearParameters Method (Prepared Statement Only)

This method is used to clear all values currently assigned to input parameters. Normally, you would simply assign new values to clear the previous value. However, this method can be used if you need to clear all values at once. This may be especially useful when working with large binary values and you need to regain some memory.

The wasNull Method

The `wasNull()` method can be used to determine if the return value of the last "get" method was null. The `wasNull()` method takes no parameters and can only determine the value of the last "get" method.

Chapter Summary

In this chapter, we convered a lot of ground. We have seen how the `Statement` object is used for static SQL statements, the `PreparedStatement` is used for procedures with IN parameters, and `CallableStatements` are used for SQL statements with OUT or IN/OUT parameters. We also explained why there are three "execute" methods and how each is different from the other, how to handle multiple results and how to cancel a query.

What's Next

In the next chapter, we will take an in-depth look at how to create and execute nearly every type of SQL statement with as many variations as possible. This will include both DML and DDL SQL statements. We will also learn more about how to use escape syntax to help create completely database-independent applications.

CHAPTER 7

Creating and Executing SQL Statements

In the previous chapter, we saw how the `Statement`, `PreparedStatement`, and `CallableStatement` objects each use one of the execute methods to send SQL statements to the database server for execution. In this chapter, we will take a closer look at the SQL statements and the subtle nuances of programming SQL statements in JDBC.

SQL Basics in JDBC

In the center of every JDBC statement object is an SQL statement or, more accurately, a string representing an SQL statement. In most cases, the SQL statement and the JDBC representation are exactly the same. However, in some instances, you must modify the JDBC string to ensure that the database receives the intended SQL statement. For our purposes, any string that is identical to the SQL statement is referred to as a *simple* SQL statement, while those requiring special handling or modification are considered *complex*.

Simple Queries

Queries are one of the most basic forms of SQL statements. They are used to return data from a table. In JDBC, all queries return results in the form of a `ResultSet` object. As we saw earlier, the most efficient way to execute a query is to use the Statement `executeQuery()` method. The `execute-Query()` method takes the SQL query string as an argument and returns a `ResultSet` containing the selected data. Here is a short example of a simple query:

```
SQL:      SELECT price, part_number FROM inventory;

JDBC:     String sqlString = "SELECT price, part_number FROM
                             inventory";
```

For simple SQL statements, the SQL and JDBC strings are identical. No special handling is required. Here is what the relevant Java code would look like:

```
String sqlString = "SELECT price, part_number FROM inventory"
Statement stmt = conn.createStatement();
ResultSet rs = stmt.executeQuery(sqlString);
```

We could just as easily have added a WHERE clause to the above example without any difficulties. For example:

```
SQL:      SELECT price, part_number FROM inventory
          WHERE price > 100;
JDBC:     String sqlString = "SELECT price, part_number
                             FROM inventory"
                           + "WHERE price > 100"
```

While SQL is a very powerful and useful language, it can be a bit verbose at times. Often you will find that SQL statements get very long and it is much easier to view and manage them when they are broken up into multiple lines. However, Java does not allow you to `carryover` a string declaration from one line to the other without explicitly concatenating the lines with a plus sign (+). For uniformity and easier readability, I prefer to put the (+) at the beginning of the second line where it is more visible. Whenever more than one clause is used in a statement, each is placed on a separate line to improve readability. Of course, this is a stylistic choice and you may choose to keep the entire statement on one line if you prefer.

Other clauses could have been added, as well. The following example shows a very complex looking SQL statement that is actually considered a simple query.

```
SQL:        SELECT * FROM employee
              WHERE salary > 100 AND NOT (salary > 1000)
              GROUP BY department_id
              ODER BY last_name;

JDBC:       String sqlString = ("SELECT * FROM employee"
                        + "WHERE salary > 100 AND NOT (salary > 1000)"
                        + "GROUP BY department_id "
                        + "ODER BY last_name ";
```

Essentially, any SQL query that does not contain any double quotes, formatting commands, or functions is simple and should not need any special handling.

Simple Updates

SQL update statements do not return data results as `ResultSets`, but rather return an integer representing the number of rows affected by that statement. Therefore, you cannot use the same method for executing a statement that returns a `ResultSet` as you do for one that returns an integer. For updates, the `Statement` object and the `executeUpdate()` method should be used. This method takes the SQL string as an argument and returns the required integer value. Here is a short example of an INSERT statement:

```
SQL:       INSERT INTO inventory (price)
             VALUES ( 101)
             WHERE price > 100;

JDBC:      String sqlString = "INSERT INTO inventory (price)"
                        + "VALUES(101)"
                        + "WHERE price > 100";
```

To execute this example above we need to use the `Statement.execute-Update()` method. Here is a code fragment showing what that would look like:

```
String sqlString = "INSERT INTO inventory (price)"
                  + "VALUES(101)"
                  + "WHERE price > 100";

Statement stmt = conn.createStatement();
int rowcount = stmt.executeUpdate(sqlString);
```

As we saw in the `executeQuery()` example, the SQL statement remains the same as its original SQL code. No modification or special handling is required for simple update statements.

Any SQL statement that modifies existing data, deletes, or inserts new data in a
table is considered an update statement.

Simple DDL Statements

Up until now, we have concentrated our efforts on DML (Data Manipulation
Language) and SQL statements. Now let's turn our attention to DDL (Data
Definition Language) statements.

Recall that DDL statements are used to modify the structure of the database. These statements create tables, add columns to existing tables, add constraints, delete tables, and a wide variety of other database management operations. Since DDL statements do not perform any query they do not return a
ResultSet. Similarily, they do not affect any rows in a table either, and therefore do not need to return a row count. However, in order to keep DDL statements consistent with all other types of SQL statements, DDL statements
always return a value of 0. This ensures that the methods for determining the
type and number of results discussed in Chapter 6 remain consistant. Here is
an example of a DDL statement that creates a new table "testtable."

```
SQL:       CREATE TABLE testtable
           ( testname VARCHAR2(24),
            testint int );

JDBC:      String sqlstring = (" CREATE TABLE testtable"
                             + "( testname VARCHAR2(24), "
                             + " testint int );
           Statement stmt = conn.createStatement()
           stmt.execute(sqlstring);
```

Since there are no meaningful results returned by a DDL statement, I simply
ignore the results. The only indication of whether or not the execution failed
will be if an SQLException was thrown.

Complex SQL Statements

Handling Double Quotes in a SQL Statement

In the previous sections, I stated that you can copy any simple SQL statement
from its original SQL form directly into a JDBC string with no modification
whatsoever. However, if the original SQL statement has double quotes in it,
the statement will need to be modified in order for it to interpreted correctly.
For example, most databases will allow you to specify a temporary column

header name for a column by placing the new column name in double quotes following the original column name.

```
SQL:      SELECT price "Retail Price" from inventory;

JDBC:     String sqlstring = ("SELECT price "Retail Price"
                              + from inventory");
          // This will not compile.
```

In cases where double quotes are used, you must "escape" the quote marks you do not want interpreted by the Java compiler. Java uses the front slash (/) as the escape character. Here is what the correct string assignment for the example above would look like.

```
JDBC:     String sqlstring = ("SELECT price "Retail Price"
                              + from inventory");
```

Java does not use single quote (' or `) marks as delimiters. Quoting of single quotes is not necessary.

SQL Statements Containing the LIKE Operator

The LIKE operator is used to compare two strings using pattern matching. In LIKE operations, the percent (%) and underbar (_) are used as pattern matching characters. The percent is used to match zero or more characters and the underbar is used to match a single character. In general, this poses no problem in JDBC applications because neither of these two characters is interpreted by Java as having any special meaning. For example:

```
SQL:      SELECT part_name FROM inventory
          WHERE part_name LIKE 'CDROM%'

JDBC:     String sqlstring = "SELECT part_name FROM inventory"
                             + "WHERE part_name LIKE 'CDROM%'";
```

The example above is perfectly legal and will compile without any problems. However, in some cases, the percent (%) or the underbar (_) need to be interpreted as a literal string. The solution to this problem is to precede the percent or underbar with an escape character. In most databases, as in Java, this is the front slash (\). For example, let's suppose that we want to find all the part names in our database that begin with an underbar:

```
SQL:      SELECT part_name FROM inventory
          WHERE part_name LIKE '\_'

JDBC:     String sqlstring = "SELECT part_name FROM inventory"
                             + "WHERE part_name LIKE '\_'"
```

While this statement looks correct and will compile, the results you get from the SQL statement and executing the JDBC statement will be vastly different. The reason for this is that the Java compiler will interpret the forward slash as a special character, and strip the character from the string. In our example, that means the string that is actually sent to the database looks like this:

```
SELECT part_name FROM inventory WHERE part_name LIKE '_'
```

Of course this is not what we had intended. This statement will only return a list of parts that match the name "_" exactly, not all the ones that begin with an underbar. So what is the solution to this particular annoyance? Actually there are two. The first is to simply change the escape character for that particular statement. Most databases will allow you to specify any character you want to be the escape character by adding the ESCAPE clause to the end of the statement. For instance, we could change the escape character to a tilde (~) in our statement as demonstrated below.

```
SQL:      SELECT part_name FROM inventory
          WHERE part_name LIKE '~_'
          ESCAPE '~'

JDBC:     String sqlstring = "SELECT part_name FROM inventory"
                    + "WHERE part_name LIKE '~_' "
                    + "ESCAPE '~' ";
```

Since Java does not affix any special meaning to the tilde, it will not attempt to strip it from the string. Once passed to the database, it is the database compiler that will interpret the meaning of the tilde.

 If your database does not use the keyword "ESCAPE," JDBC provides a database-independent method for setting the escape character. Later in this chapter, I will show you how to use JDBC *escape syntax* to set the database *escape character*.

The second method of protecting escape characters from being interpreted by Java is to escape the escape character. Here is what that would look like:

```
SQL:      SELECT part_name FROM inventory
          WHERE part_name LIKE '\\_'

JDBC:     String sqlstring = "SELECT part_name FROM inventory"
                    + "WHERE part_name LIKE '\\_'"
```

While this may seem a bit redundant, it does make sense. Java will see the first escape and interpret it to mean "treat the next character as a literal." It will then strip the first escape character from the string, leaving the second one intact. The string is then sent to the database to be interpreted. In this case, the statement sent is what we had originally intended.

```
SELECT part_name FROM inventory WHERE part_name LIKE '\_'
```

JDBC Escape Syntax

In Chapter 2, I had mentioned that JDBC does not check the SQL grammar and therefore you can send any SQL statement to a database. This means that if your particular vendor supports extended functions other than those specified in the entry level SQL92 standard, you are free to use them. I had also mentioned that a subset of these extensions is widely used by most database vendors, though each may have its own syntax for them. To support these extensions in a database independent manner, JDBC implements an ODBC-style escape syntax for many of these extensions. By using escape syntax, applications can achieve total database independence and still take advantage of the additional functionality.

Escape syntax works much like the escape character we saw earlier in this chapter. The escape syntax consists of a keyword and parameters all enclosed in curly braces(({}).

```
{ keyword [parameter], ... }
```

When JDBC finds a set of curly braces in an executable `string`, the driver maps the enclosed keyword and parameter(s) to the database-specific syntax. The new syntax is then sent to the database for execution.

JDBC escape syntax supports seven keywords, each of which indicates the type of extension that is enclosed within the braces. Table 7.1 is a listing of the keywords and their syntax.

Table 7.1
Keywords and their syntax.

Keyword	Used for	Syntax
call	Execute stored procedures.	{ call procedure_name [arg1,...] }
?= call	Execute stored functions.	{ ?= call function_name [arg1,...] }
d	Define a date.	{ d `yyyy-mm-dd`}
escape	Define the databases escape character.	{ escape `escape character`}
fn	Execute a scalar function.	{ `fn function [arg1,...] }
oj	Define an outer join.	{ oj outer-join }
t	Define a time.	{ `hh:mm:ss` }
ts	Define a time stamp.	{ `yyyy-mm-dd hh:mm:ss.f....` }

Calling Stored Procedures and Functions

Nearly all RDBMS support stored procedures and functions. To ensure that your application does not rely on a vendor-specific implementation of stored procedure calls or stored function calls, the following escape syntax should be used.

For stored procedures that have no IN or OUT parameters:

```
CallableStatement cs = conn.prepareCall ("{call get_inventory () }");
```

For stored procedures that use IN or OUT parameters, simply add the proper number of "?" as place holders:

```
CallableStatement cs = conn.prepareCall ("{call get_inventory (?, ?,
?) }");
cs.setInt(1,50);
cs.setString(2,"CDROM");
cs.setInt(3,100);
```

Stored functions are executed in the same manner, except that the returned results must be assigned to a registered OUT parameter:

```
CallableStatement cs = conn.prepareCall ("{ ? = call calculate_profit
(?, ?, ?) }");
cs.registerOutParameter(1,Types.NUMERIC);
cs.setInt(2,50);
cs.setString(3,"CDROM");
cs.setInt(4,100);
```

Note that in the stored function example, the first parameter is registered as an OUT parameter and that the first IN parameter is actually in the second position. Remember that the place holders are numbered sequentially from left to right, regardless of their position relative to the equal "=" sign.

For simplicity, examples in the previous sections used the command EXECUTE for the execution of stored procedures. However, the EXECUTE command may not be appropriate for all databases. Whenever a stored procedure or function is to be called, the appropriate escape syntax should be used.

Escape Characters

In some rare cases it may become necessary to specify a different escape character than the default value for the database. This is normally only required in instances where an escape character needs to be interpreted by the database and where the default database escape character is the same as the one in Java, e.g., the backslash ("/"). This will only occur in instances where the "%" and "_" characters are used in a LIKE clause and need to be interpreted literally rather than as special characters. In the following example, I use the JDBC escape syntax to set the database escape character to set the tilde "~." This is similar to the example earlier.

```
String sqlstring = "SELECT part_name FROM inventory"
                + "WHERE part_name LIKE '~_' {escape '~'} ";
Statement stmt = conn.createStatement();
stmt.execute(sqlstring);
```

Here, Java ignores the tilde and treats it as a literal string. The database, however, interprets the tilde as a special character and knows to escape the following underbar character.

Time and Date Literals

Obviously, all RDBMS must support time and date literals. However, as anyone who has ever done any database programming knows, there can be many variations on the format used to represent them. Here is a short list of some different date formats to illustrate my point.

July 1, 1965	7/01/65	7-1-1965
Jul 1, 1965	7/01/1965	1965-07-01
Jul 01, 1965	7-01-65	65-07-01

Which format does your database support? In many cases, all of them, while in some cases perhaps none of them. Therefore, to ensure that all JDBC applications can read and write time and dates uniformly across all databases, escape syntax for dates, times, and time/date stamps are supported. As with all escape syntax, the JDBC driver is responsible for interpreting the escape clause and converting it to the appropriate database format.

The escape syntax format for dates is:

```
{ d `yyyy-mm-dd' }
```

Where: yyyy = Four digit year
       mm = Two digit month
       dd = Two digit day

Here is an example of how you would use the date escape syntax to select all employees in the employee table hired on January 1, 1995.

```
String sqlstring = "SELECT employee_id FROM employees"
                    + "WHERE hire_date = {d `1995-01-30' }");
    Statement stmt = conn.createStatement();
    stmt.execute(sqlstring);
```

In addition to dates, JDBC also supports escape syntax for time literals. Time escape syntax uses the following format:

```
{ t `hh:mm:ss[.f.f...] ' }
```

Where hh = The hour represented in 24-hour (military) time.
      mm = Number of minutes.
      ss = Number of seconds.
(optional) f = Fraction of a second.

Time stamps are simply the concatenation of the data and time formats:

```
{ ts `yyyy -mm-dd hh:mm:ss[.f.f...]' }
```

Modifying the previous example to include the time 1:45 p.m. we have:

```
String sqlstring = "SELECT employee_id FROM employees"
                    + "WHERE hire_date =
                    {ts `1995-01-30 13:45:00.0' }");
    Statement stmt = conn.createStatement();
    stmt.execute(sqlstring);
```

Scalar Functions

Although widely implemented by RDBMS vendors, scalar functions are not quite as universal as date/time literals or stored procedures. As a result of this, JDBC drivers are not required to support scalar functions as they are other escape syntax. If you plan to use scalar functions in your application, you must first determine if your RDBMS and driver supports them. Chapter 10 details how you can use methods in the `DatabaseMetaData` class to do this.

All scalar functions use the same escape syntax:

```
{ fn FunctionName(function parameter 1, ....) }
```

The following tables (Tables 7.2–7.5) list all scalar functions and their parameters currently supported by JDBC.

Table 7.2
Numeric Scalar
Functions

ABS (number)	EXP (float)	RAND (integer)
ACOS (float)	FLOOR (number)	ROUND
(number,places)		
ASIN (float)	LOG (float)	SIGN (number)
ATAN (float)	LOG10 (float)	SIN (float)
ATAN2 (float1,float2)	MOD (integer1,integer2)	SQRT (float)
CEILING (number)	PI ()	TAN (float)
COS (float)	POWER (number,power)	TRUNCATE (number,places)
DEGREES (number)	RADIANS (number)	

Table 7.3
String Scalar
Functions

ASCII (string)	LTRIM (string)
CHAR (code)	REPEAT (string,count)
CONCAT (string1,string2)	REPLACE (string1,string2,string3)
DIFFERENCE (string1, string2)	RIGHT (string,count)
INSERT (string1,start,length,string2)	RTRIM (string)
LCASE (string)	SOUNDEX (string)
LEFT (string,count)	SPACE (count)
LENGTH (string)	SUBSTRING (string,start,length)
LOCATE (string1,string2,start)	UCASE (string)

Table 7.4
Time/Date Scalar
Functions

CURDATE ( )	HOUR (time)	SECOND (time)
CURTIME ( )	MINUTE (time)	TIMESTAMPADD (interval,count,timestamp)
DAYNAME (date)	MONTH (time)	TIMESTAMPDIFF (interval,timestamp1, timestamp2)
DAYOFMONTH (date)	MONTHNAME (time)	WEEK (date)
DAYOFWEEK (date)	NOW ( )	YEAR (date)
DAYOFYEAR (date)	QUARTER (date)	

Table 7.5
System Scalar
Functions

| DATABASE () |
| IFNULL (expression,value) |
| USER () |

The final scalar function is the CONVERT function. The CONVERT function accepts two parameters, the first is the value to be converted, and the second is the SQL type to convert the first parameter. The syntax for convert is as follows:

```
{ fn CONVERT (value,SQLtype) }
```

For example, to convert a string into a VARCHAR SQL type, you would use:

```
{ fn CONVERT ("this is a string", VARCHAR) }
```

Table 7.6 contains a list of all valid SQL types that can be used with the CONVERT function.

Table 7.6
SQL Types for
Use with CONVERT
Function

BIGINT	DOUBLE	SMALLINT
BINARY	FLOAT	TIME
BIT	INTEGER	TIMESTAMP
CHAR	LONGVARBINARY	TINYINT
DATE	LONGVARCHAR	VARBINARY
DECIMAL	REAL	VARCHAR

Outer Joins

The last SQL escape syntax to be examined is the outer join. Outer joins are considered a fairly advanced feature, but often provide the only means to retrieve certain data. Outer joins, unlike inner joins, preserve unmatched rows from one or both joined tables. For instance, suppose we have the following two tables, each with two columns:

Example: Users
Database Table 1

User_ID	User_Name
T22551	Bob
T33111	Sue
T44331	Bill

Example: Orders
Database Table 2

User_ID	Order_Num
T22551	1001
T33111	1002
T44331	1003

Now, let's say you wanted a list of all outstanding orders and wanted to include the User_Name. You might use the following inner join (simple join):

```
SELECT users.User_Name, users.User_ID,orders.Order_Num
FROM users, orders
WHERE user.User_ID = orders.User_ID;
```

The results would be:

```
Bob   T22551    1001
Sue   T33111    1002
```

As you can see, although User_ID T55555 has an outstanding order, the order does not show up in the results. This is probably not what we really wanted. The reason for this is that there is no User_Name that correlates with the User_ID T55555. To solve this problem, you must use an outer join to ensure that all unmatched rows are included in the results. (Later, I will show you an example for this.)

The syntax for outer joins is as follows:

```
{ oj outer-join-statement }
```

Outer joins come in several different flavors: FULL , LEFT, and RIGHT. LEFT outer joins preserve the unmatched rows contained in the table on the left side of the FROM clause, while RIGHT outer joins preserve data from tables on the right side; FULL preserves unmatched rows from both. For example, to preserve the unmatched rows of data in table "orders" you could use the following:

```
SELECT users.User_Name, users.User_ID,orders.Order_Num
FROM users RIGHT OUTER JOIN order
ON user.User_ID = orders.User_ID;
```

JDBC, however, only supports LEFT outer joins. While this may seem to be a fairly harsh restriction, in fact, it is not since any RIGHT or FULL outer join statement can be manipulated into a LEFT only outer join statement. All *outer join statements* in JDBC have the following syntax:

```
table LEFT OUTER JOIN { table | outer-join-statement } ON search-
                      condition
```

Using a LEFT outer join, we can rewrite our previous SQL example to retrieve a list of all outstanding orders.

```
SELECT users.User_Name, users.User_ID,orders.Order_Num
FROM orders LEFT OUTER JOIN users
ON user.User_ID = orders.User_ID;
```

The results of this statement will be:

```
Bob     T22551    1001
Sue     T33111    1002
null    T5555     1003
```

However, if we wanted to retrieve all unmatched rows from both tables, we would need to use a recursive outer join statement.

```
SELECT users.User_Name, users.User_ID,orders.Order_Num
FROM orders LEFT OUTER JOIN ON
(
SELECT users.User_Name, users.User_ID,orders.Order_Num
FROM users LEFT OUTER JOIN orders ON user.User_ID = orders.User_ID
)

ON user.User_ID = orders.User_ID;
```

The results of this statement are:

```
Bob     T22551    1001
Sue     T33111    1002
Bill    T44331    null
null    T5555     1003
```

Executing SQL outer joins within JDBC is the same as executing any other SQL. An outer join statement requires no special handling outside of using the proper escape syntax. Here is a code fragment to execute the double outer join shown above.

```
String sqlstring = "SELECT users.User_Name,
users.User_ID,orders.Order_Num"
        + "FROM orders LEFT OUTER JOIN ON ("
        +" SELECT users.User_Name, "
        +" users.User_ID,orders.Order_Num "
```

```
              +" FROM users LEFT OUTER JOIN orders"
              +" ON user.User_ID = orders.User_ID"
              +" )"

              + "ON user.User_ID = orders.User_ID "

Statement stmt = conn.createStatement();
ResultSet rs = stmt.executeQuery({ oj sqlstring });
```

Chapter Summary

In this chapter, you saw how SQL statements are used in JDBC applications. For simple queries and updates, modifications to the SQL statement string are not necessary. For statements that involve passing literal strings to the database in double quotes, the backslash must precede the double quote marks. Finally, you saw how JDBC provides escape syntax to provide uniform access to advanced features such as scalar numeric functions and outer joins. At this point, you should be very comfortable with all aspects of creating and executing SQL statements within JDBC.

What's Next

In Chapter 8, we will be examining the ResultSet objects. I will demonstrate how to use the ResultSet "get" methods to retrieve data and how to handle SQL to Java data type conversions. It's a short but very important chapter.

CHAPTER 8

Working with Results: The ResultSet Object

Now that you have learned how to create connections to the database, manage drivers and execute SQL statements, it is time to turn our attention to the details of how to process the results of these endeavors. In Chapters 6 and 7, we saw how to create `ResultSet` objects, pass IN and OUT variables and determine the number of rows affected by an update. In this chapter we will concentrate on the methods used to retrieve and process the actual data contained in the `ResultSet`. We will also take a look at the `getMetaData()` method. `ResultSet` meta data tells us vital information about our data, such as title, display width, data type and write permissions of each column of data. Armed with this information, you can create highly sophisticated and dynamic data processing algorithims for your applications.

Getting the ResultSet

As demonstrated in previous chapters, data from SQL queries is returned to your application in `ResultSet` objects. The `ResultSet` object is created by either the `executeQuery()` method or the `getResultSet()` method.

Data is stored in the `ResultSet` just as it is returned by the database, i.e., it is stored in tabular format. Each field of the database can be described by a unique combination of a row ID and column ID, much like a two-dimensional array. The `ResultSet` places no restriction as to what type of data can be retrieved into the `ResultSet` provided that all data stored in a single column is of the same data. A column therefore can be easily modeled as an `array`, since all of the data in a single column must be of the same type. Similarily, a row is a set of related data that may or may not be all of the same data type. A row therefore, is more easily represented in a `Vector`. Putting the two together, you can see that the most convenient way to model the entire table is to create an array of `Vectors`. This will come in very handy when you start retrieving data from the `ResultSet` and you need to store it in some sort of logical Java structure.

Now that we understand how we can structure data to look like a table, we are ready to begin the process of getting the data out of `ResultSet` and into our own structure. The first step in this process is to retrieve the data from the `ResultSet`.

As with many objects in JDBC, the `ResultSet` object is dependent on several other objects that must be created beforehand. A `ResultSet` cannot exist without an associated `Statement` object, just as a `Statement` object cannot exist without a `Connection`. Accordingly, each time you execute a SQL statement with a statement object, the `ResultSet` is overwritten with the new results. You must ensure that you have completely processed the current `ResultSet` before closing the `Statement` object.

Processing ResultSets

Once the `ResultSet` object is created, an appropriate `ResultSet` "get" method is used to access data. Since the data is in tabular format, any data can be retrieved by using the column and row ordinals. Columns can be referenced explicitly by an index number or by name. The row is determined by a cursor that points to the current row. In order for you to process a single row, you advance the row cursor to that row and then execute the appropriate "get" method with a column index as the argument.

Determining the Row

Each row of data must be processed in the order in which they are returned. As stated above, a cursor is used to determine the current row. The current row is the only row available to any "get" method. To navigate through the entire ResultSet and process each row, you use the next() method. The next() method moves the row pointer from its current position to the next row. The next() method will return a true value each time it advances to a row containing data. Once the the cursor points to a null row, then false is returned. Figure 8.1 demonstrates the next() method.

Figure 8.1
Row pointer
positioning diagram.

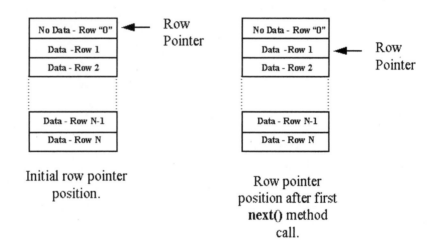

Initial row pointer
position.

Row pointer
position after first
next() method
call.

As indicated in the diagram, the row cusor is initially set just before the first row of data. Prior to accessing your first row of data, you must execute the next() method to advance the row cursor to the first row. This is done so that you can easily implement a while loop to process each row without having a special case for the first row. By calling the next() method after each row is processed, you can successively access each row in the Result-Set. Here is an example of how you would use a while loop to access all the data contained in the first column of a ResultSet.

```
ResultSet rs1 = stmt1.getResultSet();

while (rs1.next()) {
```

```
String dept_name = rs1.getString (1);

}
```

The next () *method is the only method provided to facilitate navigation through the rows. You cannot go back to a previous row once it has been passed. Before calling the* next () *method, ensure that you have retrieved all data you need from the current row.*

Determining the Column

The second step to retrieving your data from the ResultSet is to determine what column you need. Each "get" method has two forms. One form takes the column name as an argument while the other takes the column index number. For example, the following code uses the column name as the argument passed to the getString() method:

```
Statement stmt1 = conn1.createStatemtent();

stmt1.executeQuery ("select department_id, dept_name,
                          + manager from department");

ResultSet rs1 = stmt1.getResultSet();

while (rs1.next()) {

     String dept_name = rs1.getString ("dept_name");
     System.out.println(dept_name);
}
```

In this example, I explicity used the column name "dept_name" as the argument to the getString() method. Placing it in the while loop, I iterated through each row and "got" the string value contained in each row's "dept_name" coulmn. For applications that access pre-defined or well-known tables, using the column name is a very convenient method for the developer. It also ensures that, even if the structure of a table is modified, the proper row is retrieved.

Columns appear in the ResultSet in the same order in which they are listed in the SQL statmenet. If individual columns are not specified (wild cards are used), then the order in which they appear in the database is used.

In instances were the column name is not known at compile time, you can use the index number as the argement to the "get" methods. In the previous example, I could have just as easily used the column index number for the "dept_name":

```
Statement stmt1 = conn1.createStatemtent();

stmt1.executeQuery ("select department_id, dept_name,
                       + manager+ from department");

ResultSet rs1 = stmt1.getResultSet();

while (rs1.next()) {

      String deptname = rs1.getString (2);

}
```

In the above example, "department_id" has an index number of 1, "dept_name" has index number 2, and "manager" number 3. Since I only wanted the department name, I only retrieved the values from column number 1.

The `ResultSet` interface also provides a method that enables you to determine the column index number from the column name. The `findColumn()` method takes the column name as an argument and returns the index number of that column. Here is an example of the `findColumn` method:

```
Statement stmt1 = conn1.createStatemtent();

      stmt1.executeQuery ("select department_id, dept_name, manager
                             + from department");

      ResultSet rs1 = stmt1.getResultSet();
      int colNum = stmt1.findColumn(deptname);
      while (rs1.next()) {

            String deptname = rs1.getString (colNum);

      }
```

If a "*" is used as the column selection, then the index order is the same as the table itself.

Dynamic Column Names

Some databases allow you to dynamically create an alias for a selected column within the SQL statement. This is done to either simplify long column names or make the column heading more readable. Aliases are also often used in conjunction with a scalar function. For example:

```
SELECT dept_id "Department ID" from departments;
```

In JDBC, this becomes:

```
String sql = "SELECT dept_id \"Department ID\" from departments";
```

To use a "get" method to retrieve data from a column with an alias, you must either use the alias given or the column index. For example:

```
Statement stmt1 = conn1.createStatemtent();

String sql = "SELECT dept_id \"Department_ID\" from
                                    departments;"

stmt1.executeQuery (sql);

ResultSet rs1 = stmt1.getResultSet();

while (rs1.next()) {

    String deptname = rs1.getString ("Department ID");
    System.out.println(deptname);
}
```

Using the "get" Methods

Simlar to the `CallableStatement` "get" methods, each `ResultSet` "get" method is used to retrieve the value of a data field of a particular type. Each `ResultSet` "get" method can take either a column name (a string value) or an index number. The `ResultSet` "get" methods can be put into three separate catagories: primitive data type methods, object methods, and stream methods. With the exception of the `BigDecimal()` method, the syntax for all of the `ResultSet` "get" methods is the same:

```
getNNN (Integer);
```

or

```
getNNN(String);
```

Where: NNN = The data type of the feild.
        Integer = The column index number.
        String = The column name.

The `getBigDecimal()` method syntax is only slightly different, in that it specifies the scale of the value:

```
getBigDecimal (Integer,Integer2);
```

or
```
getBigDecimal(String,Integer2);
```

Where: Integer = The column index number.

String = The column name.

Integer2 = The scale of the value. (the number of digits to the
right of the decimal point)

Here is a list of all the "get" methods:

- getBoolean
- getByte
- getInt
- getLong
- getFloat
- getDouble
- getNull
- getShort
- getBigDecimal
- getBytes
- getDate
- getTime
- getString
- getObject
- getTimeStamp
- getAsciiStream
- getUnicodeStream
- getBinaryStream

Data Conversion

Each "get" method will attempt to retrieve the value of the data in a specified
column of the current row. However, there are limitations to the values that a
particular "get" can retrieve. Since not all SQL data types can be mapped to
all Java types, you must use an appropriate "get" method to retrieve the data
and convert it to a Java type. However, appropriate is a somewhat fluid term
and is not always obvious.

To determine the appropriate "get" method to use, you will need to determine three things. First, you will need to determine the SQL data type for
the column. You will then need to check and see which of the "get" methods
are capable of retrieving that particular SQL data type. (Table 8.1 shows
which get method is compatible with which SQL data types.) Finally, you will
need to decide what Java data type the application requires. Once you have
assembled all three pieces of information, you are ready to pick the appropriate "get"method.

For example, let's say I have a date column in my database. From the conversion matrix Table 8.1, I can see that an SQL date can be retrieved using
the getDate(), getString(), getTimeStamp(), or getObject()
method. This limits my choices but still does not tell us exactly which method
to use. To make our final selection, we need to look at what the application
requirements are. Let's further suppose that I intend to retrieve that date,
add a week to it, and then update the database with the new date. In this
instance, it would make sense to retrieve that date using the getDate()
method which converts the SQL data format and returns it as a Java Date
object. You can then manipulate the Date object within Java.

Now let's suppose that my application only allows me to view data (as with
the Database Browser application in Part 3). What would I gain by having a

Date object? Most likely, I will have to convert the Date object to a String before I can display it anyway. In this instance, using the get-String() method would be more appropriate.

One way around this process is to use the getObject() method. The getObject method will retrieve any SQL data type and automatically convert it to the "preferred" Java data type (indicated with an ● in the matrix). The advantage of this is that you will never have to know what SQL type the data is. The disadvantage of this is that it does not take into account the needs of your application. For example, let's assume that we again have a date column in our table and we only want to display the date as a String. If the getObject() method is used the object returned is a Date object. If your application expects a String, you will have to explicitly convert the Java Date object to a String.

Table 8.1
ResultSet "get" method to SQL data type conversions.

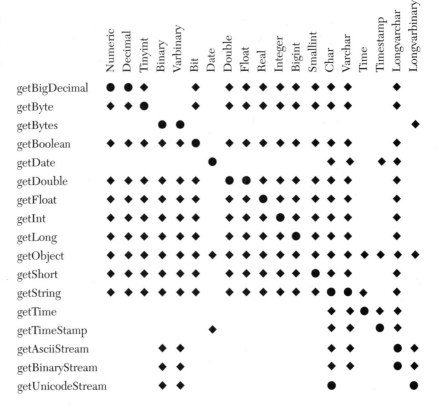

Method	Numeric	Decimal	Tinyint	Binary	Varbinary	Bit	Date	Double	Float	Real	Integer	Bigint	Smallint	Char	Varchar	Time	Timestamp	Longvarchar	Longvarbinary
getBigDecimal	●	●	◆			◆		◆	◆	◆	◆	◆	◆	◆	◆			◆	
getByte	◆	◆	●			◆		◆	◆	◆	◆	◆	◆	◆	◆			◆	
getBytes				●	●														◆
getBoolean	◆	◆	◆	◆	◆	●		◆	◆	◆	◆	◆	◆	◆	◆			◆	
getDate							●							◆	◆		◆	◆	
getDouble	◆	◆	◆	◆	◆			●	●	◆	◆	◆	◆	◆	◆			◆	
getFloat	◆	◆	◆	◆	◆			◆	◆	●	◆	◆	◆	◆	◆			◆	
getInt	◆	◆	◆	◆	◆			◆	◆	◆	●	◆	◆	◆	◆			◆	
getLong	◆	◆	◆	◆	◆			◆	◆	◆	◆	●	◆	◆	◆			◆	
getObject	◆	◆	◆	◆	◆	◆	◆	◆	◆	◆	◆	◆	◆	◆	◆	◆	◆	◆	◆
getShort	◆	◆	◆	◆	◆			◆	◆	◆	◆	◆	●	◆	◆			◆	
getString	◆	◆	◆	◆	◆			◆	◆	◆	◆	◆	◆	●	●	◆		◆	
getTime														◆	◆	●	◆	◆	
getTimeStamp							◆							◆	◆		●	◆	
getAsciiStream				◆	◆									◆	◆			●	◆
getBinaryStream				◆	◆									◆	◆			●	◆
getUnicodeStream				◆	◆									●					●

◆ = Method is capable of retrieving this SQL data type.
● = Preferred "get" method for this SQL data type.

In most cases, you will need to do some form of data conversion. You can choose to either do the conversion at data retrieval time by using one of the "get" methods that return a specific Java type or by using the getObject() method and doing the conversion after retrieval. The method for data conversion that you choose will depend on your application.

The getMetaData Method

The ResultSetMetaData object provides methods for discovering information about the structure and context of data returned to a ResultSet. To create a ResultSetMetaData object for the associated ResultSet use the getMetaData() method as shown below.

```
stmt1.executeQuery (sql);
ResultSet rs1 = stmt1.getResultSet();
ResultSetMetaData rsmd = rs1.getMetaData();
```

Information included in the ResultSetMetaData object is vital to applications that access random databases and tables. This includes the number of columns returned, the preferred column name, and the column display width. Additional information on the original context of the column such as the schema, table, and catalog form which it was retrieved from can also be discovered. As you can see, the ResultSetMetaData object has many uses. For a complete discussion on the application and implementation of the ResultSetMetaData class, please refer to Chapter 9.

ResultSet Management

As with most of the objects in the java.sql package, the ResultSet interface provides several methods for the management of the object itself. These methods are similar to methods of the same name in other classes. You should be able to deduce their usage and application from their names and previous discussions. They are:

- clearWarnings()
- close()
- getWarnings()

Chapter Summary

In this chapter, we have learned how to actually process the data returned in a `ResultSet` object. You also learned how to convert data from SQL data types to Java data types and how to use the `getObject()` method to automatically perform the conversion for you. By now, you should be very comfortable with all of the "get" methods and their syntax.

What's Next

This chapter rounded out the list of classes that were listed in Chapter 3 as being the seven essential steps of JDBC programming. While the information contained in the next chapter may not be considered a requirement for every application, it does provide invaluable information for the creation of dynamic and extensible ones. The next chapter will discuss the details of the `ResultSetMetaData` class. In it, you will learn how to uncover all of the hidden information that is so vital to creating data independent applications.

CHAPTER 9

Using Result Set Meta Data:
The ResultSetMetaData Interface

In Chapter 3, I introduced the ResultSetMetaData interface and later in Chapter 8 discussed how to create a ResultSetMetaData object. In this chapter, I will show you how to use the methods in the ResultSetMetaData object to create data source independent applications. By using the ResultSetMetaData object you will be able to dynamically discover information about the structure and properties of results. This means that your application will not require previous knowledge of the data or database structure. By using result set meta data, you can write entire applications without even knowing what RDBMS, tables, or types of data to be accessed.

The getColumnCount Method

While all of the methods in the `ResultSetMetaData` interface are useful, the `getColumnCount()` method surely ranks near the top of the "most useful methods" list. This method is used to simply return the number or columns in a `ResultSet`. Although this may seem unimportant and perhaps even a bit trivial, the impact this method has on applications is immense. For example, let's suppose we are using the following code fragment to process data from a query:

```
while (rs1.next()) {

            String deptname = rs1.getString ("dept_id");
            System.out.println(deptname);
            String dept_id = rs1.getString("dept_id");
            System.out.println(dept_id);
            String dept_manager = rs1.getString("dept_manager");
            System.out.println(dept_manager);

       }
```

In this short example, you can see that, in order to process each column of data, I must have prior knowledge of the column name of the queried table. This can be a very serious limitation. For instance, what will happen if the column name is changed? How can you write applications that allow users to enter adhoc queries?

As you may have already surmised by now, the simplest solution to this problem is to use the `getColumnCount()` method to determine the number of columns in the `ResultSet`, and then use the column index number to retrieve each column. Here is a short example:

```
ResultSetMetaData rsmd1 = rs.getMetaData

while (rs1.next()) {
    for ( int i = 1; i <= rsmd1.getColumnCount(); i ++)
        {
         System.out.println( rs1.getString (i));
        }

    }
```

Note that the `getColumnCount()` method greatly simplifies the processing of each column of data. You no longer need prior knowledge to the names or even the number of columns in the `ResultSet`. By using the `for` loop in conjunction with the `next` method within a `while` loop, you are able to dynamically process each column of every row. All of this with three lines of code!

Determining Column Titles

While the `getColumnCount()` method is extremely useful by itself, it does not solve all the problems associated with creating dynamic applications. One problem that must be addressed is how columns are to be labeled when they are displayed. While most programmers don't mind referring to columns by their index number, end users are more likely to want column headings that actually have meaning. For instance, a column labeled "1" is great for a programmer since it will work with a loop counter quite nicely, but a user might find "qty_onhand" more useful. However, to an end user, "First Name" would be much more meaningful.

To address this need, the `ResultSetMetaData` provides two methods that will return an appropriate title for a column. The first method to look at is the `getColumnName()` method. As its name would suggest, the `getColumnName()` method returns the name of a column. The `getColumnName()` method takes the column index number as an argument and returns a string representing the name of the column as defined in the database.

The second method is the `getColumnLabel()` method. This method is very similar to the `getColumnName()` method, in that it takes the column index number as an argument and returns a title for the column. However, the title returned by this method is not determined by the table structure, but rather returns any alternate name that has been assigned to that column.

Alternate names are often assigned after the creation of the table and are usually created to make column names more readable. For instance, a table might have a column name "PercTotRet." This name might have a great deal of meaning to the database administrator that created it, but an end user could understandably be confused by such a title. However, an alternate name of "Percent Total Returned " might be defined for this column. Therefore, to get the "preferred" name, you would use the `getColumnLabel()` method.

The `getColumnLabel()` will only return a value if an alternate name is defined for the column. If an alternate name is not specified, then null is returned. Thus, you cannot simply replace the `getColumnName()` method with the `getColumnLabel()` method. Only the `getColumnName()` method is guarenteed to have a non-null return value. The following example shows how to create a method called `getColumnTitle()` that will return the preferred column name for a column if it exists, and if not, returns the column name as defined in the table definition.

```
public String getColumnTitle(int columnIndex)
  {

      String colTitle = rsmd1.getColumnLabel(columnIndex);
      if ( colTitle == null )
```

```
        {
          colTitle = rsmd1.getColumnName(columnIndex);
        }
      return colTitle;
  }
```

Sizing Up a Column

In addition to knowing the title of a column, it is often required that you also know the width of the column before displaying it. There are several methods within the `ResultSetMetaData` interface that will enable you to determine the proper size of a column. The exact method used will depend on the column data type.

Columns with Text Values

For text values such as SQL types VARCHAR and LONGVARCHAR, the width is normally set to a value equal to or less than the maximum number of characters as defined in the table structure. Using the `getColumnDisplaySize()` method, you can determine what this maximum width of the column is and then use the value to determine what your display size should be. Here is an example:

```
while (rs1.next()) {
    for ( int i = 1; i <= rsmd1.getColumnCount(); i ++)
        {
         String column1 = rs1.getString (i));
         int cwidth = rsmd1.getColumnDisplaySize(i);
         System.out.println ("The column name is : " + column1 );
         System.out.println (" The column max width is : " +
                             cwidth);

        }


    }
```

It is important to remember that the width returned by `getColumn-DisplaySize()` can be much greater than what is displayed on an entire screen. If you are going to use this value to set a column width in a table component or GUI, you will need to determine the absolute maximum for any column before setting the column width, otherwise you may find only a portion of one column visable at a time. In cases where the data is larger than the displayed size, your table should allow for scrolling to the end of the end of the data.

Columns with Numeric Values

For real or floating point numbers, the width of the field is determined in a slightly different manner. Normally, the width of the columns is set to the total sum of precision (number of digits on the left of the decimal point) digits and scale (number of digits to the right of decimal point) digits plus one. (The extra one is needed for the decimal point itself.) To obtain the precision use the `getPrecision()` method. As you might guess, the `getScale()` method is used to obtain the scale. Both of these methods take the column index as an argument and return an integer representing either the precision or the scale.

```
while (rs1.next()) {
    for ( int i = 1; i <= rsmd1.getColumnCount(); i ++)
        {
        float column1 = rs1.getFloat (i));
        int pwidth = rsmd1.getPrecision(i);
        int swidth = rsmd1.getScale(i);
        int totalwidth = pwidth + swidth + 1;
        System.out.println ("The column name is : " + column1 );
        System.out.println (" The column max width is : "
                                + totalwidth);

        }

    }
```

As with text columns, the sum of the precision and scale may be larger than the maximum width practical to display. You will need to decide whether or not you want to enable scrolling or simply truncate that data to be displayed. This will depend entirely on your application.

Working with Numeric Results

In addition to the two methods discussed above, the `ResultSetMetaData` interface provides two other methods for discovering information related to numeric columns. Both of the methods take the column index as an argument and return an appropriate boolean operator.

Signed and Unsigned Numbers

The first of these two methods is the `isSigned()` method. It is used to determine if the value in a column is signed. You may recall that when signed numbers are represented in binary, a single bit is used to determine if the value is negative or not. Normally, this is the last bit on the left. This means that a signed 32-bit integer can only use 31 bits to represent the number and that the largest possible signed number for a signed number is $2^{31}-1$ (2147483647). However, in some databases an unsigned number may be used. Unsigned numbers allow the last bit to be used for the number itself rather than as a sign bit. The maximum size of an unsigned number is enlarged to $2^{32}-1$ (4294967294). While this might be good for the database because now it can represent larger numbers with the same number of bits, it can cause some difficulties in Java. Java only understands signed numbers. You will need to ensure that unsigned numbers are not misinterpreted.

For example, let's suppose that a column in our table is unsigned and that it contains the number 4294967294. If we were to retrieve that number using the `getInt()` method, the integer returned would be –2147483648. The reason for this is that the last bit on the left is interpreted to be a sign bit rather than part of the number.

While JDBC does not directly address this problem by providing methods to retrieve unsigned numbers, the `isSigned()` method can be used as the test for your own unsigned number handler method. One way to implement an unsigned number handler method without having to actually manipulate bits is to use a bit mask of a 1 followed by 31 0s. In base 10, this would be 2147483647. Now all that is left is to apply the mask to the signed `long` by adding it to the absolute value of the signed long. Here is an example:

Suppose that we have an 32 bit unsigned number.

```
2147483648 =     1000 0000 0000 0000 0000 0000 0000 0001
```

However, if we use `getLong`, the value returned is:

```
    -1 =
```

```
10000000000000000000000000000000000000000000000000000000000001
```

Therefore, we will now need to put a bit back into the 32nd place and remove the negative sign. To do this, we use the absolute value of the signed number to strip off the sign bit and then add 2147483647 to the value:

```
1 +   2147483647 = 2147483648
```

or in binary

```
  0000000000000000000000000000000000000000000000000000000000000001
+ 0000000000000000000000000000000001000000000000000000000000000000
  ----------------------------------------------------------------
  0000000000000000000000000000000001000000000000000000000000000001
```

To implement this in Java, you will need to import the java.lang.Math class and use the `abs()` method to determine the absolute value of the retrieved value. Here is an example of how you could use the `isSigned()` method to implement this strategy.

```
.
.
.
while (rs1.next()) {
    for ( int i = 1; i <= rsmd1.getColumnCount(); i ++)
        {
         long aNumber = rs1.getLong (i));
         boolean isNumSigned = rsmd1.getSigned(i);
         if (isNumSigned)
          {
            System.out.println ("The column is a signed integer : " +
                                    aNumber );
          }
         else
          {
            long newNumber = abs(aNumber) + 2147483647 ;
            System.out.println (" The column is unsigned: " +
                                    newNumber);
          }
        }

    }
```

Working with Currency

The second method provided by the ResultSetMetaData interface for handling numbers is the `isCurrency()` method. This method returns true if the column referenced by the index number contains currency figures.

```
boolean isMoney = rsmd1.isCurrency(i);
```

Unfortunately, there is no method for determining what type of currency the column represents. Therefore, if `isCurrency()` returns true, it will be up to you to attach the proper prefix or symbol to it.

Discovering SQL Data Types

As stated earlier in this chapter, one of the benefits of using meta data is that you can build dynamic applications that are independent of the data source. One of the ways to achieve this is to remove the need for all direct column name references. This was demonstrated earlier by using the `getColumn-Count()` method and substituting all the column names with an index number shown on the following page:

```
.
.
.
ResultSetMetaData rsmd1 = rs.getMetaData

while (rs1.next()) {
    for ( int i = 1; i <= rsmd1.getColumnCount(); i ++)
        {
          System.out.println( rs1.getString (i));
        }

    }
```

In this example, you can see that I have used the `getString()` method to retrieve that data from the `ResultSet`. However, you should recall from Chapter 8's discussion on the "get" methods, that the particular "get" method used is dependent on both the original SQL data type and the application of the data. In the short example above, all data retrieved is simply printed out, therefore the `getString()` method is used. In some instances, you will need to manipulate your data and will need the data in a format that is compatible with its original SQL type. One of the methods for providing the proper data conversion is to use the `getObject()` method, which will convert the data based on conversion rules set up by JDBC. In some instances however, the default data conversions rules may not be appropriate for your application. To address this, the `ResultSetMetaData` interface provides two methods that can be used to determine a column's SQL data type. These two methods `getColumnType()` and `getColumnTypeName()` can be used to create your own data conversion rules.

The getColumnType Method

The `getColumnType()` method takes the column index as an argument and returns the integer value representing the SQL data type as defined in the java.sql.Types class. The java.sql.Types class defines data type constants for each data type in the XOPEN standard. To create a conversion method of your own, you simply need to decide what Java data type you want each of the SQL data types to be converted to. For instance, let's suppose I have the following critiria:

1. Convert all numeric values to floating point numbers.
2. Convert all dates to strings.
3. Convert all binary data columns to a string stating the column contains unreadable information.

Here is a conversion chart showing some of data type mappings:

Table 9.1

Application specific
SQL to Java data
type conversion.

SQL Data Type	Java Data type	"get" method
BIGINT, INTEGER, SMALLINT, TINYINT	float	getFloat
BINARY, LONGVARBINARY	String: "Column contains binary data"	N/A
CHAR, VARCHAR, LONGVARCHAR	String	getString
FLOAT, REAL, NUMERIC	float	getFloat
DATE, TIME, TIMESTAMP	String	getString

The example below shows how you could implement the conversion in Table 9.1.

```
    .
    .
    .

ResultSet rs1 = conn1.getResultSet
ResultSetMetaData rsmd1 = rs.getMetaData

while (rs1.next()) {
    for ( int i = 1; i <= rsmd1.getColumnCount(); i ++)
        {
        switch (rsmd1.getColumnType(i))
        {
        case java.sql.Type.BIGINT:
            float data = rs1.getFloat(i);
            break;
        case java.sql.Type.INTEGER:
            float data = rs1.getFloat(i);
            break;
        case java.sql.Type.SMALLINT:
            float data = rs1.getFloat(i);
            break;
        case java.sql.Type.TINYINT:
            float data = rs1.getFloat(i);
            break;
        case java.sql.Type.FLOAT:
            float data = rs1.getFloat(i);
            break;
        case java.sql.Type.REAL:
            float data = rs1.getFloat(i);
            break;
        case java.sql.Type.CHAR:
            String data = rs1.getString(i);
            break;
        case java.sql.Type.DATE:
            String data = rs1.getString(i);
            break;
        case java.sql.Type.DATE:
            String data = rs1.getString(i);
            break;
        case java.sql.Type.VARCHAR:
            String data = rs1.getString(i);
```

```
            break;
        case java.sql.Type.LONGVARCHAR:
            String data = rs1.getString(i);
            break;
        case java.sql.Type.BINARY:
            String data = "Column contains binary data";
            break;
        case java.sql.Type.LONGVARBINARY:
            String data = "Column contains binary data;
            break;
        }
    }
}
```

The getColumnTypeName Method

Not all RDMBS use the XOPEN standard and may have data types specific
to their database. Database specific data types are therefore not in the
java.sql.Types class and cannot be determined by the `getColumnType()`
method. If a database specific data type is found, it is mapped to the data
type java.sql.Types.OTHER. In order to determine the most appropriate
"get" method to use, you must determine the database data type name.

To accomplish this, the `ResultSetMetaData` interface provides the
`getColumnTypeName()` method. This method returns the RDBMS specific data type name as a `String`. For instance, in an Oracle database a
numeric value can have a data type of *number*. (A *number* is actually a
floating point number.) However, since the data type *number* is not in the
java.sql.Types interface, the `getColumnType()` method returns OTHER
as the data type. In order to determine what "other" really means, you will
need to use the `getColumnTypeName()` method. You can then use the
returned `String` to determine the proper "get" method to use. This can be
done by adding another case clause to the previous example:

```
while (rs1.next()) {
    for ( int i = 1; i <= rsmd1.getColumnCount(); i ++)
        {
        switch (rsmd1.getColumnType(i))
        {
         case java.sql.Type.OTHER(i);
            String colType = rsmd1.getColumnTypeName(i);
            if (colType.equals("NUMBER"))
              {
                float data = rs1.getFloat(i);
              }
            else
              {
                String data = "Column Data Type Unknown"

         case java.sql.Type.BIGINT:
```

```
            float data = rs1.getFloat(i);
             break;
     .
     .
     . // more case statements
     .
     .
     case java.sql.Type.LONGVARBINARY:
        String data = "Column contains binary data;
         break;
    }
  }
}
```

One drawback to this method of data conversion is that you will need to know all of the possible database specific data types you might run into. You will also need to hard code each data type name into your code. However, since most databases use data types that are compatible with those defined in the java.sql.Types interface, you will not often have to do this.

Determining a Columns Source

In many instances, queries contain joins that combine data from different tables, schemas, and even different catalogs. In some applications, it may be necessary to discover what the original source of that column was. To facilitate this, the ResultSetMetaData interface provides three methods: getCatalogName(), getSchemaName(), and getTableName().

Each of the three methods takes the column index number as an input argument and returns a string. As you would expect, the getCatalog-Name() returns the name of the catalog that contained the original column of data. The getSchemaName() returns the schema name and the get-TableName() returns the table name. The getCatalogName() method will throw an SQLException if the RDBMS does not use catalog names.

Column Properties

The remaining methods in the ResultSetMetaData interface are used to discover particular properties that a column has. For instance a column may restrict the insertion of null values and may be read-only. Some of these properties do not have to be persistent and can change state during transactions, while some are most likely to be set once and left alone. In either case, the ResultSetMetaData provides several methods that can be used to discover the current state or properties of a column.

The isAutoIncrement Method

The `isAutoIncrement()` method is used to determine if the column referenced by the argument contains data that is automatically updated by the RDBMS, i.e., sequence numbers. Automatically updated columns that contain sequence numbers should not be modified by the user and are normally read-only. Any attempt to update, insert, or delete data from that column can result in an SQL error. As a precaution, any column that contains integer or long integer values should be checked to ensure they do not contain a sequence number before any attempt to update them is made.

The isNullable Method

As with all of the other methods in the `ResultSetMetaData` interface, the `isNullable()` method takes a column index as an argument. However, unlike all of the other "is" methods the `isNullable()` method does not return a boolean operator but rather returns an integer value.

The return value of the isNullable method can be either 0, 1, or 3.

- 0 = The column does not accept null values.
- 1 = The column does accept null values.
- 2 = It is unknown if the column will accept null values.

The isReadOnly Method

The `isReadOnly()` method is used to determine if a column is only readable by the current user. However, the particular status of a column is likely to be very transient and change very quickly since the read-only flag of a column can often be set by anyone or any application that has write permission to that column. This means that users can change the status of the column themselves. You should therefore model your application and tests of the read-only status of a column judiciously. The `isReadOnly()` method takes the column index as an argument and returns true if the column is in fact read-only.

The isSearchable Method

The `isSearchable()` method is used to determine the suitability of a particular column to be used as search criteria. The `isSearchable()` method will return `true` if the column referred to by the input argument can be used as search criteria. That is, it will return `true` for any column that can be used in a WHERE clause of a SELECT statement.

Columns may not be suitable as search criteria for many reasons. Most often the reason is that the data contained is simply too long to be useful, such as columns containing binary data or very long variable character strings.

The isWritable and isDefinitelyWritable Methods

The last two methods in the `ResultSetMetaData` interface are used to determine if you can update, insert, or delete data in a particular column. The `isWritable()` method is the exact opposite of the `isReadOnly` method. The `isWritable()` method will return true if the column referenced is not set to be read-only. Therefore, the column could be writable. However, just because a column is not set to read-only mode explicitly, it may implicitly deny updates. To truly determine if you can actually write to a column you must use the `isDefinitelyWritable()` method.

Chapter Summary

In this chapter, we took an in-depth look at the methods contained in the `ResultSetMetaData` interface and how they can be applied to write dynamic and data source independent applications. One of the key components to any application is determining the column header information such as preferred title name, column width, and data type. The `ResultSetMetaData` interface provides the means to collect this information. Additionally, you are provided with methods to dynamically discover update properties, null status, and read-only status of columns within a table.

If you intend to build applications that browse multiple databases or databases that are unknown at compile time, the `ResultSetMetaData` interface provides invaluable information.

What's Next

Now that you know how to use `ResultSetMetaData`, it is time to move onto `DatabaseMetaData`. In Chapter 10, I will show you how to use the `DatabaseMetaData` interface to help you move your applications from data independence to database simply independence.

Working with Database Meta Data
The DatabaseMetaData Interface

The `DatabaseMetaData` interface is by far the largest of the interfaces, with 137 methods. Although the interface is nearly 14 times the size of the `Driver` interface, the `DatabaseMetaData()` methods are not absolutely essential to every JDBC application. The `DatabaseMetaData` interface will primarily be of interest to those developers who are writing applications that need to be completely RDBMS-independent. The `ResultSetMetaData` class is to free the developer from needing prior knowledge of the database table structure. The `DatabaseMetaData` interface provides methods that allow you to dynamically discover properties of the RDBMS and database state itself. For instance, if your application uses some of the more advanced features of SQL such as outer joins or stored procedures, you can dynamically discover if the database supports them. Just as the `ResultSetMetaData()` methods allowed you to discover the structure of tables and properties of columns, the `DatabaseMetaData` interface will enable you to dynamically determine properties of the RDBMS.

Since the `DatabaseMetaData` interface is so large, only those that seem of particular importance or troublesome are discussed in detail here. Many of the methods do not take any argument and simply return an appropriate boolean operator. The purpose and meaning of the method are usually self evident from the method's name. It doesn't take much to figure out that if your database supports catalog names in a table definition, the `supports-CatalogsInTableDefinitions` returns true. For a complete listing with syntax of the DatabaseMetaData methods, please refer to Appendix D.

Information collected using `DatabaseMetaData()` methods is only valid for the driver and the RDBMS that you are connected to. Remember that the `DatabaseMetaData` object is created from the `Connection` object, using the `getMetaData()` method, and is therefore associated with only one `Connection`.

Product Identification Methods

Several methods in the `DatabaseMetaData` interface provide a means to discover the identity of the RDBMS and the JDBC driver. These methods can be useful if you need to build special logic in your application for handling particular tasks. For instance, you may know that your application will only work with certain revisions of a particular database. You could therefore use the `getDatabaseProductName()` and `getDatabaseProductVersion()` methods to determine if the revision number is correct for your application.

In addition to the `getDatabaseProductName()` and `getDatabaseProductVersion()` methods, the `DatabaseMetaData` interface also provides four methods to discover the JDBC Drivers version and product name. These methods are:

- `getDriverName()`
- `getDriverVersion()`
- `getDriverMajorVersion()`
- `getDriverMinorVersion()`

You may recall from Chapter 4 that these methods are normally used in lieu of the `Driver()` methods, so that you do not need to create a referenceable `Driver` object. Also, as with the methods of the same name in the `Driver` interface, each of these methods takes no arguments and returns a string representing either the name or version information requested.

Discovering Database Objects

Because most modern databases are relational databases, they use models for grouping related data together in a hierarchical format. At the highest level is the database itself. A database can contain one or more catalog objects. Each catalog may contain one or more schemas and each schema may contain one or more tables. And, of course, each table can contain one or more columns, each comprised of any number of rows. Here is a diagram of a typical RDBMS relational object tree model.

Figure 10.1
RDBMS object tree.

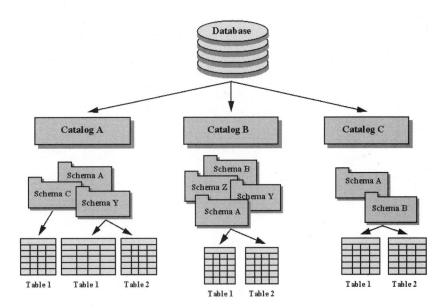

For the most part, this book has concentrated on the objects at the lowest level of the tree. That is, columns and rows of user data contained in tables. Until now, we have discussed how the tables are organized or the container objects that hold them: catalogs and schemas. However, in order to build truly robust and flexible applications, you must be able to identify and navigate through the containers in order to get at the user data you need. Fortunately, JDBC provides several methods within the DataBaseMetaData class for this purpose. The next several pages will discuss in detail each of these methods.

Working with Catalog Objects

When working with large databases, you may find that multiple catalogs are used within the RDBMS. Catalogs are top level container objects that contain related schemas. Therefore, if you need to access tables contained in multiple catalogs, you will need to explicitly specify a catalog name.

The `DatabaseMetaData` interface contains several methods for discovering catalog related information so that you can build applications that have the ability to dynamically select and use catalog objects.

To change the active catalog you can use either an appropriate SQL command (e.g., the *use* command) or you can use the `Connection.setCatalog()` method.

The getCatalogTerm Method

The first method in this category to examine is the `getCatalogTerm()` method. Since not all databases refer to catalogs as "catalogs," it may be helpful to know what the vendor specific term for them is. An example of the `getCatalogTerm()` is as follows:

```
DatabaseMetaData dbmd = conn1.getMetaData();
String catName = dbmd.getCatalogTerm();
```

The getCatalogSeperator and isCatalogAtStart Methods

The `getCatalogSeperator()` and `isCatalogAtStart()` methods often are used together. As its name implies, the `getCatalogSeperator()` method is used to discover what character string is used to separate the catalog name and the table or schema name. However, since not all databases are consistent in their naming schemes, the catalog name might be appended after or inserted in front of the table or schema name. Therefore, simply knowing what the separator is may not be enough information. The `isCatalogAtStart()` method can be used to determine if the catalog name should appear before or after the table or schema name. Armed with the catalog name, the separator character string, and the placement of the catalog name, you should be able to fully reference a database catalog object within the database. The following is a short example:

Example 10.1

```
import java.sql.*;

public class catalogselect {

    public static void main(String args[]) {
    Connection conn1;

try {
    Class.forName("weblogic.jdbc.oci.Driver");
    conn1 = DriverManager.getConnection
                    ("jdbc:weblogic:oracle:fool:",
                    "jdbcuser","jdbcisfun");

        DatabaseMetaData dbmd = conn1.getMetaData
        String separator = dbmd.getCatalogSeperator();
        System.out.println (" The database uses the \" "
                            + " \" as a separator.")
        if (dbmd.isCatalogAtStart())
          {
            System.out.println ("Insert catalog name before table or
                                schema name");
          }
          else
          {
            System.out.println("Append catalog name after table
                                name");
          }

    }
    catch (SQLException e)
      {
        System.out.println ("An SQL exception occurred" +
                            e.getMessage() + "\n");
    conn1.close();
    }
}
}
```

The getCatalogs Method

After you have discovered what the catalog separator character string is and where to place the catalog name, the last step is to determine what catalog names are. If you want to discover the current active catalog, you would use the `Connection` method `getCatalog()`. However, if you need to know all of the catalogs available in the database, you will need to use the `DatabaseMetaData` method `getCatalogs()`.

The `getCatalogs()` method takes no arguments and returns a `ResultSet` object containing a list of all catalog names available in the database. The returned ResultSet object only contains a single column named TABLE_CAT. To retrieve the list of catalogs, you will need to use the `getString()` method and either supply the column index (1) or the column name (TABLE_CAT). Here is a short example that demonstrates how you could print a list of all available catalogs and the current catalog:

Example 10.2

```
import java.sql.*;

public class catalogselect {

    public static void main(String args[]) {
    Connection conn1;

try {
    Class.forName("weblogic.jdbc.oci.Driver");
    conn1 = DriverManager.getConnection
                  ("jdbc:weblogic:oracle:fool:",
                    "jdbcuser","jdbcisfun");
        String currentCatalog = conn1.getCatalog();
        System.out.println ("The current active catalog name is: "
                            + currentCatalog );
        DatabaseMetaData dbmd = conn1.getMetaData
        ResultSet rs = dbmd.getCatalogs();
        System.out.println (" The following catalogs are available
                            in this database")
        while (rs.next())
          {
            System.out.println(getString(TABLE_CAT);
          }

    }
    catch (SQLException e)
      {
        System.out.println ("An SQL exception occurred"
                            + e.getMessage() + "\n");
    conn1.close();
  }
}
```

Catalog Name Support

Not all RDBMS allow the catalog name to be appended to all SQL statements. In some cases, you must activate or open a catalog by using the "use" clause rather than explicitly referring to the table in SQL statements while other databases may not even use catalog names at all. JDBC provides several methods to enable you to better understand the limitations set on catalog names. Some of the most common ones are:

* `supportsCatalogsInDataManipulation()`
* `supportsCatalogsInProcedureCalls()`
* `supportsCatalogsInTableDefinitions()`

The most common method for determining if catalog names are used at all within the database is to use the `supportsCatalogsInTableDefinitions()`. If this method returns false you can be reasonably assured that the database does not support catalog names.

There are several other methods of this type that can be used to discover if a particular SQL statement will allow explicit catalog names. Please refer to Appendix D for a complete list of them.

Working with Schema Objects

Schemas are used by databases to group a set of related tables, just as a catalog is used to group a set of related schemas. Most schemas are named to reflect a user login name or ID. Therefore, in most cases, all objects in a particular schema are owned by a particular user (or at least userID) and are related by ownership. This is not to say that every user has his or her own schema, but that each schema must have at least one owner. For instance, let's say I log in to a database as user "msiple" and create several tables. The newly created tables will have a schema name "msiple" and be owned by "msiple." Now let's say that I want everyone in my workgroup to use my tables. To do this, the database administrator (DBA) will specify that the default schema for all of the users in my workgroup is "msiple." The tables are all still related to a user name "msiple," but not every user name in my workgroup.

The getSchemaTerm Method

As we saw with the catalogs, not all RDBMS use the same terminology for schemas. To discover what the vendor specific term for a schema is, you can use the `getSchemaTerm()` method. As with its catalog equivalent, the `getSchemaTerm()` method takes no arguments and returns a `String` representing the vendor specific term for a schema.

Getting Schema Names

In order to determine the names of available schemas in a database, the `DatabaseMetaData` interface provides the `getSchemas()` method. The `getSchemas()` method is very similar to its catalog counterpart in that it takes no arguments and returns a `ResultSet` containing a single column listing all of the schemas available in a database.

To retrieve the names of all the schemas, you will need to use the `get-String()` method. The `ResultSet` contains a single column titled TABLE_SCHEM that contains the available schema names. Below is an example of the `getSchemas()` method:

Example 10.3

```
import java.sql.*;

public class schemaselect {

    public static void main(String args[]) {

try {
    Connection conn1;
    Class.forName("weblogic.jdbc.oci.Driver");
    conn1 = DriverManager.getConnection
                        ("jdbc:weblogic:oracle:fool:",
                         "jdbcuser","jdbcisfun");

        DatabaseMetaData dbmd = conn1.getMetaData
        ResultSet rs = dbmd.getSchemas();
        System.out.println (" The following schemas are available in
                            this database")
        while (rs.next())
          {
              System.out.println(getString(TABLE_SCHEM);
          }

    }
    catch (SQLException e)
      {
        System.out.println ("An SQL exception occurred" +
                            e.getMessage() + "\n");
    conn1.close();
  }

}
```

The `getSchemas()` method returns all schema names in a database, not just the names of schemas in the current catalog.

Determining the Current Schema Name

Unfortunately unlike catalog names, neither the `DatabaseMetaData` interface nor the `Connection` interface provides any means to discover the default or current schema name directly. To determine the current schema name, you will need to do some extra work.

One interface method that provides a means to discover schema names is the ResultSetMetaData getSchemaName(). The method getSchemaName() returns the schema name for a given column. Therefore, if you do not specify a schema name in an SQL statement, the default schema is used. You can determine the default schema name indirectly by executing an SQL statement against a table in your default schema and then determining the schema name from the returned column. Here is an outline of the steps you would follow:

1. Create a connection to the database.
2. Get a list of all tables in the current schema (Discussed later in this chapter).
3. Select a column(s) from one of the tables in the default schema.
4. Use the ResultSetMetaData method getSchema() to determine the source of one of the columns.

Schema Name Support

Not all databases support or use schemas to logically partition tables into groups, and those that do may not support the use of schema names directly in SQL statements. The DatabaseMetaData interface provides several methods for testing schema name support. These methods are very similar to the catalog methods listed in the Catalog Name Support section. Here is a short list of some of the methods available:

- supportsSchemasInDataManipulation()
- supportsSchemasInProcedureCalls()
- supportsSchemasInTableDefinitions()

For a complete list of all the schema-related methods, please refer to Appendix D.

Working with Table Objects

As we have discussed earlier, within each schema there can be one or more tables. Tables are comprised of one or more columns and rows of data. The table is the smallest container object that does not contain data elements directly. It contains columns of data of a specific data type which can be combined to form rows (or records). The DatabaseMetaData interface is used to discover names and properties of tables contained in a schema.

Getting a List of Table Types

In the previous paragraph, I said that a schema can contain one or more tables. However, the term "tables" was used somewhat loosely and can actually refer to several different types of "table-like" objects. For our purposes, a table can be a physical table, a logical view, an alias to a table, or even a collection of specific tables. The reason that each of these objects is referred to as simply "tables" is that they all behave in the same manner when interacting with SQL. For instance, a *view* can be a subset of columns from a single table. When an SQL statement selects data from the view, the SQL interacts with the view in exactly the same manner as it does a table. SQL will perform any function on a view as it does a table. Therefore for SQL, a table and a view are essentially the same. The different types of tables are simply organizational groups that make it easier for us to manage.

To allow access to all of the "table" objects and still be able to group them logically together, the `DatabaseMetaData` provides a means to list all of the available table types. To retrieve a list of all table types available in the database, use the `getTableTypes()` method. The `getTableTypes()` method takes no arguments and returns a `ResultSet` containing a single column titled TABLE_TYPE.

Getting a List of Tables

Once you have determined all of the table types, catalogs, and schemas available in the database, you are ready to get a list of all the tables themselves. You can either choose to list all tables in the database, break them down by catalog, or even group them by schema names within each catalog. The method used to retrieve the table names is the `getTables()` method. The reason you need to know the catalog, schema, and table types before executing this method is that the `getTables()` method takes each as an argument. The syntax for the `getTables()` method is as follows:

```
ResultSet tablesRS = dbmd.getTables(StringC, StringS, StringT,
                     ArrayStringT);
```

Where: `StringC` = A string containing the Catalog name to use. If you want to omit the catalog name (use the current catalog), you can use the `null` string. Also if the database does not use catalog names, a null string should be used. A null will indicate that no catalog name should be appended or inserted in the selection criteria.

StringS = A string containing the Schema name to use. If you do not want to specify a particular schema (use the current schema), you can use the null string. As with the catalog, if your database does not support schema names in table selections, you should use a null string.

StringT = A string containing a table name pattern to be matched. This can include wild cards such as the "%" and "_." For example, using the string "myTabl%" will return a list of tables that begin with "myTabl" such as "myTable1," "myTable2," etc....

ArraryStringT = An array of strings containing the table types you want to be selected.

For example, let's suppose I have two catalogs in my database and I wish to see all the tables and views in the catalog "MyCat." You would use the following statement:

```
String [] tabTypes= {"table","view"};
ResultSet tablesRS = dbmd.getTables("MyCat","","%", tabTypes);
```

After execution, the ResultSet object contains five columns. Each of the returned column names and a brief description of them is in Table 10.1 below:

Table 10.1
Table name ResultSet
columns

Column Name	Column Description
TABLE_CAT	The catalog that contains the table.
TABLE_SCHEM	The Schema that contains the table.
TABLE_NAME	The table name .
TABLE_TYPE	The type of table. (e.g., VIEW,TABLE,ALIAS etc.)
REMARKS	A brief comment or description given the table when created.

As we saw with the catalog and schema result sets, each of the columns in the table name ResultSet can be retrieved using the getString() method.

Getting Table Privileges

The last table-related method we will look at in this chapter is the get-TablePrivileges() method. This method is used to determine a user's privileges such as access rights and granting others privileges on the table.

The getTablePrivileges method takes three arguments: the catalog, the schema, and the table name. As demonstrated above, the catalog name can be null, indicating that either catalogs are not used by the database or that the current catalog is to be used. Similarly, the schema name can be null. The getTablePrivileges method returns a ResultSet containing seven columns. Table 10.2 describes each column.

Table 10.2
Table privileges
ResultSet columns

Column Name	Column Description
TABLE_CAT	The catalog that contains the table.
TABLE_SCHEM	The schema that contains the table.
TABLE_NAME	The table selected.
GRANTOR	Who granted the rights to the table (usually the owner)?
GRANTEE	Who was granted these rights? This could be a user or a group of user (e.g., PUBLIC).
PRIVILEGE	What rights were granted?
IS_GRANTABLE	Can the user grant them to someone else?*

*A YES or NO string is returned—not a boolean.

A Dynamic Table Tree Example

The following example demonstrates how to combine the getCatalogs(), getSchemas(), getTableTypes(), and getTables() methods to dynamically discover all of table objects available to in a database. It also uses the getTablePriviliges() method to determine the table privileges:

Example 10.4

```
import java.sql.*;
import java.util.Vector;

public class getTables {

 public static void main(String argv[])
  throws Exception
 {
  int numberOfCatalogs;
  int numberOfSchemas;
  int numberOfTableTypes;
  boolean supportsCatalogs = false;
  boolean supportsSchemas = false;
  String thisCatalog;
```

```
String thisSchema;
Vector catNames = new Vector();
Vector schemaNames = new Vector();

Class.forName("weblogic.jdbc.oci.Driver");
Connection conn = DriverManager.getConnection
                  ("jdbc:weblogic:oracle:fool", "scott", "tiger");

DatabaseMetaData dbmd = conn.getMetaData();

if (dbmd.supportsCatalogsInTableDefinitions())
 {
   supportsCatalogs = true;
   catNames = new Vector();
   ResultSet catNamesRS = dbmd.getCatalogs();
   while (catNamesRS.next())
     {
        String catalog = catNamesRS.getString("TABLE_CAT");
        catNames.addElement(catalog);
     }
   numberOfCatalogs = catNames.size();
 }
else
 {
   supportsCatalogs = false;
   numberOfCatalogs = 1;
    System.out.println ("Database does not support catalogs");
 }
if (dbmd.supportsSchemasInTableDefinitions())
 {
   supportsSchemas = true;
   schemaNames = new Vector();
   ResultSet schemaNamesRS = dbmd.getSchemas();
   while (schemaNamesRS.next())
     {
        String schema = schemaNamesRS.getString("TABLE_SCHEM");
        schemaNames.addElement(schema);
     }
   numberOfSchemas = schemaNames.size();
 }
else
 {
   supportsSchemas = false;
   numberOfSchemas = 1;
  System.out.println("Database does not support schema names");
 }

ResultSet tabTypesRS = dbmd.getTableTypes();
Vector tabTypes = new Vector();
while (tabTypesRS.next())
 {
   String tabType = tabTypesRS.getString("TABLE_TYPE");
   tabTypes.addElement(tabType);
 }

// getTables() wants list of types as an array not a vector

numberOfTableTypes = tabTypes.size();
String[] tableTypes = new String[numberOfTableTypes];
```

```
      for ( int i=0; i<tabTypes.size(); i++ )
       {
         tableTypes[i] = (String)tabTypes.elementAt(i);
       }

    for ( int cats=0; cats<numberOfCatalogs; cats++ )
      {
        if (supportsCatalogs)
         {
           thisCatalog = (String)catNames.elementAt(cats);
           System.out.println("Catalog: " + thisCatalog);

         }
        else
         {
           thisCatalog = "";
           System.out.println("Catalog name not used");
         }
         for ( int schems=0; schems<numberOfSchemas; schems++ )
          {
          if (supportsSchemas)
          {
           thisSchema = (String)schemaNames.elementAt(schems);
           System.out.println("--> Schema: " + thisSchema);
          }
          else
           {
           thisSchema = "";
           System.out.println("Schema names not used");
           }

        ResultSet tableNamesRS = dbmd.getTables(thisCatalog,
                                       thisSchema,"%",
                                       tableTypes);
        while (tableNamesRS.next())
         {
            System.out.println("--->" +
tableNamesRS.getString("TABLE_TYPE") + ": " + tableNamesRS.
                                         getString("TABLE_NAME"))
                                         ;

           try {
               ResultSet tablePrivs = dbmd.getTablePrivileges(this
                               Catalog,thisSchema,tableNamesRS.
                               getString("TABLE_NAME"));
              while (tablePrivs.next())
              {
               System.out.println("---->" +
               tableNamesRS.getString("TABLE_NAME") +" Privileges: " +
               tablePrivs.getString("PRIVILEGE"));
               System.out.println("----->Grantor: " + tablePrivs.
               getString("GRANTOR"));
               System.out.println("----->Grantee: " + tablePrivs.
               getString("GRANTEE"));
               System.out.println("---->Is Grantable: " +
               tablePrivs.getString("IS_GRANTABLE"));
              }
            }
          catch (SQLException e)
            {
              System.out.println ("Could not get privileges for this
```

```
                                            table.");
                    }


            }
          }
        }

      conn.close();
    }

  }
```

Getting More Table Information

In addition to getting table privileges, the `DatabaseMetaData` interface provides many more methods that provide detailed information about tables. This information ranges from maximum column sizes to imported key lists. Nearly all of the remaining methods follow the same format as those already discussed. For a complete list of all the table methods, please refer to Appendix D.

Stored Procedures

The `DatabaseMetaData` interface also provides several methods for discovering the names and structure of stored procedures. However, since many of these methods are very similar to those discussed earlier and share the same basic syntax, I will only list them in Table 10.3.

Table 10.3
Procedure-related methods.

Column Name	Column Description
getProcedureTerm()	Returns a string representing the database specific term for procedures.
supportsStoredProcedures()	Returns true if the database supports stored procedures.
getProcedures()	Returns a ResultSet object containing a list of all procedure names and types (See Appendix D for description of procedure types).
getProcedureColumns()	Returns a ResultSet containing a description of a procedures parameters and column names.

Each procedure's results can be processed in the same manner outlined above. For a complete list of methods and the column names of their associated `ResultSet` please, refer to Appendix D.

Supported Features

Throughout this book, I have shown you how to take advantage of many advanced database functions. However, we have not discussed how to determine if your particular database actually supports those functions. Stored procedures, outer joins, and transaction locking are all advanced functions (or features) and may not be fully supported. The `DatabaseMetaData` interface provides many methods for determining just about everything you will need to know about your database's capabilities. All of these methods fall into a single category and can best be described as the "supports" methods.

Each method in this category begins with the keyword "supports" followed by the feature name. For instance, if you would like to know if your database supports outer joins, you will find there is a `supportsOuterJoins()` method. In fact, there are `supportsFullOuterJoins()` and `supportsLimitedOuterJoins()`, too. All of the methods take no arguments and return a boolean operator indicating if the feature is supported.

More than one-third of the `DatabaseMetaData()` methods fits into this category. Therefore, since the syntax is nearly all the same and processing the results is trivial, I will simply refer you to Appendix D for the complete list of supported features.

Supported Syntax

Within the supported features there are four methods that I thought should be pointed out. These four methods are: `supportsANSI92EntryLevel-SQL()`, `supportsANSI92FullSQL()`, `supportsANSI92IntermediateSQL()`, and `supportsCoreSQLGrammar()` methods. The first three are self explanatory, as we have already discussed what each of these levels of SQL92 is in Chapter 1. However, the last method can be a bit confusing and will be examined more closely.

The `supportsCoreSQLGrammar()` method is used to determine if the database supports the Core SQL grammar as defined by ODBC. It is not necessarily true that if a database is SQL92 Entry Level compliant (and, therefore, JDBC COMPLIANT) it must also support the ODBC Core. If you rely on ODBC Core SQL grammar, you should verify that the database supports it.

Database Limitations

The last category of `DatabaseMetaData` methods to be looked at is the "limitations" category. I have grouped all of the methods that are used to determine the set maximum values of database parameters. These methods all take the same form. Each begins with the phrase "getMax" and is followed by the parameter name. Each returns an integer value representing the maximum value for that parameter. For instance, the `getMaxColumnsIn-Index()` method is used to determine the maximum number of columns that can be used in an index.

While not as numerous as the supported features category, the limitations category contains a fair number of methods. Please refer to Appendix D for a complete list of all of the limitations methods.

Chapter Summary

In this chapter, we looked at the `DatabaseMetaData` interface and some of its most useful methods. Unlike some of the other interfaces or classes discussed, the shear magnitude of this interface has prevented us from looking at every method in detail. However, one of the more important topics covered was how to use the `DatabaseMetaData` interface to dynamically discover all of the database objects available to us. This chapter demonstrated how to find the names of catalogs, schemas, table types, and tables, all on the fly. As discussed later in the chapter, many of the remaining methods in the interface provide information on the features and limitations of the database.

Odds and Ends

This last chapter in Part Two will wind up our discussions on the JDBC API. It will take a look at the few remaining classes and exceptions: the `Time`, `TimeStamp`, `Types`, and `DriverPropertyInfo`. Each of these is very small and primarily extend existing core Java classes. Also, we will examine `SQLException`, `SQLWarning`, and `DataTruncation` exceptions.

The Time Class

The `Time` class extends the java.util.Date class and provides a subset of the methods in that class. Unlike the java.util.Date class which requires a minimum of a year, month, date, hour, and minute arguments to represent a time, the java.sql.Time class allows you to create a `Time` object with only the hour, minute and second. This allows for easy access to the SQL TIME data type, since the SQL TIME does not contain year, month, or day information.

The `Time` class has only two methods and a single constructor. The constructor takes the three arguments hour, minute, and seconds as integers following the format listed below:

- Hour: 0 to 23 (0 = midnight, 23 = 11pm)
- Minute: 0 to 59
- Second: 0 to 59

`Time` objects can be retrieved from either a `ResultSet` or an OUT parameter using the appropriate `getTime()` method. The example below shows how the `ResultSet.getTime()` method could be used:

```
ResultSet rs = stmt.executeQuery("SELECT User_ID, my_time from
                                  accts");
while (rs.next());
 {
     System.out.println("User " + rs.getString(User_ID) + "
                         logged in at: "
                      + rs.getTime(my_time);
 }
```

Time Class Methods

The `Time` class only has two methods. The first method, `toString()`, is used to convert a `Time` object to a `String` object. The second method, `valueOf()`, is used to convert a `String` value to a `Time` object. Here is a short example demonstrating the two methods:

```
Time time = valueOf("01:30:00");
String timeString = time.toString ();
```

The `ValueOf()` method takes a `String` argument comprised of the hour, minute and seconds separated by colons. The `toString()` method takes no arguments and simply returns a `String` value with the time as a series of three double digit numbers separated by colons.

The TimeStamp Class

The `TimeStamp` class also extends the java.util.Date class, but instead of removing fields such as the day and year from the constructor method, the `TimeStamp` class adds a seventh field to represent nano seconds. A comparison of the java.util.Date object and the java.sql.TimeStamp object is shown below:

```
java.util.Date:
        YY-MM-DD HH:MM:SS
```

```
java.sql.TimeStamp:
```

```
        YY-MM-DD HH:MM:SS.F
```

Where YY = Years: Number of years since 1900
       MM = Month: 0-11
       DD = Day of month:1-31
       HH = Hours: 0 -23
       MM = Minutes: 0 - 59
       SS = Seconds: 0 - 59
       F = Fraction of seconds: 0 - 999,999,999

The constructor method for a `TimeStamp` takes seven double-digit integer values as arguments. Here is an example of how to create a new `TimeStamp` representing July 23, 1997 1:30:05.30pm:

```
TimeStamp ts = new TimeStamp(97,07,23,01,30,05,30);
```

As with the `Time` class, the `TimeStamp` class is provided in order to access SQL TIMESTAMPS easier. Without these two methods, values retrieved via SQL will not exactly match any Java type and therefore would require special handling.

TimeStamp Class Methods

The `TimeStamp` class has five methods. Similar to the `Time` class, it has two methods used to convert `String` and `TimeStamp` objects back and forth between each other. In addition to these two methods, the `TimeStamp` class adds a third and fourth method to set or retrieve nano second values. The fifth method is used to compare `TimeStamp` objects for equality.

The valueOf Method

The `valueOf()` method is used to convert a `String` to a `TimeStamp` object. The format for the `String` must conform to the following:

```
YYYY-MM-DD HH:MM:SS.f
```

For example:

```
TimeStamp ts = valueOf("1997-07-23 01:30:05.30");
```

Note that this format is not the same as the constructor method. The constructor method takes seven double-digits and represents the date as the number of years since 1900. The `ValueOf()` method uses dashes, colons, and periods to separate the numbers and uses the four-digit year. This can be very useful since many databases represent dates in this format.

The toString Method

The `toString()` method is used to reverse the process shown above. The `toString()` method converts the `TimeStamp` into a `String` of the format:

```
YYYY-MM-DD HH:MM:SS.f
```

Obviously, this format is much easier to understand than a series of seven double digit numbers.

The setNanos and getNanos Methods

Since the `TimeStamp` class is an extension of the java.util.Date class, all of the methods in the java.util.Date class can be used on `TimeStamps`. This includes the java.util.Date methods `set/getDay()`, `set/getMonth()`, `set/getDay()`, `set/getMinute()`, and `set/getSeconds()` methods. However, since the java.util.Date object does not have to contain a nanosecond field, the java.sql.TimeStamp method must provide these methods. As you would expect, the `getNanos()` method is used to retrieve the nano second field of a `TimeStamp` and the `setNanos()` method is used to set the nano second field value. Below are two short examples demonstrating how to use the `getNanos()` and `setNanos()` methods:

```
TimeStamp ts = new TimeStamp(97,07,23,01,30,05,00);
ts.setNanos(30);
int nanoseconds = ts.getNanos();
```

The Equals Method

Also as a result of changing the format of the `TimeStamp` to include the nano second field, the java.sql.TimeStamp method must override the java.util.Date `equals()` method. The `equals()` method is used to compare two `TimeStamp` or `Date` objects. If the java.util.Date equals method is used, that method would not know how to handle the extra field, and therefore would result in an error. The java.sql.TimeStamp `equals()` method is therefore overriding the java.util.Date method in order to allow for the nano seconds field and to ensure it is included in the comparison of the `TimeStamps`. Here is an example of how to compare two `TimeStamps`:

```
TimeStamp ts1 = new TimeStamp(97,07,23,01,30,05,30);
TimeStamp ts2 = valueOf("1997-07-23 01:30:05.30");
boolean timeIsEqual = ts1.equals(ts2);
```

The Types Class

The Types class contains no methods other than its constructor. The Types class sole function is to define a set of constants that is used to identity SQL data types. Each SQL92 standard data type is defined as a static integer constant. This allows other methods to refer to these data types by name rather than some arbitrary number.

An example of how these data types can be used is found in the Discovering SQL Data Types section of Chapter 9.

The DriverPropertiesInfo Class

The DriverPropertiesInfo class is used to dynamically determine what properties are used by the database to complete a connection to a database. The DriverPropertiesInfo object is created by calling the Driver method getDriverPropertiesInfo() class and each object provides information about one of the connection properties. The property information is contained in five variables: choices, description, name, required, and value. Since there normally is more than one property per connection, the getDriverProperties() method creates an array of DriverProperties objects that represent all of the properties a database may accept.

Table 11.1 outlines and gives a brief description of each of the five variables. A complete example of how the getDriverProperties method is used can be found in the More Driver Methods section of Chapter 4.

Table 11.1
DriverPropertyInfo
Variables

Variable Name	Description
choices	An array containing possible choices for this property.
description	A brief description of what the property represents.
name	The name of the property (e.g., userid, password).
required	Boolean value to determine if you must provide a value for this property.
value	Returns the value of the property if the property has been already set.

Error Handling

The JDBC API provides three classes of error handling, each of which extends the java.lang.Exception class. At the top of the inheritance chain is the SQLException. Below the SQLException is the SQLWarning and below the SQLWarning is the DataTruncation class. However, only an SQLException objects must be caught. If you choose to, you can ignore both SQLWarnings and DataTruncation errors.

The SQLException Class

The first type of error to examine is the SQLException. The SQLException is thrown by nearly all of the methods in JDBC and can be caused by any one of hundreds of reasons. The SQLException class is used to provide information to assist in determining the root cause of the error.

SQLExceptions are caught in the same manner as any Java exception. They can be either caught by adding a *throws* clause at the class declaration or by using a *try* and *catch* pair.

The getErrorCode Method

The getErrorCode() method is used to retrieve the vendor-specific error code. If you have a reference to tell you what that error code is, this is often the best way to determine what caused the error.

All of the exceptions in JDBC are extensions of the java.lang.Exception class. Therefore you can use all of the Exception methods such as getMessage() to assist you in decoding error messages.

The getSQLState Method

The getSQLState() method is used with X/OPEN error code which identifies the error. Since each vendor can have its own error messages, the same problem can generate very different error messages. The X/OPEN error code is a standard error message that is used across all compliant databases to simplify database error handling. This is especially useful in environments where multiple RDBMS are used. The X/OPEN code is primarily used when you need to identify a single problem that occurs across multiple vendor databases.

To learn more about the X/OPEN standard you can visit its web site at
http://www.rdg.opengroup.org.

The getNextException Method

In many cases, a single error can throw multiple exceptions. In situations where this occurs, `SQLExceptions` objects can be chained together. This will allow you to keep track of all the error messages and trace the entire exception chain down to its root cause. The method provided to navigate the chain is the `getNextException()` method. It is used to retrieve the next (if any exist) `SQLException` object in the chain.

The setNextException Method

The `setNextException()` method is primarily of interest to those who are writing methods that throw their own `SQLException`. This methods allows you to add your own `SQLException` to the end of the chain.

An SQLException Handling Example

The following code fragment can be used to print out all the information about any SQLException that has occurred. While it is probably a bit too verbose for most situations it certainly can be useful when debugging a problem in applications.

```
catch SQLException exception {

System.out.println ("\n WARNING SQL Exception (s) caught: \n"

while (exception != null ) {
    System.out.println ( "Java SQL Exception: " +
                          exception.getMessage () );
    System.out.println (" Vendor Error Code: " +
                          exception.getErrorCode () );
    System.out.println (" SQL State: " + exception.getSQLState
                          ());
    exception = exception.getNextException
    }
```

The SQLWarning Class

The `SQLWarning` class is very specialized. The `SQLWarning` object is created when a database itself issues a warning. Most database warnings are only issued at login or statement execution time and do not block database access.

SQLWarnings do not interrupt the application flow and you must specifically test for them in order to process them.

If a database issues a warning, the warning is chained to the object that
caused the error. To retrieve the error you would use that object's getWarn-
ings() method. For instance, both the Connection and the Statement
objects contain getWarnings() methods. If you need to determine if an
SQLWarning object has been created and chained to one of the objects, you
would need to call both of their getWarnings methods as shown below:

```
Connection conn = DriverManager.getConnection(".......");
Statement stmt = conn.createStatement();
ResultSet rs = stmt.executeQuery(sqlString)
SQLWarning sqlWarnConn = conn.getWarnings();
SQLWarning sqlWarnState = stmt.getWarnings();
SQLWarning sqlWarnRS = rs.getWarnings();
```

As you can see, in order to ensure that none of the database access or connection requests generated an SQLWarning, you must check each object individually. You also should note that the ResultSet was checked, too.

SQLWarning Methods

The SQLWarning class has only two methods of its own. As we saw with
SQLExceptions, SQLWarnings can be chained together. This means
that the SQLWarning class must provide a means to navigate and add SQL-
Warnings to a chain. The two methods to do this are getNextWarn-
ing() and setNextWarning(). From their names, you should be able to
determine what each is used for.

The DataTruncation Class

Occasionally an error will occur when reading or writing data that results in
data being truncated or lost. When this occurs a DataTruncation error is
created and chained to the object that was performing the read or write. The
DataTruncation() class provides methods to discover the cause of the
truncation and the effect it had on the data.

The getDataSize and getTransferSize Methods

The getDataSize() method is used to determine the number of bytes
that should have been transferred by the operation. The getTransfer-
Size() method is used to determine the number of bytes that were actually
transferred. These methods might be useful in determining the extent of the
data loss.

The number returned by these methods is an integer representing the number of single bytes.

The getIndex Method

The `getIndex()` method is used to determine either the column index number where the data truncation occurred, or in the case of an IN or OUT parameter being truncated, the relative position of the parameter that was truncated. The `getIndex()` method returns an integer value.

If the `getIndex()` method returns a −1, this means that the index number could not be determined.

The getParameter Method

The `getParameter()` method returns a boolean operator indicating whether or not the truncation occurred on a column or a parameter. If the error occurred when reading or writing a column, then the `getParameter()` method will return false.

If the `getIndex()` method returned a −1 value, the results of the `getParameter()` method are not valid and should be ignored.

The getRead Method

The `getRead()` method returns true if the truncation error occurred during a data read.

If the `getIndex()` method returned a −1 value, the results of the `getRead()` method are not valid and should be ignored.

Handling DataTruncation Objects

Since `DataTruncation` errors occur very infrequently, none of the JDBC objects contains a "getDataTruncation" method. Therefore, in order to retrieve and process `DataTruncation` errors, you must use one of the

getWarning methods and then determine if the object is an SQLWarning
or DataTruncation. The example below shows how to explicitly cast an
SQLWarning object to a DataTruncation object and then use the
results of the cast to determine the object type:

```
ResultSet rs = stmt.executeQuery(sqlString);
SQLWarning sqlWarn = stmt.getWarnings();
while (sqlWarn != null )
{

    try {
        DataTruncation dataTrunc = (DataTruncation) sqlWarn;
        System.out.println ("DataTruncation occurred ! ");
        System.out.println ("Error occurred on Column: "
                                + dataTrunc.getIndex());
        System.out.println ("Number of bytes lost:
                        + (dataTrunc.getDataSize() -
                            getTransferSize()));
        }
    catch (Exception e)
        {
        System.out.println ("A SQL Warning occurred !);
        System.out.println ( "Java SQL Warning: "
                                + sqlWarn.getMessage () );
        }
sqlWarn = sqlWarn.getNextWarning();
}
```

Chapter Summary

In this chapter, I attempted to clean up all the loose ends of the JDBC API.
The classes and methods included in this chapter are by no means unimportant, but were placed here simply because they did not logically belong with
any other chapter and were too small to warrant a chapter of their own.

By now, you should have a complete understanding of how to handle any
type of error which may come your way. You should also be comfortable with
using both Time and TimeStamp objects. The examples given in this chapter have also illustrated how to incorporate some of these new classes and
methods into our applications.

PART
3

Building Reusable Database Objects

The DataBeans Objects

This chapter begins a new part of the book. Now that we have looked at all the design considerations, learned how the JDBC API is laid out, and the inner workings of each of the classes and methods of the JDBC API, we are ready to begin assembling these into reusable software components. This chapter begins this process by building new components that are used to simplify accessing the database. These components build on the foundation classes discussed in the previous sections of the book and extend them to a higher level of functionality and ease of use. The components in this chapter only deal with data extraction and session management. Later in Chapter 13 we will build components that will handle all of the data manipulation and results. Once completed, the components built in these two chapters form the basis of "DataBeans" package.

JDBC and JavaBeans

One of the many reasons that Java has become so popular is that it promotes the use of reusable software components. The framework for defining these reusable objects is the JavaBeans API. The JavaBeans API specifies how software should be designed and written so that it can be manipulated with visual tools. This ensures that components are usable by the widest range of programmers and developers. To this end, the components developed in this section of the book all conform to the JavaBeans specifications. This will allow you to integrate these components into nearly any development environment.

You will need to create your own manifest and `jar` file before using them in a visual development tool such as the Bean Box.

One of the requirements of JavaBeans components that must be addressed is that of *thread safety*. In order for a bean to be fully compliant with the specifications, it must be thread safe. That is, the bean must be able to be manipulated by several threads at a time without any unwanted side effects. However, in our application, data is normally manipulated in a sequential fashion. For example, to open and read a table, you would issue the SQL command, retrieve the results, retrieve any meta data required for that table, and then close the statement. If multiple threads were used, you could not guarantee that the steps would be followed in order. If you plan to incorporate these components in a multi-threaded application, you will need to synchronize the methods. This will ensure that data integrity can be guaranteed at least within each method. Synchronizing each method cannot guarantee that you will not attempt to access that data in the wrong order, such as trying to open a table before you have opened the connection.

The DataBeans Goals

The DataBeans classes will contain all of the methods necessary to build our database browser application. By taking advantage of the flexibility provided by meta data, the data browser application will be able to interact with any database, regardless of the vendor, type of driver, and whether or not your application is stand-alone or an applet.

The DataBeans classes will incorporate the following functionalities:

- More flexible database login procedure
- Improved error handling

- Random access to single row or column of data
- Provide automatic column sizing and title information
- Single method to discover database features
- Single method to discover database limitations
- Provide dynamic catalog, schema, table type and table information
- Automatic data type conversions

The DataBeans package contains eight separate classes. However, only three of the components interact directly with JDBC. The remaining five components build on the first three JDBC-related components to build a three-tier, RMI-based application. Here is a brief description of the first three components:

- **The DriverListManager class.** This class is a small, simple, yet powerful class which maintains a persistent list of drivers to be loaded by your application. This allows you to create applications that have absolutely no vendor dependence whatsoever by eliminating the hard-coding of driver names.
- **The DBAccess class.** This class contains methods that interact directly with the database and use the JDBC API classes and methods. Results of queries are passed to the DataTable class for handling.
- **The DataTable class.** This class contains methods for the manipulation and management of the data. All data are placed in tabular format and manipulated by either row, column, or field access methods. This class does not interact with the database. The DataTable class is developed in Chapter 13.

The DriverListManager Class

The `DriverListManager` class provides several methods for the storing and retrieving of JDBC driver names from a single configuration file. The purpose of this class is to provide a means for users or system administrators to determine what drivers should be loaded at run time rather than the developer deciding what drivers should be loaded at compile time. To accomplish this, the `DriverListManager` class simply writes the list of driver names to a file called *drvList.cfg*. At application run time, you can then simply call the `getList()` method to retrieve the stored list. To save a new list of drivers, you would call the `saveList()` method.

The `main()` method of the `DriverListManager` class is a simple command line interface and allows you to add to, delete from, or print the list of available drivers. This is the only method that actually manipulates the contents of the driver list.

Being a UNIX hack, I prefer simple command line interfaces whenever possible. I leave the development of a GUI front end to this class as an exercise for the reader.

The rest of the methods in the `DriverListManager` method are primarily used for debugging and error handling. The *debug* variable can be set to true if you wish to print out error messages I have embedded in the code.

A few last words about programming style. You will note that the `msg()` method simply checks to see if the *debug* variable has been set, and if so, prints the message passed to it. When writing and developing the code, I always add statements to be printed out to the screen during test runs to assist in debugging. This is a personal habit I have developed and found to be very useful in application development. While it is not absolutely necessary, it does come in handy on many occasions. For this reason, I have left the statements and *debug* routines in. You can certainly remove them if you desire.

```
/*

This Class provides the methods to
save and restore the names of JDBC drivers to
a file. The file can then be read by other applications
to load the drivers.  To change the configuration file name,
modify the value of the String "fileName".

*/

package DataBeans;

import java.sql.*;
import java.io.*;
import java.util.Vector;

public class DriverListManager
{

  static boolean debug = false;
  static String fileName = "drvList.cfg";

  /*
   * This method is used to print out any status
   * or user information. This method could be modified
   * to send this information to a status line in
   * a GUI if desired.
   */

  public static void printMsg (String message)
  {
      System.out.println (message);
  }


  /*

  * This method is used to print embedded error messages or
```

```
   * information you may want to use for debugging.  You
   * can turn off all debug messages by changing
   * the value of debug to true to turn this feature on.
   * You can also modify this method to redirect the messages.
   */

  public static void msg (String message)
  {
    if (debug)
      {
       System.out.println (message);
      }
  }

  /*
   * This method is similar to to the previous two, but handles
   * all system error messages. You can modify it to conform to
   * you specific error handling requirements.
   */

  public static void errorMsg (String message)
  {
      System.out.println (message);
  }

  /*
   * This method returns a Vector containing a list of all driver
   * names that have been saved in the configuration
file(drvList.cfg).
   */

  public static Vector getList ()
  {
  FileInputStream listFile;

  Vector driverList = new Vector();
    try {
        listFile = new FileInputStream(fileName);
        ObjectInputStream objectIn = new ObjectInputStream(listFile);
        driverList = (Vector)(objectIn.readObject());
      msg("Opened configuration file");
      }
      catch (Exception e)
      {
       errorMsg (e.getMessage());
     printMsg ("Could not read drvList.cfg");
      }
    return driverList;
  }

  /*
   * Used to write the current list of drivers to the configuration
   * file.
   */

  public static void saveList (Vector driverList)
  {
    try {
        FileOutputStream fileOut = new FileOutputStream (fileName);
        ObjectOutputStream objectOut = new ObjectOutputStream (file-
```

```
                                                                            Out);
            objectOut.writeObject(driverList);
            objectOut.flush();
            objectOut.close();
            fileOut.close();
            }
      catch (Exception e)
       {
        errorMsg (e.getMessage());
        printMsg("Save List Error" );
        }

      printMsg ("\n Driver List Updated ! \n ");
      printList(driverList);
}

/*
 * used to print the current list of drivers. (may or
 * may not be saved to disk).
 */

public static void printList (Vector driverList)
{
 for (int i = 0; i < (driverList.size()); i++)
   {
    int lineNumber = i + 1;
    printMsg(lineNumber + ".  " + driverList.elementAt(i));
   }
}

/*
 * Prints the usage message if the class is executed with
 * improper or missing commands.
 */

public static void printUsage ()
{
  printMsg("DiveListManager Usage:");
  printMsg("  driverListManager add <driver name>");
  printMsg("  driverListManager list");
  printMsg("  driverListManager delete \n");
}

/*
 * The main method is a command line interface to the
 * methods in this class. A GUI can be used to replace
 * this method.
 */

public static void main (String argv[])
{
 Vector driverList = new Vector();

 if (argv.length < 1)
   {
    printUsage();
   }
 else
   {
    if (argv[0].equals("add"))
```

```
                        {
                         driverList = getList();
                         driverList.addElement(argv[1]);
                         saveList(driverList);
                        msg ("Argument is add");
                        }
                        else
                         if (argv[0].equals("delete"))
                           {
                          msg ("Argument is delete");
                          driverList = getList();
                          printList(driverList);
                          System.out.print ("Which driver number do you wish to delete ?
                                          ");
                              int lineNumber = 0;
                           int elementNumber = 0;
                           try {
                              InputStreamReader inRead = new InputStreamReader(System.in);
                              BufferedReader lineIn = new BufferedReader(inRead);
                              String line = lineIn.readLine();
                                 lineNumber = (java.lang.Integer.parseInt(line));
                                 elementNumber = lineNumber -1;
                                 msg ("Line number" + lineNumber);
                              }
                                 catch (Exception e)
                                   {
                                    errorMsg(e.getMessage());
                                    printMsg ("Error Reading file: "+ fileName);
                                   }
                           if (lineNumber <= driverList.size())
                            {
                              printMsg("Deleting driver at line: " + lineNumber );
                              driverList.removeElementAt(elementNumber);
                              saveList(driverList);

                            }
                           else
                            {
                            printMsg("\nLine number" + lineNumber + " is invalid !");
                            }

                        }
                         else
                          if (argv[0].equals("list"))
                        {
                         msg ("Argument is list");
                         driverList = getList();
                         printList(driverList);
                            }
                          else
                        {
                         printMsg("Command " + argv[0] + " not found.");
                         printUsage();
                            }
                    }

                 }

              }
```

The DBAccess Class

The DBAccess class methods are used to interact with the database. These methods simplify database access by grouping several related JDBC method calls into single methods and by providing a single structure for all data to be returned. The DBAccess method takes care of loading all the available drivers (listed in the drvList.cfg file) at creation time. Once instantiated, the user simply needs to login and issue an SQL command to be executed. To further simplify things, common tasks such as opening a table, getting database product information, and driver product information are all automated for the user. Each of these tasks can be accomplished with a single command such as openTable() or getDriverInfo(). All data, regardless of origin, are then returned as a DataTable object. Later you will see that the Data-Table object will allow you to retrieve data as individual rows, columns, or fields. The DBAccess method does not provide any means to access the tabular data itself.

The getSchema(), getCatalog(), and getTables() methods are the only methods that will return data directly to the caller. This is because in most instances this data will be used to build some sort of selection list rather than simply displayed as a table. (In Chapter 14 we will use this data to build a browsable tree structure.) Each of these methods returns a Vector containing the list of the associated names.

The main method of the DBAccess class is used only to test some of DBAccess and DataTable methods. You can eliminate this method if you wish. The following is a list and brief description of the methods implemented in the DBAccess class.

Error and exception handling methods include:

- public static void msg (String message)
  The msg method prints out embedded debugging information. It is controlled by the debug variable. Setting the debug variable to false will disable this method.

- public void setErrorMessage (String message)
  The setErrorMessage is used whenever a method throws an exception. The error can then be handled appropriately by the calling routine. This ensures that SQLExceptions do not halt the execution of the application.

- public void appendErrorMessage (String message)
  The appendErrorMessage appends an error message to an existing

error message. This allows you to chain exceptions together to ensure you can trace them to their root causes.

- `public String getErrorMessage ()`
  The getErrorMessage method returns the string of error/exception messages currently in the chain. If the autoClearErrorMessages variable has been set, then the getErrorMessages method will also clear the error message string once they have been retreived.

- `public void setAutoClearErrorMessage (boolean autoClear)`
  The setAutoClearErrorMessage method sets the AutoClearErrorMessage variable that is used by the getErrorMessage method to determine if error messages should be cleared once they have been retrieved.

- `public void clearErrorMessage ()`
  The clearErrorMessage method sets the current error message string to null. It can be called directly by the application or indirectly through the getErrorMessage method.

Session management and connection related methods include:

- `private void setLoginProperties (String url, String user, String passwd)`
  The setLogin properties method sets the value of the login properties to be used for the current session. Currently, the method is private and is only called by the getSession method and getLoginProperties.

- `public DataTable getLoginProperties ()`
  The getLoginProperties method returns the URL and user ID that have been set for the current session. The information is returned in a DataTable and is expected to be displayed in tabular format. Note that this method does not require a Connection object to be passed as an argument as with the rest of the methods in this category. This is because the information returned is the local login information that will be used to connect to the database.

- `public DataTable getDBInfo (Connection conn)`
  The getDBInfo method returns information related to the database product. This information includes the database product name, version, and URL. The data is collected from the DatabaseMetaData class and returned in the DataTable object.

- `public DataTable getDriverInfo (Connection conn)`
  The getDriverInfo method is similar to the getDBInfo except that the

information returned is specific to the JDBC driver instead of the database product. It is important to remember that the information returned is only for the driver that is used to make the current connection. It does not return information about drivers that are loaded but not used.

- `public DataTable getSQLLevelInfo (Connection conn)`
  The getSQLLevelInfo method returns a DataTable containing information on the SQL92 level supported by the current database.

- `public Connection getSesssion (String url, String user, String passwd)`
  The getSession method logs the user into the database and, if successful, returns the Connection object for that session. The getSession method is primarily a wrapper method for the getConnection method which provides Exception handling automatically. This method is the only method that returns a java.sql object.

SQL execution and table navigation methods include:

- `public String[] getCatalogNames (Connection conn)`
  The getCatalogNames method returns a list of all the catalogs available in the current database. If your database does not support catalogs, then a null is returned.

- `public String[] getSchemaNames (Connection conn)`
  The getSchemaNames method returns a list of all the schemas available in the current database.

The list returned by the `getSchemaNames()` method contains all schema names found in the database. It is not possible to get a list of schemas limited to a particular catalog.

- `public String[] getTableTypes (Connection conn)`
  The getTableTypes method returns a list of all the table "types" that are available in the database. Some of the more common types are: tables, views, system, and aliases.

- `public Vector getTableNames (Connection conn, String catalog, String schema, String tableType)`

- `public Vector getTableNames (Connection conn, String catalog, String schema, String[] tableTypes)`

The getCatalogNames methods return a list of all the tables available in the current database within the catalog, schema, and type(s) referenced. As indicated, the method is overloaded so that it can take either a list of table types or a single table type as an argument. If the database does not support catalogs, then a null value should be passed as the catalog argument. If you do not want to limit the list to those in a particular schema then a null value can also be used in place of the schema name.

- ```
  public DataTable[] executeSQL (Connection conn,
  String sqlString)
  ```
  The executeSQL method is used to execute any arbitrary SQL statement against the current database. Since some databases allow for multiple results, the executeSQL method returns an array of Data-Table objects, each containing separate result sets from the statement execution. However, in most cases the length of the DataTable string will be only one.

- ```
  public DataTable openTable (Connection conn,
  String tableName)
  ```
  The openTable method is provided as a quick and easy way to select all the data from a particular table and return it as a DataTable object. Unlike the executeSQL method that had to accommodate the possibility of multiple results, only one table name can be passed in at a time to the openTable method, and therefore only one DataTable object can be returned at a time.

```
/*

The DBAccess class provides methods used to interact with the data-
base. The primary purpose of these methods is to simplify the process
of accessing data in the database and retrieving associated meta data.

*/


package DataBeans;

import java.sql.*;
import java.util.*;
import java.lang.Integer;
import java.lang.Boolean;
import java.util.Vector;

public class DBAccess
{

 String errorMessage;
 String dbURL;
 Properties loginProps;
 ResultSet rs;
```

```
Connection conn;

static boolean debug = true;
boolean autoClearErrorMessages;

 /*
  * This method is used to print embedded error messages or
  * information you may want to use for debugging. You
  * can turn off all debug messages by changing
  * the value of debug to true to turn this feature on.
  * You can also modify this method to redirect the messages.
  */

private static void msg (String message)
{
 if (debug)
  {
  System.out.println (message);
  }
}

/*
 * All exceptions are handled by setting the errorMessage string
 * variable using this method.
 */

private void setErrorMessage(String message)
{
 errorMessage = (message);
 msg (message);
}                                       // end setErrorMessage method

/*
 * Multiple exceptions that need to be chained together, can be
 * appended to the existing errorMessage string using the
 * appendErrorMessage method.
 * /

private void appendErrorMessage (String message)
{
 errorMessage += ("\n" + message);
 }                                      // end appendErrorMessage
                                           method

/*
 * Error messages are retrieved by the getErrorMessages method.
 */

public synchronized String getErrorMessage ()
{
 String thisErrorMessage = errorMessage;
 if (autoClearErrorMessages)
 {
  clearErrorMessages();
 }
 return thisErrorMessage;
 }                                      // end getErrormessage method

 /*
  * The default is to have error messages automatically cleared when
```

```
 * they are retrieved by the getErrorMessage method. This method
 * can be used to toggle this feature on or off.
 */

public synchronized void setAutoClearErrorMessages (boolean auto)
  {
    autoClearErrorMessages = auto;
  }

/*
 * Error messages are cleared manually by calling this method or
 * can be automatically cleared  using this method.
 */

public synchronized void clearErrorMessages()
{
 errorMessage=null;
}                                    // end clearErrormessage
                                        method
```

The constructor method primarly gets the list of drivers currently listed in the driver configuration file by calling the `DriverListManager getList` method and then attempts to load each of the drivers listed.

```
public DBAccess ()
{
  setAutoClearErrorMessages(false);
  Vector driverNames = DriverListManager.getList();
  if (driverNames.isEmpty())
   {
    setErrorMessage("Driver list is null - add driver names. ");
   }
  else
   for (int i = 0; i < driverNames.size(); i++)
    {
     try {
       Class.forName((String)driverNames.elementAt(i));
          msg ("Driver loaded: " + driverNames);
     }                                // end try
        catch (ClassNotFoundException e)
          {
          setErrorMessage ("Error: " +  e.getMessage());
          }                                // end catch
    }                                      // end for loop
}                                          // end driverNames method
```

Login properties are needed by several methods and therefore are made public throught the class. This next method takes the three most common login properties and sets the appropriate class variables. This method is only called internally and is therefore private.

```
private void setLoginProperties ( String url,
                        String user,
                        String passwd)
{
 loginProps = new Properties();
 dbURL=url;
```

```
loginProps.put("user",user);
loginProps.put("password",passwd);
}                                              // end setLoginProperties
                                               method
```

The `getLoginProperties` method is used to provide information related to the current session. All information is returned as a `DataTable` object to allow the information to be displayed in table format without any special handling by an application.

```
public synchronized DataTable getLoginProperties ()
{
Vector[] props = new Vector[3];
props[0] = new Vector();
props[1] = new Vector();
props[2] = new Vector();

props[0].addElement("The database URL:");
props[0].addElement(dbURL);
props[1].addElement("The user ID:");
props[1].addElement(loginProps.getProperty("user"));
props[2].addElement("The user password:");
props[2].addElement("-------");
String[] headings = new String[2];
headings[0] = ("Login property  ");
headings[1] = ("Current Value  ");
DataTable dt = new DataTable(props,headings);

msg ("Login properties: " + props);
return dt;
}

/*
 * This method returns a DataTable object containing information
 * related to the RDBMS product itself.
 */

public synchronized DataTable getDBInfo ()
{
Vector[] dbInfo = new Vector[4];
dbInfo[0] = new Vector();
dbInfo[1] = new Vector();
dbInfo[2] = new Vector();
dbInfo[3] = new Vector();

try {
  DatabaseMetaData dbmd = conn.getMetaData();

      dbInfo[0].addElement("DataBase Product Name");
      dbInfo[0].addElement(dbmd.getDatabaseProductName());
      dbInfo[1].addElement("DataBase Version Number");
      dbInfo[1].addElement(dbmd.getDatabaseProductVersion());
      dbInfo[2].addElement("DataBase URL");
      dbInfo[2].addElement(dbmd.getURL());
       }
      catch (SQLException e)
       {
          setErrorMessage ("getDBInfo Failed: " + e.getMessage());
```

```
                        appendErrorMessage ("Vendor ErrorCode: " + e.getErrorCode());
                            }

                String[] headings = new String[2];
                headings[0] = ("Database Information ");
                headings[1] = ("Current Value   ");
                DataTable dt = new DataTable(dbInfo,headings);
                return dt;

        }
```

The `getDriverInfo()` method is used to return information related to the driver that used by the connection. This enables you to determine which driver is being used if you are unsure or if multiple drivers have been loaded.

```
    public synchronized DataTable getDriverInfo ()
    {
    Vector[] dbInfo = new Vector[2];
    dbInfo[0] = new Vector();
    dbInfo[1] = new Vector();

    try {
            DatabaseMetaData dbmd = conn.getMetaData();

            dbInfo[0].addElement("Driver Name");
            dbInfo[0].addElement(dbmd.getDriverName());
            dbInfo[1].addElement("Driver Version Number");
            dbInfo[1].addElement(dbmd.getDriverVersion());
             }
            catch (SQLException e)
             {
                setErrorMessage ("getDriverInfo Failed: " +
                                    e.getMessage());
                appendErrorMessage ("Vendor ErrorCode: " +
                                        e.getErrorCode());
             }

            String[] headings = new String[2];
            headings[0] = ("Description ");
            headings[1] = ("Current Value   ");
            DataTable dt = new DataTable(dbInfo,headings);
            return dt;

    }

    /*
     * Provides information regarding the supported SQL level of the
     * RDBMS that you are connected to.
     */

    public synchronized DataTable getSQLLevelInfo ()
     {
     Vector[] dbInfo = new Vector[4];
     dbInfo[0] = new Vector();
     dbInfo[1] = new Vector();
     dbInfo[2] = new Vector();
     dbInfo[3] = new Vector();
```

```
try {
    DatabaseMetaData dbmd = conn.getMetaData();

    dbInfo[0].addElement("SQL92 Entry Level");
    dbInfo[0].addElement (new Boolean
                         (dbmd.supportsANSI92EntryLevelSQL()));
    dbInfo[1].addElement("SQL92 Intermediate Level ");
    dbInfo[1].addElement(new Boolean (dbmd.supportsANSI92-
                                     IntermediateSQL()));
    dbInfo[2].addElement("SQL92 Full Level ");
    dbInfo[2].addElement(new Boolean (dbmd.supportsANSI92Full-
                                     SQL()));
    }
catch (SQLException e)
    {
       setErrorMessage ("getDriverInfo Failed: "
                       + e.getMessage());
       appendErrorMessage ("Vendor ErrorCode: "
                          + e.getErrorCode());
    }

    String[] headings = new String[2];
    headings[0] = ("SQL92 Level Supported");
headings[1] = (" ");
DataTable dt = new DataTable(dbInfo,headings);
return dt;

}
```

The getCatalogNames() method returns a Vector containing a list of
all the catalogs available in the current database. If catalogs are not supported
by the database, a null list is returned. Since the most likely application of this
data will be to create a tree or pick list of all available catalogs, the data is not
returned as a DataTable.

```
public synchronized Vector getCatalogNames()
{
 Vector catalogName= new Vector();
 try {
     DatabaseMetaData dbmd = conn.getMetaData();
     if (dbmd.supportsCatalogsInTableDefinitions())
       {
        ResultSet catalogRS = dbmd.getCatalogs();
        while (catalogRS.next())
          {
            catalogName.addElement(catalogRS.getString("TABLE_CAT"));
          }
       }
     else
       {
         catalogName.addElement("");
         msg ("Catalog names not supported.");
       }
     }
 catch (SQLException e)
   {
     setErrorMessage ("GetCatalogNames Failed: "
                     + e.getMessage());
```

```
                     appendErrorMessage ("Vendor ErrorCode: " +
                                       e.getErrorCode());
         }
   return catalogName;
}

/*
 * This method returns a list of all schemas available in the database.
 */

public synchronized Vector getSchemaNames()
{
 Vector schemaNames = new Vector ();
 try {
       DatabaseMetaData dbmd = conn.getMetaData();
       ResultSet schemaNameResultSet = dbmd.getSchemas();
       while ( schemaNameResultSet.next() )
         {
            schemaNames.addElement(schemaNameResultSet.getString
                                ("TABLE_SCHEM"));
         }
       }
       catch (SQLException e)
         {
            setErrorMessage ("GetSchema  Failed: "
                               + e.getMessage());
            appendErrorMessage ("Vendor ErrorCode: "
                                  + e.getErrorCode());
         }
   return schemaNames;
 }

/*
 * This method returns an array of Strings containing the names
 * of all the table types the database accepts.
 */

public synchronized String[] getTableTypes()
{
 Vector tableTypes= new Vector();
 try {
       DatabaseMetaData dbmd = conn.getMetaData();
       ResultSet tableTypesRS = dbmd.getTableTypes();
       while (tableTypesRS.next())
         {
          tableTypes.addElement(tableTypesRS.getString("TABLE_TYPE"));
         }
       }
       catch (SQLException e)
         {
          setErrorMessage ("GetTableTypes Failed: " + e.getMessage());
          appendErrorMessage ("Vendor ErrorCode: "
                               + e.getErrorCode());
         }
 // Convert Vector to an Array of Strings
 String [] types = new String[tableTypes.size()];
 for (int i=0; i<tableTypes.size(); i++)
   {
      types[i] = (String)tableTypes.elementAt(i);
      msg ("Table Type: " + types[i]);
```

```
        }
   return types;
  }
```

The `setTableNames()` method is used to return a list of all tables that are contained in the catalog and schema specified and are of a single table type.

```
public synchronized Vector getTableNames(String catalog,
                                  String schema, String tableType)
{
 Vector tableNames = new Vector();
 String[] tableTypes = new String[1];
 tableTypes[0] = tableType;

 try {
      DatabaseMetaData dbmd = conn.getMetaData();
      ResultSet tableNamesRS =
                    dbmd.getTables(catalog,schema,"%",tableTypes);
      while (tableNamesRS.next())
       {
        tableNames.addElement(tableNamesRS.getString
                                      ("TABLE_NAME"));
       }
      }
      catch (SQLException e)
       {
        setErrorMessage ("SetTableNames Failed: "
                            + e.getMessage());
        appendErrorMessage ("Vendor ErrorCode: "
                              + e.getErrorCode());
       }
   return tableNames;
  }
```

The `getTableNames()` method is also used to return a list of tables contained in the specified catalog and schema. However, this method takes an array listing the tableTypes.

```
public synchronized Vector getTableNames( String catalog,
                   String schema,
                   String[] tableTypes)
 {
  Vector tableNames = new Vector();

  try {
       DatabaseMetaData dbmd = conn.getMetaData();
       ResultSet tableNamesRS = dbmd.getTables(catalog,schema,
                                        "%",tableTypes);
       while (tableNamesRS.next())
        {

tableNames.addElement(tableNamesRS.getString("TABLE_NAME"));
        }
       }
       catch (SQLException e)
        {
         setErrorMessage ("SetTableNames Failed: "
                            + e.getMessage());
```

```
                    appendErrorMessage ("Vendor ErrorCode: "
                                         + e.getErrorCode());
        }
  return tableNames;
 }

/*
 * Creates the connection to the database and sets the login
 * properties.
 */

public synchronized void getSession ( String url,
                      String user,
                      String passwd )
{
 Connection conn = null;

 setLoginProperties(url,user,passwd);
 try {
      conn = DriverManager.getConnection(dbURL,loginProps);
      msg ("Logged in OK" );
     }
      catch (SQLException e)
        {
          setErrorMessage ("Connection Failed: " + e.getMessage());
          appendErrorMessage ("Vendor Error Code: " +
                              e.getErrorCode());
        }                                    // end catch

 }                                          // end getSession
```

The `executeSQL()` method executes any SQL statement and returns at least one DataTable containing either the data from the subsequent Result-Set or a one row table contianing the number of rows affected by the update. Because some RDBMS support multiple results from a single SQL statement there may be multiple DataTables returned in an array. In most cases only the DataTable[0] will be used by your applications.

```
public synchronized DataTable[] executeSQL ( String sqlString)
{
msg ("sqlString" + sqlString);
DataTable[] dataTables;
Vector vDataTables = new Vector();
boolean isMoreResults = true;
try {
     Statement stmt = conn.createStatement();
     stmt.execute(sqlString);
     int rowCount = stmt.getUpdateCount();
    // while ((rowCount > 0 ) || (isMoreResults = true )) put this
                                  back for book
     //   {
     if ( rowCount != -1 )
        {
          Vector[] updatedRowCount = new Vector[1];
          updatedRowCount[0].addElement(sqlString);
          updatedRowCount[0].addElement(new Integer(rowCount));
          String[] headings = new String[2];
```

```
            headings[0] = ("Statement Executed");
            headings[1] = ("Number of Rows effected");
            vDataTables.addElement(new DataTable(updatedRowCount,
                                            headings));
      isMoreResults = stmt.getMoreResults();
        rowCount = stmt.getUpdateCount();
        msg ("Got Row Count");
       }
      else
       {
        rs = stmt.getResultSet();
      vDataTables.addElement(new DataTable(rs));
      msg ("Got ResultSet");
        isMoreResults = stmt.getMoreResults();
        rowCount = stmt.getUpdateCount();

       }                                // end else(rs)
      //}                               // end while(moreResults)
    }
    catch (Exception e)
      {
        // setErrorMessage ("Execution Error: " +
                           e.printStackTrace());
        e.printStackTrace();
      }
    /* Convert the Vector containg the results to an array now
     * that we know how many elements (results) there are.
     */

    dataTables = new DataTable[vDataTables.size()];
    for (int i = 0; i < vDataTables.size(); i++)
      {
       dataTables[i] = (DataTable)vDataTables.elementAt(i);
      }
   return dataTables;
}

  /*
   * This method is provided since it is very common to select all the
   * elements from a table. This provides a shortcut for this common
   * task.
   */


public synchronized DataTable openTable (String tableName)
{
 DataTable[] dt = executeSQL("select * from " + tableName);
 return dt[0];
}

public synchronized void closeSession ()
  {
   try
     {
      conn.close();
     }
     catch (SQLException e)
       {
         setErrorMessage ("Close Failed: " + e.getMessage());
         appendErrorMessage ("Vendor Error Code: " + e.getErrorCode());
```

```
        }                                              // end catch
    }

    /*
     * The main method is used only to test the DBAccess class methods.
     */

    public synchronized static void main (String args[] )
    {
    try
    {
    DBAccess db1 = new DBAccess();
    db1.getSession("jdbc:weblogic:oracle","scott","tiger");
    DataTable[] dt = db1.executeSQL("select * from  employee");
    msg("Number of results of Query: " + dt.length);
    int columns = dt[0].getNumberOfColumns();
    int rows = dt[0].getNumberOfRows();
    msg("Number of Rows: " + rows );
    msg("Number of Cols: " + columns);

    //Print out a list of column titles (names).
    System.out.print("Titles");
    for (int i=1; i<=columns; i++)
      {
        System.out.print (dt[0].getColumnTitle(i) + " ");
      }
    System.out.println("");

    //Print out a list of column sizes.
    System.out.print ("Sizes");
    for (int i=1; i<=columns; i++)
      {
        System.out.print(dt[0].getColumnSize(i) + " ");

      }
    System.out.println ("");

    //Print out all the data in the table.
    for (int i=1; i<=rows; i++ )
      {
        for (int k=1; k<=columns; k++)
          {
            System.out.print( dt[0].getObjectAt(i,k) + " ");
          }
          System.out.println ("");
      }

    }
    catch (Exception e) { e.printStackTrace(); }
    }                                              // end main method
}                                                  // end DBAccess class
```

Chapter Summary

In this chapter, you were presented two new data components to provide access to a database. The first component, the DriverListManager class is used for the sole purpose of keeping a persistent list of JDBC drivers that can be read by your application. The second component, the DBAccess component, is used to login to the database, access the data, and return a DataTable object that can then be used to access the actual data. Once we have completed the data handling components, we will then be ready to move on to the next step of building a remote interface to these components so that they may be accessed by applets as well as stand-alone applications.

Buiding Data Handling Components

The DataBeans Package: DataTable Class

In Chapter 12, we developed the DBAccess components for our data browser. However, one of the drawbacks of JDBC is that it only allows for the seqential access of data in ResultSets and does not allow for multiple reads of the same data. Additionally, results that are not ResultSets must be handled separately. Therefore, to simplify access and provide a more flexible method of accessing results of all types, we will create the DataTable class.

The DataTable Class

The `DataTable` class is used to provided a common way to access all data. This data can be actual `ResultSets`, row counts or even groups of related meta data such as "database vendor information." Conceptually, you can think of all data being placed in an array of vectors, and having a row and column index. Each column of data has a certain amount of header information associated with it (meta data). Header information describes properties of that column, such as preferred display width, the SQL data type, and if it is a currency figure. Once the data is stored in our "two-dimensional array," you can then access it simply by referring to its row and column field pair. This allows for random access to any field, row, or column of data. This is much more flexible than using a row pointer and accessing all data sequentially. Additionally, we want to be able to access all of our results in the same manner. Row counts therefore are returned as a single row of data as in database meta data objects. This creates a consistent and uniform method for all data access.

Additionally, the standard JDBC methods provide no means for determining the number of rows returned by a query or in a `ResultSet`. The `DataTable` class extracts this information and allows direct access to it.

Below is a list and brief description of the methods in the DataTable class.

Error and exception handling methods include:

- `public static void msg (String message)`
  The msg method is used to print out embedded debugging information. It is controlled by the debug variable. Setting the debug variable to false will disable this method.

Constructor methods include:

- `public DataTable (ResultSet rs) throws Exception`
- `public DataTable (Vector[] metaTable, String[] columnNames) throws Exception`
- `public DataTable ()`

As you can see, there are three `DataTable` constructor methods. The first one accepts a `ResultSet` as an argument and will most likely be the most commonly used form. It is used whenever you have executed an SQL query.

The second form excepts an array of `Vectors` and an array of `Strings`. This form of the constructor is provided so that you can create `DataTable` objects out of non `ResultSet` data. This gives you the flexibility to convert any type of data into a `DataTable` object. By doing this, you can then access any type of data in a consistent and uniform manner.

The third form of the constructor is provided solely for the use of visual development tools. Many such tools, such as the BeanBox, require that there be a constructor defined which takes no arguments.

Data retrieval methods include:

- ```
  public Object[] getColumn (int index) throws
                            SQLException
  ```
- ```
  public Object[] getColumn (String columnTitle)
                            throws SQLException
  ```

The `getColumn()` method returns an array of `Objects` referenced by the index number argument or the column name. Since all data in a single column are of the same data type, they are returned as an array of `Objects`.

All tables begin with column index number 1. However, all arrays begin with index number 0. As a result of this, it is easy to confuse the column index and array index numbers and retrieve the wrong column of data.

- ```
  public Vector getRow (int index) throws
  SQLException
  ```

The getRow method returns the row of data referenced by the index number argument. Since a row can contain various data types, the data is returned in a Vector.

- ```
  public Object getObjectAt (int row, int column)
                            throws SQLException
  ```
- ```
  public Object getObjectAt (int row, String
                            column) throws
                            SQLException
  ```

The `getObjectAt()` method returns a single field of data referenced by the row and column arguments. As with the `getColumn()` method, a column can be referenced by index number or by name.

Header information and row count retreival methods include:

- ```
  public String getColumnTitle (int index) throws
                              SQLException
  ```
- ```
  public String getColumnTitle (String colName)
                              throws SQLException
  ```
- ```
  public String[] getColumnTitles () throws
                              SQLException
  ```

These three `getColumnTitle()` methods are used to retrieve either a single preferred column name (title) or a list of column names within the table. In most instances, the preferred name will be the same as the column name, however, in instances where aliases have been assigned to column or an alternate column label has been assigned, the alternate name is considered the preferred name. A column name is the actual name known to the database and bound to the table. The title is the name of the column for display purposes.

- `public int getColumnSize (int index) throws`
  `SQLException`
- `public int getColumnSize (String colName) throws`
  `SQLException`
- `public int[] getColumnSizes () throws`
  `SQLException`

These three methods return either a single or list of integer(s) representing the display width for a given column. If the actual width of the column exceeds the maximum value set, then the maximum size is returned.

- `public String getColumnType (int index) throws`
  `SQLException`
- `public String getColumnType (String colName)`
  `throws SQLException`
- `public String[] getColumnTypes () throws`
  `SQLException`

The `getColumnTypes()` methods return the SQL data type for the indicated column.

- `public int getColumnPrecision (int index) throws`
  `SQLException`
- `public int getColumnPrecision (String colName)`
  `throws`
  `SQLException`
- `public int[] getColumnPrecisions () throws`
  `SQLException`
- `public int getColumnScale (int index) throws`
  `SQLException`
- `public int getColumnScale (String colName)`
  `throws SQLException`
- `public int[] getColumnScales () throws SQLException`

These methods return the scale or precision associated with the referenced column. If the column does not contain numeric data, then a null value is returned.

- ```
  public boolean getColumnCaseSensitive (int index)
                                          throws
                                          SQLException
  ```
- ```
  public boolean getColumnCaseSensitive (String col-
                                          Name) throws
                                          SQLException
  ```
- ```
  public boolean[] getColumnCaseSensitive () throws
                                             SQLexcep-
                                             tion
  ```
- ```
  public boolean getColumnIsCurrency (int index)
                                       throws
                                       SQLException
  ```
- ```
  public boolean getColumnIsCurrency (String col-
                                       Name) throws
                                       SQLException
  ```
- ```
  public boolean[] getColumnIsCurrency () throws
                                           SQLException
  ```

These methods return a boolean indicating whether or not the referenced column contains currency or is case sensitive.

- ```
  public int getNumberOfRows ()
  ```
- ```
  public int getNumberOfColumns()
  ```

The last two methods in the DataTable class return the number of rows or number of columns of data in the result table.

The DataTable class contains the ResultData in a more usable format. The DataTable class provides methods for retreiving data in rows, columns or feilds. It will also provide information such as the number of columns, rows and column header information. All data results (ResultSets, Row Counts and MetaData) should be converted to DataTable(s) before being presented to the user.

All methods throw Exceptions to allow for the main calling application to handle all error messages.

```
package DataBeans;

import java.util.Vector;
import java.sql.*;

public class DataTable
    {
    Vector[] dataTable;
    ResultSet rs;
    ResultSetMetaData rsmd;
    String[] mColumnNames;
    String errorMessage;
```

```
boolean isMetaTable = false;
int numberOfColumns;
int numberOfRows;
int maxColumnSize = 32;
static boolean debug = false;
boolean autoClearErrorMessages;

 /*
  * This method is used to print embeded error messages or
  * information you may want to use for debugging. You
  * can turn off all debug messages by changing
  * the value of debug to true to turn this feature on.
  * You can also modify this method to redirect the messages.
  */

 private static void msg (String message)
 {
   if (debug)
    {
     System.out.println (message);
    }
 }
 /*
  * All exceptions are handled by setting the errorMessage string
  * variable using this method.
  */

 private void setErrorMessage(String message)
 {
  errorMessage = (message);
  msg (message);
 }                                        // end setErrorMessage method

 /*
  * Multiple exceptions that need to be chained together, can be
  * appended to the existing errorMessage string using the
  * appendErrorMessage method.
  */

 private void appendErrorMessage (String message)
 {
  errorMessage += ("\n" + message);
 }                                        // end appendErrorMessage
                                                    method

 /*
  * Error messages are retrieved by the getTableErrorMessages method.
  */

 public synchronized String getTableErrorMessage ()
 {
  String thisErrorMessage = errorMessage;
  if (autoClearErrorMessages)
   {
     clearTableErrorMessages();
   }
   return thisErrorMessage;
 }                                          // end getErrormessage method

 /*
```

```
 * The default is to have error messages automatically cleared when
 * they are retrieved by the getTableErrorMessage method. This
 * method can be used to toggle this feature on or off.
 */

public synchronized void setTableAutoClearErrorMessages (boolean
                                                            auto)
 {
   autoClearErrorMessages = auto;
 }

/*
 * Error messages are cleared manually by calling this method or
 * can be automatically cleared  using this method.
 */

public synchronized void clearTableErrorMessages()
{
  errorMessage=null;
}                                          // end clearErrormessage
                                              method
```

This first constructor method is called when a ResultSet is to be converted to a DataTable object. If data contained in Vectors is to be used to
create the DataTable object, the second constructor method is called.

```
public DataTable (ResultSet rs)
{
 this.rs = rs;
 try
  {
    rsmd = rs.getMetaData();

 Vector tmp = new Vector();
 Vector row = null;
 Object data = null;

 numberOfColumns = rsmd.getColumnCount();
 while (rs.next())
  {
  row = new Vector();
  for(int i=1;i<= numberOfColumns;i++)
    {
    switch (rsmd.getColumnType(i))
        {
        case java.sql.Types.BINARY:
          data = "Binary Data Truncated";
              row.addElement(data);
             break;
        case java.sql.Types.LONGVARBINARY:
          data = "Binary Data Truncated";
              row.addElement(data);
             break;
        default:
              row.addElement(rs.getObject(i));
          }
      }
      tmp.addElement(row);
```

```
    }
    numberOfRows = tmp.size();
    dataTable = new Vector[numberOfRows];
    for (int k=0; k< numberOfRows; k++)
       {
       dataTable[k] = new Vector();
       for (int j=0; j < (((Vector)tmp.elementAt(k)).size()); j++)
          {
          dataTable[k].addElement(((Vector)tmp.elementAt(k)).
                                     elementAt(j));
          }
       }
    }
    catch (SQLException e)
     {
     setErrorMessage ("Error: " +  e.getMessage());
     }
   }
```

This constructor method is used whenever "meta data" or other data not contained in a `ResultSet` is used to create the `DataTable`.

```
public DataTable ( Vector[] metaTable,
            String[] columnNames)
{
 dataTable = metaTable;
 mColumnNames = columnNames;
 numberOfColumns = metaTable[0].size();
 numberOfRows = metaTable.length;
 rs = null;
 isMetaTable = true;
}

/*
 * This method will return the column "title" for the column
 * referenced by the index value. This method is called by the
 * getColumnTitles method to create an array containing titles
 * for all of the columns.
 */

public synchronized String getColumnTitle(int index)
{
 String colTitle = new String();
 if (isMetaTable)
  {
    colTitle = mColumnNames[index];
    }
  else
    {
    try
     {
     colTitle = rsmd.getColumnLabel(index);
     if ( colTitle == null )
    {
    colTitle = rsmd.getColumnName(index);
    }
 }
    catch (SQLException e)
     {
```

```java
              setErrorMessage ("Error: " +  e.getMessage());
          }
      }
  return colTitle;
}

/*
 * Returns a complete list of all column "titles".
 */

public synchronized String[] getColumnTitles()
 {
  String[] data = new String[numberOfColumns];
  if (isMetaTable)
   {
    data = mColumnNames;
   }
  else
   {
    for (int i=0; i < (numberOfColumns); i++)
     {
      data[i] = getColumnTitle(i+1);
     }
   }
  return data;
 }

/*
 * Returns the width (in characters) of the referenced column.
 * This method is called by the getColumnSizes method to create
 * a list of all column sizes.
 */


public synchronized int getColumnSize (int index)
{
 int data = -1;
 if (isMetaTable)
      {
        data = maxColumnSize;
        msg ("Is Meta Table Data Size");
      }
      else
      {
       try
        {
        int tmp = rsmd.getColumnDisplaySize(index);
        msg ("Temp Display Size" + tmp);
        if (tmp < maxColumnSize)
           {
            data = tmp;
            msg ("Is Real Data Size");
           }
        else
          {
           data = maxColumnSize;
           msg ("Is Tuncated (max) Data Size");
          }
        }
       catch (SQLException e)
```

```
            {
        setErrorMessage ("Error: " +  e.getMessage());
            }
          }
    return data;
  }

/*
 * Returns a complete list of the width of all columns in an array.
 */
public synchronized int[] getColumnSizes ()
{
 int[] data = new int[numberOfColumns];
 data = null;
 for (int i=0; i < (numberOfColumns); i++)
    {
    data[i] = getColumnSize(i+1);
      }
    return data;
  }



/*
 * Returns the SQL data type of the column referenced. Called
 * by getColumnTypes.
 */


public synchronized String getColumnType (int index)
{
String data = null;
if (isMetaTable)
    {
      data = null;
    }
  else
    {
      try
        {
         data = rsmd.getColumnTypeName(index);
        }
        catch (SQLException e)
          {
          setErrorMessage ("Error: " +  e.getMessage());
            }
          }
    return data;
  }

/*
 * Returns a list of all SQL Data Types for all columns.
 */


public synchronized String[] getColumnTypes ()
{
 String[] data = new String[numberOfColumns];
 for (int i=0; i < (numberOfColumns); i++)
    {
```

```
      data[i] = getColumnType(i+1);
      }
   return data;
   }

   /*
   * Get the precision (number of digits to the right of decimal
   * point for the column. If the column is not a numeric column
   * and has no precision associated with it, null is return. Called
   * by getColumnPrecisions.
   */

   public synchronized int getColumnPrecision (int index)
   {
    int data = 0;
    if (isMetaTable)
      {
       data = 0;
      }
    else
      {
       try
         {
          data = rsmd.getPrecision(index);
         }
         catch (SQLException e)
          {
          setErrorMessage ("Error: " +  e.getMessage());
          }
        }
    return data;
   }

   /*
   * Return the precision for all columns.
   */

   public synchronized int[] getColumnPrecisions ()
   {
   int data[] = new int[numberOfColumns];
   for (int i=0; i < (numberOfColumns); i++)
    {
      data[i] = getColumnPrecision(i+1);
    }
   return data;
   }

   /*
   * Return the scale ( number to left of decimal point) for the
   * column referenced. Called by getColumnScales
   */

   public synchronized int getColumnScale (int index)
   {
    int data = 0;
    if (isMetaTable)
      {
       data = 0;
      }
    else
```

```
      {
       try
         {
          data = rsmd.getScale(index);
          }
        catch (SQLException e)
          {
        setErrorMessage ("Error: " +  e.getMessage());
           }
        }
       return data;
      }

   /*
    * Returns the scale for all columns.
    */

   public synchronized int[] getColumnScales ()
   {
    int data[] = new int[numberOfColumns];
    for (int i=0; i < (numberOfColumns); i++)
       {
          data[i] = getColumnScale(i+1);
          }
    return data;
   }

   /*
    * Returns true if the database requires that the column name
    * match the case exactly. Called by getColumnCaseSensitivities.
    */

   public synchronized boolean getColumnCaseSensitive (int index)
   {
    boolean data = false;
    if (isMetaTable)
      {
       data = false;
      }
    else
      {
       try
         {
          data = rsmd.isCaseSensitive(index);
          }
        catch (SQLException e)
          {
        setErrorMessage ("Error: " +  e.getMessage());
           }
       }
      return data;
   }

   /*
    * Returns a list of case requirments for each column.
    */

   public synchronized boolean[] getColumnCaseSensitivities ()
   {
    boolean data[] = new boolean[numberOfColumns];
```

```
    for (int i=0; i < (numberOfColumns); i++)
     {
       data[i] = getColumnCaseSensitive(i+1);
     }
   return data;
 }

/* Returns true if the referenced column contains currency figures.
 * Called by the getColumnisCurrencies method.
 */

public synchronized boolean getColumnIsCurrency (int index)
 {
 boolean data = false;
 if (isMetaTable)
    {
     data = false;
    }
   else
    {
    try
     {
      data = rsmd.isCurrency(index);
     }
     catch (SQLException e)
      {
      setErrorMessage ("Error: " +  e.getMessage());
       }
    }
  return data;
 }

 /*
  * Return list of the currency status of all columns.
  */

 public synchronized boolean[] getColumnIsCurrencies ()
 {
  boolean data[] = new boolean[numberOfColumns];
  for (int i=0; i < (numberOfColumns); i++)
    {
      data[i] = getColumnIsCurrency(i+1);
    }
  return data;
 }

 public synchronized int getNumberOfColumns ()
 {
  return numberOfColumns ;
 }

 public synchronized int getNumberOfRows()
 {
  return numberOfRows;
 }

 public synchronized Vector getRow (int index)
 {
   return dataTable[index-1];
 }
```

```
public synchronized Object[] getColumn (int index)
{
  Object data[] = new Object[numberOfRows];
  for (int i=0; i < numberOfRows; i++ )
   {
    data[i] = dataTable[i].elementAt(index-1);
   }
  return data;
}

/*
 * Return an individual data (field)object referenced
 * by the row and column.
 */

public synchronized Object getObjectAt (int row, int column)
{
  return (dataTable[row-1].elementAt(column-1));
}
}
```

Chapter Summary

In this chapter, I demonstrated how to build software components that are used to simplify access to data results. The new functionality added by these components provide a solid foundation from which to build data access applications and removes some of the bottlenecks and difficuties that arise from using the JDBC methods directly. As we saw in Part One of the book, the goal of JDBC is to provide the base functionality for accessing the data and it is up to the developer to create higher level interfaces to the data as we have done here. With both the DBAccess and DataTable components, you can now build database applications more quickly than before.

The complete source code for all of the DataBeans components are on the CD-ROM. They are located in the /source/**platform**/DataBeans directory.

RMI and JDBC

Building Remote Database Access Components

Part One of this book introduced RMI as a means to build three-tier client/server environments. Three-tier environments help overcome some of the limitations of two-tier environments and some of the current limitations of JDBC drivers. In this chapter, we will build four new components to add to our existing components built in Chapters 12 and 13. This will enable any RMI-enabled web browser to access a remote database. Furthermore, we will actually improve performance by removing the need for the driver to be downloaded and lessening the size of the objects transferred between the client and the server.

Overview of RMI Framework

To begin the process of adapting our database access components for remote client use, we will need to build the necessary framework for RMI. This framework consists of four new components. The three server-side components are discussed in detail in this chapter, while the final chapter is dedicated to the fourth component—the client application. Here is an overview of each of these four new components.

The Remote Interface

The first component to be built is the remote interface. This component, like all interfaces, only describes the methods and variables available to the client. The interface does not implement any methods. In our case, since we have both the `DBAccess` and `DataTable` classes with methods that we want to make available to the clients, the DataAcecess interface will contain an entry for every public method in both of these classes.

The Remote Interface Implementation

After you have completed writing the remote interface, it is time to implement the interface. The implementation is a server-side component that will act as a proxy for the client. Remember that with RMI, remote objects are not actually downloaded to the client, but rather only references (handle) to the object. When executed, they execute on the server, not the client. Results and return values are first serialized and then sent back to the client.

The implementation will also be used to generate the client-side stubs and server-side skeleton. It is the stubs and skeletons that actually perform communications between ther server and the client. To generate them, you will need to run the *rmic* command against the implementations class file. For example, our remote interface implementation will be called RemoteDBAccess. The command to generate the stubs and skeletons is:

```
rmic DataBeans.RemoteDBAccess
```

If you have included your implementation in a package, as we have here, you will need to copy the stubs and skeletons into the package directory after running *rmic*. The default behavior of *rmic* is to place the skeletons and stubs in the current directory.

The RMI Server

The last server-side component is the RMI server application. This is a small stand-alone application that binds the remote objects to the RMI registry. The registry is a process run on the server that contains a list of objects available to clients. The server application contains a single instance of the implementation and binds this instance to the registry. When a client needs access to the remote object, he or she contacts the registry which in turn will return a reference to the instance. However, it is important to note that this single instance is shared by all remote clients and therefore must be written in such a way as to accommodate multiple users.

To start up the server application and bind it to a registry, you will first need to start the registry process itself. Depending on your platform, you will need to do one of the following:

For Windows95 and WindowsNT:

```
start rmiregistry
```

For Solaris:

```
rmiregistry &
```

The registry will listen for requests on the default port number 8099. If you wish to change this port number, you can simply append it to the startup command. For instance, to tell the registry to listen on port 8088 instead use the following:

For Windows95 and WindowsNT:

```
start rmiregistry 8088
```

For Solaris:

```
rmiregistry 8088 &
```

The Client Applet

The client applet is the last piece to our puzzle. Now that all the server-side components are in place, the client applet simply needs to obtain a reference to the remote object. Once the client has the reference to the object, you are on your way and can begin using the objects made available through the remote interface.

Figure 14.1 is a diagram outlining the four components and how they interact with each other.

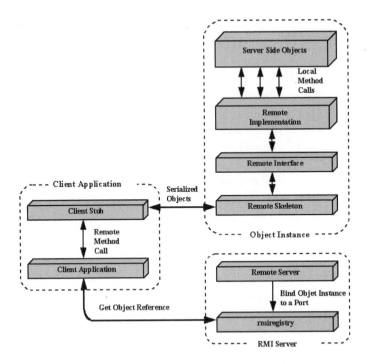

The DataBeans Remote Interfaces

In order for any remote client to access our `DBAccess` or `DataTable` components, we will first need to complete the remote interface. The interface will define all the methods and their arguments that are available to the clients. Therefore, all public methods (other than the constructors) contained in the `DBAccess` and `DataTable` classes will have a remote interface entry.

You will note that nearly all of the methods listed in the interface have an additional argument being passed to them. The additional argument is a reference ID. Since there is only a single instance of the remote interface implementation, the implementation itself must be able to create multiple instances of the `DBAccess` and `DataTable` objects. Otherwise we would only be able to have a single client. Since there may be multiple instances of the `DBAccess` or `DataTable` object within the remote implementaion, the reference ID is nessessary to determine which object is to be used. The object reference ID will be discussed more in the section on the remote implementation component "RemoteDBAccess."

The code for both the `DBAccess` and `DataTable` remote interfaces follows:

```
package DataBeans;

import java.rmi.*;
import java.sql.*;
import java.util.*;

public interface DataAccess extends java.rmi.Remote
{

  public String getErrorMessage (int sessionID) throws
                          RemoteException;
  public void setAutoClearErrorMessages (boolean auto,int sessionID)
                                throws RemoteException;
  public void clearErrorMessages(int sessionID) throws
                          RemoteException;
  public int getLoginProperties (int sessionID) throws
                          RemoteException;
  public int getDBInfo (int sessionID) throws RemoteException;
  public int getDriverInfo (int sessionID) throws RemoteException;
  public int getSQLLevelInfo (int sessionID) throws RemoteException;
  public Vector getCatalogNames(int sessionID) throws RemoteException;
  public Vector getSchemaNames(int sessionID) throws RemoteException;
  public String[] getTableTypes(int sessionID) throws RemoteException;
  public Vector getTableNames( String catalog, String schema, String
                          tableType, int sessionID) throws
                          RemoteException;
  public Vector getTableNames( String catalog, String schema, String[]
                          tableTypes, int sessionID) throws
                          RemoteException;
  public int getSession ( String url, String user, String passwd)
                     throws RemoteException;
  public int[] executeSQL ( String sqlString, int sessionID) throws
                     RemoteException;
  public int openTable ( String tableName, int sessionID) throws
                     RemoteException;
  public void closeSession (int sessionID) throws RemoteException;
  public String getTableErrorMessage (int tableID) throws
                          RemoteException;
  public void setTableAutoClearErrorMessages (boolean auto,int
                                tableID) throws
                                RemoteException;
  public void clearTableErrorMessages(int tableID) throws
                          RemoteException;
  public String getColumnTitle(int columnIndex, int tableID) throws
                     RemoteException;
  public String[] getColumnTitles(int tableID) throws RemoteException;
  public int getColumnSize (int columnIndex, int tableID) throws
                     RemoteException;
  public int[] getColumnSizes (int tableID) throws RemoteException;
  public String getColumnType (int columnIndex, int tableID) throws
                     RemoteException;
  public String[] getColumnTypes (int tableID) throws RemoteException;
  public int getColumnPrecision (int columnIndex,int tableID) throws
                          RemoteException;
  public int[] getColumnPrecisions (int tableID) throws
                               RemoteException;
  public int getColumnScale (int columnIndex,int tableID) throws
                          RemoteException;
  public int[] getColumnScales (int tableID) throws RemoteException;
```

```
    public boolean getColumnCaseSensitive (int columnIndex,int tableID)
                                          throws RemoteException;
    public boolean[] getColumnCaseSensitivities (int tableID) throws
                                          RemoteException;
    public boolean getColumnIsCurrency (int columnIndex,int tableID)
                                          throws RemoteException;
    public boolean[] getColumnIsCurrencies (int tableID) throws
                                          RemoteException;
    public int getNumberOfColumns (int tableID) throws RemoteException;
    public int getNumberOfRows(int tableID) throws RemoteException;
    public Vector getRow (int columnIndex,int tableID) throws
                        RemoteException;
    public Vector getColumn (int columnIndex, int tableID) throws
                        RemoteException;
    public Object getObjectAt (int row, int column, int tableID) throws
                        RemoteException;
    public String getColumnTitle (String colName,int tableID) throws
                        RemoteException;
     public int getColumnSize (String colName,int tableID) throws
                        RemoteException;
    public String getColumnType (String colName,int tableID) throws
                        RemoteException;
    public int getColumnPrecision (String colName,int tableID) throws
                        RemoteException;
    public int getColumnScale (String colName,int tableID) throws Remo-
                        teException;
    public boolean getColumnCaseSensitive (String colName,int tableID)
                                          throws RemoteException;
    public boolean getColumnIsCurrency (String colName,int tableID)
                                          throws RemoteException;
    public Vector getColumn (String colName,int tableID) throws
                        RemoteException;

    public Object getObjectAt (int row,String column,int tableID) throws
                        RemoteException;
}
```

The Remote Interface Implementation

After creating the remote interface we are ready to implement it. The implementation code is simply a multi-user wrapper that goes around our existing components. The `RemoteDBAccess` component accomplishes this by creating two stacks containing integers. Each integer is a reference ID for either a `DBAccess` object or `DataTable` object. Next, an array of each object is initialized to the same number of object ID numbers on each stack. When a client requests access to one of these objects, an ID number is popped off the appropriate stack, a new instance of the object is created and placed in the object array using the ID number as the array index. Now, whenever the client needs to access that object, it can easily be referenced by using the ID number as the array index. Figure 14.2 shows how this might look.

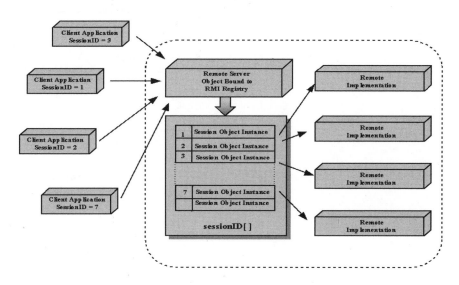

When the user is done with the object, the object is disposed of and the
ID number is pushed back on the stack. The ID number can then be used
again by the next user.

The code for the remote implementation follows:

```
package DataBeans;

import java.rmi.*;
import java.sql.*;
import java.util.*;
import java.rmi.server.UnicastRemoteObject;

public class RemoteDBAccess extends UnicastRemoteObject implements
DBAccessInterface,DataTableInterface
  {
  public int maxSessions = 25;
  public int maxOpenTables = 100;

  private DBAccess[] session = new DBAccess[maxSessions];
  private DataTable[] table = new DataTable[maxOpenTables];
  private Stack sessionStack = new Stack();
  private Stack tableStack = new Stack();

  private static boolean debug = true;

  public static void msg (String message)
  {
    if (debug)
      {
      System.out.println (message);
      }
  }
```

```
public RemoteDBAccess () throws RemoteException
{
   for (int i = 0; i < session.length; i++ )
   {
     sessionStack.push(new Integer(i));
     msg ("Pushed session ID " + i + " on stack. ");
   }
   for (int i = 0; i < table.length; i++ )
    {
       tableStack.push(new Integer(i));
       msg ("Pushed Table ID " + i + " on stack. ");
    }
}

public String getErrorMessage (int sessionID) throws RemoteException
{
 return session[sessionID].getErrorMessage();
 }

public void setAutoClearErrorMessages (boolean auto,
                            int sessionID) throws RemoteException
  {
    session[sessionID].setAutoClearErrorMessages(auto);
   }

public void clearErrorMessages(int sessionID) throws RemoteException
  {
    session[sessionID].clearErrorMessages();
   }

public int getLoginProperties (int sessionID) throws RemoteException
  {
    int tableID;
    if (tableStack.empty())
   {
    msg ("Table Stack Empty");
    tableID = -1;
    }
   else
      {
       tableID = (((Integer)(sessionStack.pop())).intValue());
       table[tableID] = session[sessionID].getLoginProperties();
       }
    return tableID;
   }

public int getDBInfo (int sessionID) throws RemoteException
  {
    int tableID;
    if (tableStack.empty())
   {
    msg ("Table Stack Empty");
    tableID = -1;
    }
   else
      {
      tableID = (((Integer)(sessionStack.pop())).intValue());
       table[tableID] = session[sessionID].getDBInfo();
       }
```

```
      return tableID;
    }

public int getDriverInfo ( int sessionID) throws RemoteException
  {
    int tableID;
    if (tableStack.empty())
    {
     msg ("Table Stack Empty");
     tableID = -1;
    }
    else
       {
     tableID = (((Integer)(sessionStack.pop())).intValue());
        table[tableID] = session[sessionID].getDriverInfo();
        }
    return tableID;
    }

public int getSQLLevelInfo ( int sessionID ) throws RemoteException
  {
    int tableID;
    if (tableStack.empty())
    {
     msg ("Table Stack Empty");
     tableID = -1;
    }
    else
       {
     tableID = (((Integer)(sessionStack.pop())).intValue());
        table[tableID] = session[sessionID].getSQLLevelInfo();
        }

    return tableID;
    }

public Vector getCatalogNames(int sessionID) throws RemoteException
  {
    return session[sessionID].getCatalogNames();
  }

public Vector getSchemaNames(int sessionID) throws RemoteException
  {
    return session[sessionID].getSchemaNames();
  }

public String[] getTableTypes(int sessionID) throws RemoteException
  {
    return session[sessionID].getTableTypes();
  }

public Vector getTableNames(String catalog, String schema,
                            String tableType, int sessionID)
                            throws RemoteException
  {
    return session[sessionID].getTableNames(catalog, schema,
                                            tableType);
  }
```

```java
public Vector getTableNames(String catalog, String schema,
                            String[] tableTypes, int sessionID)
                            throws RemoteException
  {
     return session[sessionID].getTableNames(catalog, schema,
                                             tableTypes);
  }

public int getSession ( String url, String user, String passwd)
                        throws RemoteException
  {
    int sessionID;
     if (sessionStack.empty())
     {
       msg ("Session Stack empty");
       sessionID = -1;
      }
     else
         {
          sessionID = (((Integer)(sessionStack.pop())).intValue());
          session[sessionID] = new DBAccess();
          session[sessionID].getSession(url,user,passwd );
         }
      msg ("Session Stack Number assigned :" + sessionID );
         return sessionID;
  }

public int[] executeSQL ( String sqlString, int sessionID ) throws
                        RemoteException
  {
    int tableID;
    int[] tableIDs;
    DataTable[] tempTables;

    tempTables = session[sessionID].executeSQL(sqlString);
    tableIDs = new int[tempTables.length];

    for (int i = 0; i < tempTables.length; i++ )
    {
    if (tableStack.empty())
    {
      msg ("Table Stack Empty");
      tableID = -1;
     }
    else
        {
         tableID = (((Integer)(sessionStack.pop())).intValue());
         table[tableID] = tempTables[tableID];
         tableIDs[i] = tableID;
         }
     }
     return tableIDs;
  }

public int openTable (String tableName, int sessionID) throws
                       RemoteException
  {
    int tableID;
    if (tableStack.empty())
    {
```

```
      msg ("Table Stack Empty");
      tableID = -1;
     }
    else
       {
         tableID = (((Integer)(sessionStack.pop())).intValue());
         table[tableID] = session[sessionID].openTable(tableName);
       }

    return tableID;
   }

public void closeTable (int tableID) throws RemoteException
  {
    table[tableID] = null;
    tableStack.push(new Integer(tableID));
    msg("Table ID pushed back on stack:" + tableID);
  }

public void closeSession (int sessionID) throws RemoteException
   {
    session[sessionID].closeSession();
    sessionStack.push(new Integer(sessionID));
    msg("Session ID pushed back on stack:" + sessionID);
   }

public String getTableErrorMessage (int tableID)
                                    throws RemoteException
 {
  return table[tableID].getTableErrorMessage();
 }

public void setTAbleAutoClearErrorMessages (boolean auto,
                                            int tableID) throws
                                            RemoteException
  {
    table[tableID].setTableAutoClearErrorMessages(auto);
   }

public void clearTableErrorMessages(int tableID)
                                    throws RemoteException
  {
    table[tableID].clearTableErrorMessages();
   }

public String getColumnTitle(int columnIndex, int tableID)
                            throws RemoteException
 {
  return table[tableID].getColumnTitle(columnIndex);
 }

public String[] getColumnTitles(int tableID) throws RemoteException
{
  return table[tableID].getColumnTitles();
 }

public int getColumnSize (int columnIndex, int tableID)
                         throws RemoteException
{
  return table[tableID].getColumnSize(columnIndex);
```

```
  }

public int[] getColumnSizes (int tableID) throws RemoteException
{
  return table[tableID].getColumnSizes();
  }

public String getColumnType (int columnIndex, int tableID)
                            throws RemoteException
{
  return table[tableID].getColumnType(columnIndex);
  }

public String[] getColumnTypes (int tableID) throws RemoteException
{
  return table[tableID].getColumnTypes();
  }

public int getColumnPrecision (int columnIndex,int tableID)
                              throws RemoteException
{
  return table[tableID].getColumnPrecision(columnIndex);
  }

public int[] getColumnPrecisions (int tableID)
                                throws RemoteException
{
  return table[tableID].getColumnPrecisions();
  }

public int getColumnScale (int columnIndex,int tableID)
                          throws RemoteException
{
  return table[tableID].getColumnScale(columnIndex);
  }

public int[] getColumnScales (int tableID) throws RemoteException
{
  return table[tableID].getColumnScales();
  }

public boolean getColumnCaseSensitive (int columnIndex,int tableID)
                                      throws RemoteException
{
  return table[tableID].getColumnCaseSensitive(columnIndex);
  }

public boolean[] getColumnCaseSensitivities (int tableID)
                                            throws RemoteException
{
  return table[tableID].getColumnCaseSensitivities();
  }

public boolean getColumnIsCurrency (int columnIndex,int tableID)
                                   throws RemoteException
{
  return table[tableID].getColumnIsCurrency(columnIndex);
  }
```

```
         public boolean[] getColumnIsCurrencies (int tableID)
                                              throws RemoteException
         {
           return table[tableID].getColumnIsCurrencies();
         }

         public int getNumberOfColumns (int tableID) throws RemoteException
         {
           return table[tableID].getNumberOfColumns();
         }

         public int getNumberOfRows(int tableID) throws RemoteException
         {
           return table[tableID].getNumberOfRows();
         }

         public Vector getRow (int rowIndex,int tableID)
                           throws RemoteException
         {
           return table[tableID].getRow(rowIndex);
         }

         public Object[] getColumn (int columnIndex, int tableID)
                           throws RemoteException
         {
           return table[tableID].getColumn(columnIndex);
         }

         public Object getObjectAt (int rowIndex, int columnIndex,
                               int tableID) throws RemoteException
         {
           return table[tableID].getObjectAt (rowIndex,columnIndex);
         }

    }
```

The RMI Server Object

As mentioned earlier, the server object is a small application that simply creates a single instance of the remote implementation object and binds that object to a name in the registry. When clients need access to that object, they obtain a reference to the bound object through the registry. In this example, I create a single instance of `RemoteDBAccess` and bind it to the name "RemoteDB" in the registry. Once bound, clients can begin obtaining references to that instance of the `RemoteDBAccess` object. Below is the `RemoteDBServer` application code:

```
package DataBeans;

import java.rmi.*;

public class RemoteDBServer
  {
  public static void main (String args[])
```

```
        {
    System.out.println ("Starting Remote DBAccess Server...");
    System.setSecurityManager(new RMISecurityManager());
    try {
        RemoteDBAccess remoteServer = new RemoteDBAccess();
        //Naming.rebind("rmi://localhost:1099/RemoteDB",remoteServer);
        Naming.rebind("RemoteDB",remoteServer);
        String names[] = (Naming.list("RemoteDB"));
        System.out.println ("RMI Server Started and Bound to:"
                            + names[0]);
        System.out.println ("RMI Server Started");
        }
    catch (Exception e)
    {
      System.out.println ("Error in RMI Server Startup:"
                          + e.getMessage());
      //e.printStackTrace();
      }

    }
}
```

Chapter Summary

This chapter began with a whirlwind tour of RMI and demonstrated how to implement the key components of any RMI application. In the latter part of the chapter, we developed the interface, interface implementation, and RMI server to interact with the database components built in Chapters 12 and 13. With these three new components we are now ready to complete our project of building a database browser capable of accessing any remote database. In Chapter 15, we will build that last component; the client applet.

Building the Database Browser Client

In three previous chapters, we created several new components to help simplify database access with JDBC. The `DBAccess` and `DataTable` components provide the actual interaction with the database while the `DataAccess` interface, as implemented by the `RemoteDBAccess` class, provides the necessary wrappers to allow for remote access via RMI. In this final chapter, we will shift our attention away from the data access and server portion of our client/server model and concentrate on the client portion. Also in this chapter, we will build a client application that uses many of the new components built in earlier chapters.

The DBClient Application

The DBClient class is a stand-alone application which provides a user interface for browsing tables in a database. The DBClient main window is broken into two major elements. On the left-hand side, we will build a node tree that displays all of the available catalogs (if supported), schemas, and tables. From the tree, you can select a table node and have its contents displayed on the right-side portion of the screen. Each table is fitted with appropriate scroll bars and headers, and is placed in a "tab folder" so that you can quickly navigate among mulitiple tables. While the data browser does not use all of our data components, it does demonstrate how to incorporate these new elements into your own applications.

Figure 15-1 shows what the Database Browser window looks like.

Figure 15-1
Database Browser
app. screen shot.

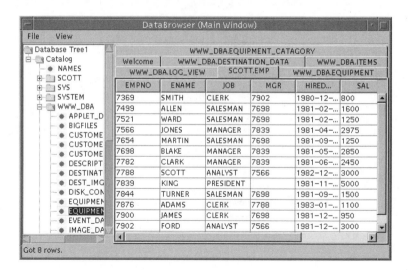

A Word about Java Fondation Classes

Before we jump into the code, there are a few items that need to be mentioned. First is that this application uses class libraries from JavaSoft's pre-release of the Java Fondation Classes Version 0.41 (JFC). The JFCs are not available on the accompanying CD-ROM. You can, however, download them from java.sun.com. The reason they are not incuded is that since JFCs are a pre-release, they are subject to change at any time. At this point, you may be wondering why I have based the example on them?

For this answer, you have to understand a bit about the goals and philosophy that I have for this book. First, I wanted to make sure that all of the code and examples could be tested and run by anyone on any platform. This means 100% pure Java. Also, I get very irritated when I purchase a computer programming book because of some slick screen shot inside, only to find out that if I want to acually build that nifty application, I will need to plunk down more cash and buy somone else's code. Therefore, for this book, I wanted to find a way to create the Database Browser from libraries that are freely available to everyone on every platform. This essentially left JavaSoft as the only option. Since neither JDK 1.0 nor JDK 1.1 has the capabilities to build the types of components I was looking for, I had to look ahead to JDK 1.2. Although it is not here yet, as of the time this book was written, the pre-release JFCs provide an excellent advance look of things to come. When it finally arrives, the example code in this chapter should be easily retrofitted to conform to any changes made to the libraries.

The DBClient Source Code

The `DBClient` application is the client portion of the Database Browser application. It implements the user interface and interacts with the DBAccess class and DataTable class via RMI and the DataAccess interface. (The DataAccess interface is implemented by RemoteDBAccess on the server side.)

```
package DataBeans;

import java.awt.event.*;
import com.sun.java.swing.event.*;
import com.sun.java.swing.*;
import com.sun.java.swing.table.*;
import java.rmi.*;
import java.util.*;
import java.awt.*;




public class DBClient {

  static boolean debug = false;

  public static Color lightGray = Color.lightGray;
  public static Color darkGray = Color.darkGray;
  public static Color blue = Color.blue;
  public static int initalWidth = 645;
  public static int initalHeight = 525;


  JTabbedPane tabbedPane;
```

```
JPanel bigPanel;

int sessionID;
int tableID;
int maxTabPanels = 25;
DataAccess db1 = null;

/*
 * This method is used to print embeded error messages or
 * information you may want to use for debugging.  You
 * can turn off all debug messages by changing
 * the value of debug to true to turn this feature on.
 * You can also modify this method to redirect the messages.
 */

public static void msg (String message)
  {
    if (debug)
      {
       System.out.println (message);
      }
  }                      // end msg

 /*
  * The printError method is used to print out any fatal
  * errors.  Warnings and non fatal errors can be sent
  * to the status line.
  */

 public static void printError (String message)
   {
     System.out.println (message);
   }

 /*
  * The main method instantiates a simply sets the security manager
  * and calls the constructor method DBClient.
  */

public static void main (String[] args )
  {
    System.setSecurityManager(new RMISecurityManager());
    new DBClient();
  }               // end main
```

The constructor for the client has only three lines. The first call is to the loginWindow constructor. The login window is a dialog window used to get the user login and password. Only when the login is correct will the Main-Window method be called.

```
/*
  * The constructor for the client has only three lines. The first
  * call is to the loginWindow constructor. The login window
  * is a dialog winodow used to get the user login and password.
  * Only when  the login is correct will the MainWindow method
  * be called.
  */
```

```
public DBClient()
 {
   loginWindow lw = new loginWindow();
   MainWindow mw = new MainWindow();
 }               // end DBClient constructor
/*
 * Provide a method to exit the application.
 */

public void doExit ()
 {
   System.exit(0);
 }

/*
 * The setSessionID method is used to set the remote session Id for
 * this instance.
 */

protected void setSessionID (int id)
 {
   sessionID = id;
 }
            // end setSession
 /*
  * The getSessionID method is used to connect to the RMI server and
  * obtain the reference to the remote objects. The sessionID number
  * will beused for every remote method call.
  */

protected int getSessionID (String url, String user, String passwd)
 {
  int sessionID = -1;            // Initialize the sessionID.
  int[] dt = null;               // Applications must have their
                                 // own security manager.
  try {
       String registryname = ("//" + "tigger" + "/" + "remoteDB");
       msg("Registry Name: "+ registryname);
       db1 = (DataAccess)Naming.lookup(registryname);
     msg("Connected to registry");
     }
     catch (Exception e)
    {
      printError ("Cannot connect to the registry !");
      return -1;
    }
    try {                        // If we can connect to the registry
                                 // try to get a session with the db.
       sessionID = db1.getSession(url,user,passwd);
       if (sessionID == -1)
         {
           printError("Ran out of session ID's !");
         }
       else
         {
           msg("Remote Connection OK");
         }
    }
    catch (Exception e)
```

```
      {
        System.out.println ("Error in DBClient:\n"
                            + e.getMessage());
        return -1;
      }
    return sessionID;

  }                                                // end getSession
```

The `loginWindow` class provides the GUI front end to the `getSession()` method. It is used to collect the URL, user name and user password and then call the `getSessionId()` method. Note also that the loginWindow class is actually an inner-class of the `DBClient` class. This is to help keep the application more organized and to reduce redundant variable declarations. Note that the `loginWindow` class implements the ActionListener class. This allows the `loginWindow` to handle all its own events locally.

```
class loginWindow extends Frame implements ActionListener
  {
    int sessionID;
    Dialog dialog;
    TextField userField,passField,connField;
    Label statusLine;

    public loginWindow ()
      {                                      // Create a new frame for
        Frame f = new Frame();          //   the dialog window.
        f.setFont(new Font("DialogInput",Font.PLAIN , 12));
        dialog = new Dialog (f,"Database Login Window",true);
                                        // Set the window to modal.
        dialog.setLayout(new BorderLayout());

        Panel lpanel = new Panel();



        GridBagLayout gbl = new GridBagLayout();
        GridBagConstraints gbc = new GridBagConstraints();
        lpanel.setLayout (gbl);


        gbc.gridwidth = 1;
        gbc.gridheight = 1;
        gbc.gridx = 0;
        gbc.gridy=0;
        gbc.anchor = GridBagConstraints.EAST;
        gbc.fill = GridBagConstraints.NONE;
        Label cLabel = new Label( "Database URL:",Label.RIGHT);
        lpanel.add(cLabel,gbc );

        gbc.gridx = 1;
        connField = new TextField( 30 );
        lpanel.add(connField,gbc);


        gbc.gridx = 0;
        gbc.gridy++;
```

```java
Label uLabel = new Label( "User Name:" ,Label.RIGHT);
lpanel.add( uLabel,gbc );

gbc.gridx = 1;
userField = new TextField( 30 );
lpanel.add( userField,gbc);



gbc.gridx = 0;
gbc.gridy++;
Label pLabel = new Label ("Password:",Label.RIGHT);
lpanel.add( pLabel,gbc );

gbc.gridx = 1;
passField = new TextField( 30 );
passField.setEchoChar( "*".charAt( 0 ) );  // Hide the password.
lpanel.add( passField,gbc );



dialog.add("Center",lpanel);

GridBagLayout gbl2 = new GridBagLayout();
GridBagConstraints gbc2 = new GridBagConstraints();

Panel buttonpanel = new Panel(gbl2);
gbc2.weightx = 1;
gbc2.weighty = 1;
gbc2.gridwidth = 1;
gbc2.gridheight = 1;
gbc2.gridy = 0;
Button exit = new Button ("Exit");
buttonpanel.add(exit,gbc2);

gbc2.gridy = 1;
Button clear = new Button ("Clear");
buttonpanel.add(clear,gbc2);

gbc2.gridy = 2;
Button connect = new Button ("Connect");
buttonpanel.add(connect,gbc2);

exit.addActionListener(this);
clear.addActionListener(this);
connect.addActionListener(this);

statusLine = new Label("   ",Label.CENTER);


Label headerLine = new Label("Please Enter Login Information");
headerLine.setFont(new Font("Welcome",Font.BOLD, 14));
headerLine.setForeground(darkGray);
Panel headerPanel = new Panel();
headerPanel.add(headerLine);

dialog.add("South",statusLine);
dialog.add("North",headerPanel);
dialog.add("East",buttonpanel);
dialog.setSize (440,220);
```

```
      dialog.setVisible(true);

   }                                   // end loginWindow constructor

   /*
    * If a non fatal login error occurs, update the status line
    * and allow user to try again.
    */

   public void setStatus (String message)
    {
   statusLine.setText(message);
   }

   /*
    * All Login Window button events are handled here.
    */

public void actionPerformed (ActionEvent e)
 {
   Button selected = (Button)(e.getSource());
   String label = selected.getLabel();

   if (label.equals("Clear"))                    // Clear the existing
    {                                             // text.
       System.out.println ("Clear the text");
       connField.setText("");
       passField.setText("");
       userField.setText("");
    }
   if (label.equals("Connect"))
       {
       System.out.println ("connect to db");
       sessionID = getSessionID(connField.getText(),
           userField.getText(),passField.getText());
       if (sessionID == -1)             // If login fails, do
        {                               // not close login window.
          setStatus("Login Failed: Please Try Again !");

        }
        else
        {
          setStatus ("Connecting to database...");
          setSessionID(sessionID);
         dialog.setVisible(false);
          dialog.dispose();
        }
     }
    if (label.equals("Exit"))           // Close window and exit.
     {
     dialog.setVisible(false);
       dialog.dispose();
       System.exit(0);
     }

   }                   // end ActionPerformed

 }                     // end loginWindow class
```

The `MainWindow` is an inner class of `DBClient` that performs most of the duties of the application. The main window has three main components:

- The treePanel: The treePanel contains a list (tree) of catalogs, schemas, and tables available to the user.
- The tabbedPane: When opened tables are placed in a "Tab Folder" to allow users to switch between tables easily.
- The menuBar: The menu bar contains the main window controls such as exit.

Each major component has its own action listener class. Each are implemented as an inner class of the `MainWindow`. This way, the listeners can call methods inside `MainWindow` and perform functions on other parts of the window.

```
class MainWindow extends JFrame {

  JTree aTree;
  JPanel dbTreePanel;
  JFrame frame;

  Label statusLine;
  public Font defaultFont = new Font("Dialog", Font.PLAIN,12);
  public Font bigFont = new Font("bigDialog", Font.PLAIN,16);
  /*
   * Status updates are displayed at the bottom of the screen and
   * are set via the setStatus method.
   */

    public void setStatus (String message)
     {
       statusLine.setText(message);
     }

    /*
     * The MainWindow constructor builds the frame to house the rest
     * of the components. It contains the menu bar, tree panel and
     * tabbed pane.
     */

 public MainWindow()
   {
     frame = new JFrame("DataBrowser (Main Window)");
     frame.setForeground(Color.black);
     frame.setBackground(Color.lightGray);

     JMenuBar menuBar = initMenuBar();
                          // Create the menu bar by calling
                          // initMenuBar().
     bigPanel = new JPanel();   // bigPanel contains the tree panel
                                // and the tabbed pane.
     GridBagLayout gb = new GridBagLayout();
     GridBagConstraints gc = new GridBagConstraints();
     bigPanel.setLayout(gb);
     gc.anchor =GridBagConstraints.WEST;
```

```
gc.weightx = 1;
gc.weighty = 1;
gc.gridx = 0;
gc.gridy =0;
gc.fill = GridBagConstraints.BOTH;

dbTreePanel = dbTree();            // Create the tree panel
bigPanel.add(dbTreePanel);         // and add to bigPanel.

tabbedPane = new JTabbedPane();    // Create the tabbed pane
                                          container.
Label welcome = new Label("Welcome to the Database
                        Browser",Label.CENTER);
welcome.setFont(bigFont);

addTabPanel("Welcome",welcome);    // Add the first tabbed
                                          folder.
tabbedPane.setSelectedIndex(0);

gc.weightx = 4;
gc.weighty = 1;
gc.gridx = 1;
gc.gridy = 0;
gb.setConstraints(tabbedPane,gc);
bigPanel.add(tabbedPane);
                   // Add the tabbed pane to the bigPanel.

frame.add("Center",bigPanel);
                   // Add bigPanel to the main window.
frame.add("North",menuBar);
                   // Add the menu bar.
statusLine = new Label("",Label.LEFT);
frame.add("South",statusLine);          // Add the status line.
setStatus ("Login complete...");

frame.setSize(initalWidth,initalHeight);
frame.show();

}                              // end MainWindow constructor

/* The first object built inside the main window is the menu bar.
 * This is done with the initMenuBar class.
 */


public JMenuBar initMenuBar()
 {

  JMenu fileMenu, viewMenu, helpMenu;
  JMenuItem menuItem;
  JMenuBar menuBar = new JMenuBar();

  fileMenu = new JMenu("File   "); // Create the "File menu"
  menuBar.add(fileMenu);
  JMenuItem login = new JMenuItem("Login");
  fileMenu.add(login);
  login.setActionCommand("Login");
  JMenuItem logout = new JMenuItem ("Logout");
  fileMenu.add(logout);
  logout.setActionCommand("Logout");
```

```
        fileMenu.addSeparator();
        JMenuItem exit = new JMenuItem("Exit");
        fileMenu.add(exit);
        exit.setActionCommand("Exit");

        viewMenu = new JMenu("View");      // Create the "View menu"
        menuBar.add(viewMenu);
        JMenuItem dbInfo = new JMenuItem("Database Info");
        viewMenu.add(dbInfo);
        dbInfo.setActionCommand("DBInfo");
        JMenuItem driverInfo = new JMenuItem("Driver Info");
        viewMenu.add(driverInfo);
        driverInfo.setActionCommand("DriverInfo");

        MenuListener ml = new MenuListener();
        exit.addActionListener(ml);           // Add the action listener.
        logout.addActionListener(ml);
        login.addActionListener(ml);
        dbInfo.addActionListener(ml);
        driverInfo.addActionListener(ml);

        return menuBar;
    }                              // end initMenuBar method



/* The MenuListener class is an inner class to MainWindow
 * that keeps track of menu bar selections.
 */

class MenuListener implements ActionListener
 {

  public void actionPerformed (ActionEvent e)
  {
   if (e.getActionCommand().equals("Exit"))
    {
      System.exit(0);
    }
   else
    if (e.getActionCommand().equals("Login"))
     {
          frame.dispose();
          new DBClient();
     }
     else
      if (e.getActionCommand().equals("Logout"))
      {
        try {
                db1.closeSession(sessionID);
                setSessionID(-1);
                }
                catch (RemoteException re)
                 {
                   setStatus("Unable to logout");
                 }


        }
      else
     if (e.getActionCommand().equals("DBInfo"))
```

```
                                {
                                 addDBInfoTable();
                                     }
                                else
                                 if (e.getActionCommand().equals("DriverInfo"))
                                  {
                                        addDriverInfoTable();
                                      }
                              }                          // end actionPerformed
                     }                                   // end MenuListener class
```

The `dbTree()` method is responsible for building and setting up the catalog tree. It calls `RemoteMethods` to determine what catalogs are available and then all schemas for each catalog. Next, a list of tables available in each schema is retrieved and added to the tree as a leaf node.

```
                    public JPanel dbTree ()
                     {

                    Vector schemaNames = null;
                    Vector catalogNames = null;
                    Vector tableNames = null;

                    TreeNode[] catalogNodes ;
                    TreeNode[] schemaNodes ;
                    TreeNode root = null;
                    String[] tableTypes = {"TABLE","VIEW"};
                                            // We only care about tables and
                                            // views for now.
                    try
                      {
                       catalogNames = db1.getCatalogNames(sessionID);
                                            // Determine catalog names.

                        int numCatalogs = catalogNames.size();
                        catalogNodes = new TreeNode[numCatalogs];
                          schemaNames = db1.getSchemaNames(sessionID);
                          int numSchemas = schemaNames.size();

                          schemaNodes = new TreeNode[numSchemas];
                          if (((String)catalogNames.elementAt(0)).equals(""))
                                                    // If there are no catalogs
                              {                      // then create a fake node
                                                    // to attach all schemas to.
                            root = new TreeNode("Database Tree1");
                            catalogNodes[0] = new TreeNode("Catalog");
                            root.add(catalogNodes[0]);
                            numCatalogs = 1;
                          }        // end if
                        else
                            {
                            for (int i=0; i < numCatalogs; i++)
                              {
                                root = new TreeNode("Database Tree");
                                catalogNodes[i] = new TreeNode((String)catalogNames.
                                         elementAt(i));
                              }                              //end i for
                        }                                    // end else
```

```
            for (int l=0; l < numCatalogs; l++)
            {
              if (numSchemas > 0)                      // For every schema
                                                                  listed
                {                                 // determine what tables are
                  for (int i =0; i < (numSchemas); i++)
                                                  // available and add them to
                    {                             // the tree.
                      schemaNodes[i] = new TreeNode((String)schemaNames.
                                    elementAt(i));
                      catalogNodes[l].add(schemaNodes[i]);
                      tableNames = dbl.getTableNames((String)catalogNames.
                                    elementAt(l),
                        (String)schemaNames.elementAt(i),tableTypes,sessionID);
                      for ( int k =0; k < tableNames.size(); k++ )
                        {
                          TreeNode table = new TreeNode((String)(tableNames.
                                        elementAt(k)));
                          schemaNodes[i].add(table);

                        }          // end k for
                    }              // end i for
                }                      // end if schemas > 0
            }                  // end l for

          }
          catch (RemoteException re)
            {
              setStatus("Remote Error in getCatalognames");
            }
          aTree = new JTree(root);        // Add all the tree node
                                          // to a tree.
          JPanel treePanel = new JPanel(true); // Create a scroll
                                                          panel
          treePanel.setLayout(new BorderLayout());      // for the
                                                          tree.
          treePanel.setSize(initalWidth/4,initalHeight*4);
          ScrollPane sPane = new ScrollPane
                  (java.awt.ScrollPane.SCROLLBARS_ALWAYS);
          sPane.setSize(initalWidth/4,initalHeight);
          sPane.add(aTree);
          treePanel.add(sPane);
          TreeSelectionListener tl = new treeAction();
          TreeExpansionListener te = new treeExpansion();
          aTree.addTreeExpansionListener(te);
          aTree.addTreeSelectionListener(tl);
          treePanel.validate();
          return treePanel;                        // Return the tree in
                                                            a nice
                                                  // neat package.
        }                                          // End dbTree

    /*
     * When a tree selection is detected, this method is called to
     * return what node was selected.
     */

    protected TreeNode getSelectedNode()
      {
```

```
                             JTreePath selPath = aTree.getSelectionPath();
                             if (selPath != null)
                                 return (TreeNode)selPath.getLastPathComponent();
                             return null;
                          }
                                                      // end getSelectedNode

                   /* Once the tree has been built we must create listeners to
                    * determine when a node was selected or when the tree was
                    * expanded or collapsed.
                    */

                   class treeAction extends Object implements TreeSelectionListener
                     {
                      public void valueChanged(TreeSelectionEvent e )
                        {
                         TreeNode lastItem = getSelectedNode();
                         if (lastItem!=null)              // If the parent is null
                          {                               // then it is not a table
                           if (lastItem.isLeaf())         // that has been selected.
                           {                              // If it is a table name
                                                          // then get it's parents
                                                          // name (the schema) and
                                                          // attempt to open it.
                             setStatus(lastItem + "Table Selected");

                             TreeNode parent = lastItem.getParent();
                                 String tableName = (parent + "." +lastItem);
                                 JButton butt = new JButton("TestButton");
                                 try {
                                     tableID = db1.openTable(tableName,sessionID);
                                     setStatus ("Opening Table: " + tableName);
                                     }
                                     catch (RemoteException re)
                                     {
                                 msg ("Error in open Table");
                                     }
                                                          // Add the new table to a tab.
                                 addTabPanel(tableName, new
                                 buildTable(tableName,tableID));

                           }                 // End if lastitem.isLeaf
                          }                  // End if lastItem != null
                        }                    // End valueChanged method
                     }                       // End treeAction method.

                   /* We also need to look for other tree events to ensure that
                    * when folders are expanded or closed we can re-validate the
                    * the main window. This is another inner-class. The rest of
                    * the actions needed to redraw are handled by JTree.
                    */

                   class treeExpansion extends Object
                               implements TreeExpansionListener
                     {
                      public void treeCollapsed (TreeExpansionEvent e)
                        {
                         doRepack();
                        }
```

```
        public void treeExpanded (TreeExpansionEvent e)
        {
         doRepack();
        }
    }                      // End treeExpansion lister class.

    /*
     * Whenever an item is added to the frame it should
     * be re-validated.
     */

    protected void doRepack ()
      {
       frame.validate();
      }

    /*
     * The addTabPanel method is used to add a component to a
     * tabbed folder and then add the folder to the tabbed.pane.
     */

   public void addTabPanel (String title, Component obj)
     {
      tabbedPane.setFont(defaultFont);
      tabbedPane.addTab(title,null,obj);
      tabbedPane.setSelectedIndex((tabbedPane.getTabCount())-1);
     }

 /* The addDBInfoTable method is called by the menu listener
  * whenever the View.DBInfo item is selected. It builds a table
  * from the DBInfo on the remote server and adds a tab folder
  * containing the table. The driver info is nearly identical.
  */

    public void addDBInfoTable()
       {
        try {
                 tableID = db1.getDBInfo(sessionID);
                 addTabPanel("Database Info",
                      new buildTable("DBInfo",tableID));
                 }
                 catch (RemoteException re)
                  {
                    setStatus("Could not get DBInfo");
                  }
        }

    public void addDriverInfoTable()
       {
        try {
                 tableID = db1.getDBInfo(sessionID);
                 addTabPanel("Driver Info",
                      new buildTable("DBInfo",tableID));
                 }
                 catch (RemoteException re)
                  {
                    setStatus("Could not get DriverInfo");
                  }
        }
```

The `buildTable` class is called whenever a table node is selected from the tree. The `buildTable` class then opens a table from the database and puts the contents of the table in a `Vector[]`. Whenever a repaint occurs, the `dataModeler` class then retrieves only the data needed to repaint the visable portion of the screen from the `Vector[]`. Without caching the data locally, each time the screen is refreshed the data would have to be retrieved across the network. The table modeler class is only used by the build table class, therefore it is an inner-class of `buildTable`.

```
class buildTable extends JPanel
 {

  Vector[] dataCache = null;
  String[] titleCache = null;
  int numCols = 0;
  int numberOfRows = 0;
  int thisTableID;

  /* The buildTable constructor creates the JTable and
   * the tableDataModeler for the table. The tableID
   * is associated withe the object and stored with it
   * since the global tableId will change but in order
   * to repaint, the modeler must know that table ID.
   */

  public buildTable(String TableName, int tableID)
   {
    super(true);
    thisTableID = tableID;
    JTableColumn newCol = null;  // Create the modeler
     tableDataModeler dataModel = new tableDataModeler();

    try {     // Determine the number of rows and then
              // retreive them into a local Vector[]
              // to be used as a data cache.

      numberOfRows = db1.getNumberOfRows(thisTableID);
      dataCache = new Vector[numberOfRows];
      for (int i =0; i < numberOfRows; i++)
       {
         dataCache[i] = db1.getRow(i+1,thisTableID);
       }
     }
    catch (RemoteException re)
     {
      setStatus ("Remote exeception in getting Rows.");
     }
   setStatus ( "Got " +numberOfRows + " rows.");
   JTable table = new JTable(dataModel);
   try {
       numCols = db1.getNumberOfColumns(thisTableID);
                        // Build a cache of the column names
                        // also since the modeler will call
                        // for them each time it repaints.
       titleCache = new String[numCols];  for (int i = 0; i <
       numCols; I++)
       {
```

```
                         titleCache[i] = (String)db1.getColumnTitle
                                              (i+1,thisTableID);
                         newCol = new JTableColumn(titleCache[i]);
                         newCol.setMaxWidth(170); table.addColumn(newCol);
          }
          }
        catch (RemoteException re)
         {
              setStatus ("Error in setting up Columns");
              }


    JScrollPane sPane = new JScrollPane();
                   // Create the scroll pane and associated
                   // view ports.
    JTableHeader tableHeader = table.getTableHeader();

    JViewport headerViewport = new JViewport();
    headerViewport.setLayout(new BoxLayout(headerViewport,
                                 BoxLayout.X_AXIS));
    headerViewport.add(tableHeader);
    sPane.setColumnHeading(headerViewport);
    JViewport mainViewPort = sPane.getViewport();
    tableHeader.setUpdateTableInRealTime(false);

    JPanel tablePanel = new JPanel(true);
    setLayout(new BorderLayout());
    add("Center",sPane);
    mainViewPort.add(table);
    validate();              // Add the table to
                             // the view port.
    }                        // End buildTable constructor method.

/*
 * The tableDataModeler requires that all the methods in the
 * interface be implemented, but since we are not
 * implementing any editing functins the setValueAt()
 * is a dummy method.
 */

class tableDataModeler extends JTableDataModelAdapter
 {
    public int getRowCount()
     {
     try {
       return db1.getNumberOfRows(thisTableID);
           }
      catch (RemoteException re)
             {
        msg ("Error in getRows");
              }
          return -1;

    }                      //End getRowCount method
 public Object getValueAt(Object columnIdentifier,
                                    int rowIndex)
   {
    int colNumber =0;
    colNumber = getColumnNumber(columnIdentifier);
```

```
                        Object data = (dataCache[rowIndex].elementAt
                                        (colNumber));
                        if (data != null)
                          {
                   return(data);
                 }
                        else
                        {                               // The Jtable class does not
                                                        // handle nulls. Return a
                                                        // blank value for nulls.
                              return (" ");
                        }

          }
      public int getColumnNumber (Object columnIdentifier)
        {
          for (int i=0; i < numCols; i++)
          {
                if (titleCache[i].equals(columnIdentifier))
                  {
            return i;
          }
                }
              return -3;
        }

      public void setValueAt(Object aValue,
                              Object colIdent, int rowindex)
        {
         msg ("setting value");
        }
     }                    // End tableDataModeler

     }                    // End buildTable class

   }               // end MainWindow class

 }             // end DBClient class
```

Chapter Summary

This final chapter rounds out our discussion on building JDBC clients. The Database Browser by no means is meant to be a full scale production quality application, but a means to demonstrate how you could put all the pieces and components we have built together. In addition, I hope it has given you some new ideas and perhaps a different perspective on the usefulness of JDBC.

What's Next

Now that you have completed the "JDBC" whirlwind tour, you are ready to go build your own applications. What's next for you? I hope it is a Java Database application.

APPENDIX **A**

ODBC Call to JDBC Method Mappings

The Driver Interface   Table 1

JDBC Method	ODBC Call
acceptsURL	none
connect	SQLDriverConnect
getMajorVersion	none
getMinorVersion	none
getPropertyInfo	SQLBrowseConnect
jdbcCompliant	none

The DriverManager Interface   **Table 2**

JDBC Method	ODBC Call
deregiserDriver	none
getConnection	none
getDriver	none
getDrivers	none
getLoginTimeout	none
getLogStream	none
println	none
registerDriver	none
setLoginTimeout	none
setLogStream	none

The Connection Interface   **Table 3**

JDBC Method	ODBC Call	ODBC Option
clearWarnings	none	
close	SQLFreeConnect	
commit	SQLTransact	fType=SQL_COMMIT
createStatement	none	
getAutoCommit	SQLGetInfo	fInfoType=SQL_CURSOR_ COMMIT_ BEHAVIOR & fInfoType=SQL_CURSOR_ ROLLBACK_BEHAVIOR
getCatalog	SQLGetInfo	fOption=SQL_CURRENT_ QUALIFIER
getMetaData	none	
getTransactionIsolation	SQLGetConnectOption	fOption=SQL_TXN_ISOLATION
getWarnings	none	
isClosed	none	
isReadOnly	SQLGetConnectOption	fOption=SQL_ACCESS_MODE
nativeSQL	none	
prepareCall	SQLPrepare	
prepareStatement	SQLPrepare	
rollback	SQLTransact	fOption=SQL_ROLLBACK
setAutoCommit	SQLSetConnectOption	fOption=SQL_AUTOCOMMIT
setCatalog	SQLSetConnectOption	fOption=SQL_CURRENT_ QUALIFIER
setReadOnly	SQLSetConnectOption	fOption=SQL_ACCESS_MODE
setTranactionIsolation	SQLSetConnectOption	fOption=SQL_TXN_ISOLATION

The Statement Interface
Table 4

JDBC Method	ODBC Call	ODBC Option
cancel	SQLCancel	
clearWarnings	none	
close	SQLFreeSmt	fOption=SQL_CLOSE
execute	SQLExecDirect	
executeQuery	SQLExecute	
executeUpdate	SQLExecute	
getMaxFieldSize	SQLGetStmtOption	fOption=SQL_MAX_LENGTH
getMaxRows	SQLGetStmtOption	fOption=SQL_MAX_ROWS
getMoreResults	SQLMoreResults	
getQueryTimeout	SQLGetStmtOption	fOption=SQL_QUERY_TIMEOUT
getResultSet	none	
getUpdateCount	SQLRowCount	
getWarnings	none	
setCursorName	SQLSetCursorName	
setEscapeProcessing	SQLSetStmtOption	fOption=SQL_NOSCAN
setMaxFieldSize	SQLSetStmtOption	fOption=SQL_MAX_LENGTH
setMaxRows ·	SQLSetStmtOption	fOption=SQL_MAX_ROWS
setQueryTimout	SQLSetStmtOption	fOption=SQL_QUERY_TIMEOUT

The Prepared Statement Interface
Table 5

JDBC Method	ODBC Call	ODBC Option
clearParameters		
execute	SQLExecute	
executeQuery	none	
executeUpdate	none	
setAsciiSTream	none	
setBigDecimal	none	
setBinaryStream	SQLBindParameter	fParamType=SQL_PARAM_INPUT
setBoolean	none	
setByte	none	
setBytes	none	
setDate	none	
setDouble	none	
setFloat	none	
setInt	none	
setLong	none	

continued

JDBC Method	ODBC Call	ODBC Option
setNull	SQLBindParameter	fParamType=SQL_PARAM_INPUT
setObject	none	
setShort	none	
setString	none	
setTime	none	
setTimeStamp	SQLBindParameter	fparamType=SQL_PARAM_INPUT
setUnicodeStream	none	

The CallableStatement Interface   Table 6

JDBC Method	ODBC Call	ODBC Option
getBigDecimal	none	
getBoolean	none	
getByte	none	
getBytes	none	
getDate	none	
getDouble	none	
getFloat	none	
getInt	none	
getLong	none	
getObject	none	
getShort	none	
getString	none	
getTime	none	
getTimeStamp	none	
registerOutParameter	SQLBindParameter	ParamType=SQL_PARAM_OUTPUT
wasnull	none	

The ResultSet Interface   Table 7

JDBC Method	ODBC Call	ODBC Option
clearWarnings	none	
close	SQLFreeStmt	fOption=SQL_CLOSE
findColumn	none	
getAsciiStream	SQLGetData	
getBigDecimal	none	
getBinaryStream	none	

continued

JDBC Method	ODBC Call	ODBC Option
getBoolean	none	
getByte	none	
getBytes	none	
getCursorName	none	
getDate	none	
getDouble	none	
getFloat	none	
getInt	none	
getLong	none	
getMetaData	none	
getObject	none	
getShort	none	
getString	none	
getTime	none	
getTimestamp	SQLGetData	
getUnicodeStream	none	
getWarnings	none	
next	SQLFetch	
wasNull	none	

ResultSetMetaData Interface

Table 8

JDBC Method	ODBC Call	ODBC Option
getCatalogName	SQLColAttributes	fDescType=SQL_COLUMN_ QUALIFIER_NAME
getColumnCount	SQLNumResultCols	
getColumnDisplaySize	SQLColAttributes	fDescType=SQL_COLUMN_ DISPLAY_SIZE
getColumnLabel	SQLColAttributes	fDescType=SQL_COLUMN_LABEL
getColumnName	SQLColAttributes	fDescType=SQL_COLUMN_NAME
getColumnType	SQLColAttributes	fDescType=SQL_COLUMN_TYPE
getColumnTypeName	SQLColAttributes	fDescType=SQL_COLUMN_TYPE_ NAME
getPrecision	SQLColAttributes	fDescType=SQL_COLUMN_ PRECISION
getScale	SQLColAttributes	fDescType=SQL_COLUMN_SCALE
getSchemaName	SQLColAttributes	fDescType=SQL_COLUMN_ OWNER_NAME

continued

JDBC Method	ODBC Call	ODBC Option
getTableName	SQLColAttributes	fDescType=SQL_COLUMN_ TABLE_NAME
isAutoIncrement	SQLColAttributes	fDescType=SQL_COLUMN_ AUTO_INCREMENT
isCaseSensitive	SQLColAttributes	fDescType=SQL_COLUMN_ CASE_SENSITIVE
isCurrency	SQLColAttributes	fDescType=SQL_COLUMN_ MONEY
isDefinitelyWritable	SQLColAttributes	fDescType=SQL_COLUMN_ UPDATABLE
isNullable	SQLColAttributes	fDescType=SQL_COLUMN_ NULLABLE
isReadOnly	SQLColAttributes	fDescType=SQL_COLUMN_ UPDATABLE
isSearchable	SQLColAttributes	fDescType=SQL_COLUMN_ SEARCHABLE
isSigned	SQLColAttributes	fDescType=SQL_COLUMN_ UNSIGNED
isWritable	SQLColAttributes	fDescType=SQL_COLUMN_ UPDATABLE

The DatabaseMetaData Interface   Table 9

JDBC Method	ODBC Call	ODBC Option
allProcedures AreCallable	SQLGetInfo	fInfoType=SQL_ACCESSABLE_ PROCEDURES
allTablesAreSelectable	SQLGetInfo	fInfoType=SQL_ACCESSABLE_ TABLES
dataDefinitionCause TransactionCommit	SQLGetInfo	fInfoType=SQL_TXN_CAPABLE
dataDefinitionIgnored InTransactions	SQLGetInfo	fInfoType=SQL_TXN_CAPABLE
doesMaxRowSize IncludeBlobs	SQLGetInfo	fInfoType=SQL_MAX_ROW_SIZE_ INCLUDES_LONG
getBestRowIdentifier	SQLSpecial Column	fColType=SQL_BEST_ROW_ID
getCatalogs	SQLTables	
getCatalogSeparator	SQLGetInfo	fInfoType=SQL_QUALIFIER_ NAME_SEPARATOR

continued

JDBC Method	ODBC Call	ODBC Option
getCatalogTerm	SQLGetInfo	fInfoType=SQL_QUALIFIER_TERM
getColumnPrivileges	SQLColumnPrivileges	
getColumns	SQLColumns	
getCrossReference	SQLForeign Keys	
getDatabaseProductName	SQLGetInfo	fInfoType=SQL_DBMS_NAME
getDatabaseProductVersion	SQLGetInfo	fInfoType=SQL_DBMS_VER
getDefaultTransactionIsolation	SQLGetInfo	fInfoType=SQL_DEFAULT_TXN_ISOLATION
getExportedKeys	SQLForeign Keys	
getExtraNameCharacters	SQLGetInfo	fInfoType=SQL_SPECIAL_CHARACTERS
getIdentifierQuoteString	SQLGetInfo	fInfoType=SQL_QUOTE_CHAR
getImportedKeys	SQLForeign Keys	
getMaxBinaryLiteralLength	SQLGetInfo	fInfoType=SQL_MAX_BINARY_LITERAL_LEN
getMaxCatalogNameLength	SQLGetInfo	fInfoType=SQL_MAX_QUALIFIER_NAME_LEN
getMaxCharLiteralLength	SQLGetInfo	fInfoType=SQL_MAX_CHAR_LITERAL_LEN
getMaxColumnNameLength	SQLGetInfo	fInfoType=SQL_MAX_COUKMN_NAME_LEN
getMaxColumnsInGroupBy	SQLGetInfo	fInfoType=SQL_MAX_COLUMNS_IN_GROUP_BY
getMaxColumnsInIndex	SQLGetInfo	fInfoType=SQL_MAX_COLUMNS_IN_INDEX
getMaxColumnsInOrderBy	SQLGetInfo	fInfoType=SQL_MAX_COLUMNS_IN_ORDER_BY
getMaxColumnsInSelect	SQLGetInfo	fInfoType=SQL_MAX_COLUMNS_IN_SELECT
getMaxColumnsInTable	SQLGetInfo	fInfoType=SQL_MAX_COLUMNS_IN_TABLE
getMaxConnections	SQLGetInfo	fInfoType=SQL_ACTIVE_CONNECTIONS

continued

JDBC Method	ODBC Call	ODBC Option
getMaxCursor NameLength	SQLGetInfo	fInfoType=SQL_MAX-CURSOR_ NAME_LEN
getMaxIndexLength	SQLGetInfo	fInfoType=SQL_MAX_INDEX_SIZE
getMaxProcedure NameLength	SQLGetInfo	fInfoType=SQL_MAX_ PROCEDURE_NAME_LEN
getMaxRowSize	SQLGetInfo	fInfoType=SQL_MAX_ROW_SIZE
getMaxSchema NameLenth	SQLGetInfo	fInfoType=SQL_MAX_OWNER_ NAME_LEN
getMaxStatement Length	SQLGetInfo	fInfoType=SQL_MAX_ STATEMENT_LEN
getMaxStatements	SQLGetInfo	fInfoType=SQL_ACTIVE_ STATEMENTS
getMaxTable NameLength	SQLGetInfo	fInfoType=SQL_MAX_TABLE_ NAME_LEN
getMaxTablesInSelect	SQLGetInfo	fInfoType=SQL_MAX_TABLES_ IN_SELECT
getMaxUserName Length	SQLGetInfo	fInfoType=SQL_MAX_USER_ NAME_LEN
getNumericFunctions	SQLGetInfo	fInfoType=SQL_NUMERIC_ FUNCTIONS
getPrimaryKeys	SQLPrimary Keys	
getProcedures	SQLProcedures	
getProceduresColumns	SQLProcedureColumns	
getProcedureTerm	SQLGetInfo	fInfoType=SQL_PROCEDURE_ TERM
getSchemas	SQLTables	
getSchemaTerm	SQLGetInfo	fInfoType=SQL_OWNER_TERM
getSearchStringEscape	SQLGetInfo	fInfoType=SQL_SEARCH_ PATTERN_ESCAPE
getSQLKeywords	SQLGetInfo	fInfoType=SQL_KEYWORDS
getStringFunctions	SQLGetInfo	fInfoType=SQL_STRING_ FUNCTIONS
getSystemFunctions	SQLGetInfo	fInfoType=SQL_SYSTEM_ FUNCTIONS
getTablePrivileges	SQLTable Privileges	
getTables	SQLTables	
getTableTypes	SQLTables	
getTimeDateFunctions	SQLGetInfo	fInfoType=SQL_TIMEDATE_ FUNCTIONS

continued

JDBC Method	ODBC Call	ODBC Option
getTypeInfo	SQLGetTypeInfo	fSQLType=SQL_ALL_TYPES
getUserName	SQLGetInfo	fInfoType=SQL_USER_NAME
getVersionColumns	SQLSpecialColumns	fColType=SQL_ROWVER
isCatalogAtStart	SQLGetInfo	fInfoType=SQL_QUALIFIER_ LOCATION
isReadOnly	SQLGetInfo	fInfoType=SQL_DATA_SOURCE_ READ_ONLY
nullAreSortedAtEnd	SQLGetInfo	fInfoType=SQL_NULL_ COLLATION
nullPlusNonNullsIsNull	SQLGetInfo	fInfoType=SQL_CONCAT_NULL_ BEHAVIOR
nullsAreSorted	SQLGetInfo	fInfoType=SQL_NULL_COLLATION
nullsAreSortedAtStart	SQLGetInfo	fInfoType=SQL_NULL_COLLATION
nullsAreSortedLow	SQLGetInfo	fInfoType=SQL_NULL_COLLATION
storesLowerCase Identifiers	SQLGetInfo	fInfoType=SQL_INDENTIFIER_ CASE
storesLowerCase QuotedIdentifiers	SQLGetInfo	fInfoType=SQL_QUOTED_ IDENTIFIER_CASE
storesMixedCase Identifiers	SQLGetInfo	fInfoType=SQL_INDENTIFIER_ CASE
storesMixedCase QuotedIdentifiers	SQLGetInfo	fInfoType=SQL_QUOTED_ IDENTIFIER_CASE
storesUpperCase Identifiers	SQLGetInfo	fInfoType=SQL_INDENTIFIER_ CASE
storesUpperCase QuotedIdentfiers	SQLGetInfo	fInfoType=SQL_QUOTED_ IDENTIFIER_CASE
suportsMixedCase QuotedIdentifiers	SQLGetInfo	fInfoType=SQL_QUOTED_ IDENTIFIER_CASE
supportsAlterTable WithAddColumn	SQLGetInfo	fInfoType=SQL_ALTER_TABLE
supportsAlterTable WithDropColumn	SQLGetInfo	fInfoType=SQL_ALTER_TABLE
supportsCatalogs InDataMinipulations	SQLGetInfo	fInfoType=SQL_QUALIFIER_ USAGE
supportsCatalogs InIndexDefintions	SQLGetInfo	fInfoType=SQL_QUALIFIER_ USAGE
supportsCatalogsIn PrivilegeDefinitions	SQLGetInfo	fInfoType=SQL_QUALIFIER_ USAGE

continued

JDBC Method	ODBC Call	ODBC Option
supportsCatalogs InProcedures	SQLGetInfo	fInfoType=SQL_QUALIFIER_ USAGE
supportsCatalogsIn TableDefinitions	SQLGetInfo	fInfoType=SQL_QUALIFIER_ USAGE
supportsColumn Aliasing	SQLGetInfo	fInfoType=SQL_COLUMN_ALIAS
supportsConvert	SQLGetInfo	fInfoType=SQL_CONVERT_ FUNCTIONS
supportsCore SQLGrammar	SQLGetInfo	fInfoType=SQL_ODBC_SQL_ CONFORMANCE
supportsCorrelated Subqueries	SQLGetInfo	fInfoType=SQL_SUBQUERIES
supportsDataDefinition AndDataManipulation Transactions	SQLGetInfo	fInfoType=SQL_TXN_CAPABLE
supportsData Manipulation TranactionsOnly	SQLGetInfo	fInfoType=SQL_TXN_CAPABLE
supportsDifferent TableCorrelation Names	SQLGetInfo NAMES	fInfoType=SQL_CORRELATION_
supportsExpressions InOrderBy	SQLGetInfo	fInfoType=SQL_EXPRESSIONS_ IN_ORDER_BY
supportsExtended SQLGrammar	SQLGetInfo	fInfoType=SQL_ODBC_SQL_ CONFORMANCE
supportsFullOuterJoins	SQLGetInfo	fInfoType=SQL_OUTER_JOINS
supportsGroupBy	SQLGetInfo	fInfoType=SQL_GROUP_BY
supportsGroupBy BeyondSelect	SQLGetInfo	fInfoType=SQL_GROUP_BY
supportsGroup ByUnrelated	SQLGetInfo	fInfoType=SQL_GROUP_BY
supportsIntegrity EnhancementFacility	SQLGetInfo	fInfoType=SQL_ODBC_ SQL_OPT_IEF
supportsLike EscapeClause	SQLGetInfo	fInfoType=SQL_LIKE_ESCAPE_ CLAUSE
supportsLimited OuterJoins	SQLGetInfo	fInfoType=SQL_OUTER_JOINS
supportsMinimum SQLGrammarSQLGrammar	SQLGetInfo	fInfoType=SQL_ODBC_SQL_ CONFORMANCE

continued

JDBC Method	ODBC Call	ODBC Option
supportsMixed CaseIdentifiers	SQLGetInfo	fInfoType=SQL_INDENTIFIER_ CASE
supportsMultiple ResultSets	SQLGetInfo	fInfoType=SQL_MULT_RESULT_ SETS
supportsMultiple Transactions	SQLGetInfo	fInfoType=SQL_MULTIPLE_ ACTIVE_TXN
supportsNon NullableColumns	SQLGetInfo	fInfoType=SQL_NON_ NULLABLE_COLUMNS
supportsOpenCurso rAcrossCommit	SQLGetInfo	fInfoType=SQL_CURSOR_ COMMIT_BEHAVIOR
supportsOpen CursorsAcrossRollback	SQLGetInfo	fInfoType=SQL_CURSOR_ ROLLBACK_BEHAVIOR
supportsOpen StatementsAcross Commit	SQLGetInfo	fInfoType=SQL_CURSOR_ COMMIT_BEHAVIOR
supportsOpen StatementsAcross Rollback	SQLGetInfo	fInfoType=SQL_CURSOR_ ROLLBACK_BEHAVIOR
supportsOrder ByUnrelated	SQLGetInfo	fInfoType=SQL_ORDER_BY_ COLUMNS_IN_SELECT
supportsOuterJoins	SQLGetInfo	fInfoType=SQL_OUTER_JOINS
supportsPositioned Delete	SQLGetInfo	fInfoType=SQL_POSITIONED_ STATEMENTS
supportsPositioned Update	SQLGetInfo	fInfoType=SQL_POSITIONED_ STATEMENTS
supportsSchemasIn DataManipulation	SQLGetInfo	fInfoType=SQL_OWNER_USAGE
supportsSchemasIn ProcedureCalls	SQLGetInfo	fInfoType=SQL_OWNER_USAGE
supportsSchemasIn TableDefinitions	SQLGetInfo	fInfoType=SQL_OWNER_USAGE
supportsSchemasIn IndexDefinitions	SQLGetInfo	fInfoType=SQL_OWNER_USAGE
supportsSchemasIn PrivilegeDefinitions	SQLGetInfo	fInfoType=SQL_OWNER_USAGE
supportsSelect ForUpdate	SQLGetInfo	fInfoType=SQL_POSITIONED_ STATEMENTS
supportsStored Procedures	SQLGetInfo	fInfoType=SQL_PROCEDURES

continued

JDBC Method	ODBC Call	ODBC Option
supportsSubqueries InComparisons	SQLGetInfo	fInfoType=SQL_SUBQUERIES
supportsSubqueries InQuantifieds	SQLGetInfo	fInfoType=SQL_SUBQUERIES
supportsSubqueries InIns	SQLGetInfo	fInfoType=SQL_SUBQUERIES
supportsTable CorrelationNames	SQLGetInfo	fInfoType=SQL_CORRELATION_ NAMES
supportsTransaction IsolationLevel	SQLGetInfo	fInfoType=SQL_TXN_ ISOLATION_OPTION
supportsTransactions	SQLGetInfo	fInfoType=SQL_TXN_CAPABLE
supportsUnion	SQLGetInfo	fInfoType=SQL_UNION
supportsUnionAll	SQLGetInfo	fInfoType=SQL_UNION
usesLocalFilePerTable	SQLGetInfo	fInfoType=SQL_FILE_USAGE
usesLocalFiles	SQLGetInfo	fInfoType=SQL_FILE_USAGE

Data Type Mappings

Java Primitive Data Types Mapped to SQL Data Types

Java Type	SQL Data Type
boolean	BIT
byte[]	VARBINARY or LONGVARBINARY
Double	DOUBLE
float	REAL
int	INTEGER
java.lang.Bignum	NUMERIC
java.sql.Date	DATE
java.sql.Time	TIME
java.sql.Timestamp	TIMESTAMP
Long	BIGINT
String	VARCHAR or LONGVARCHAR

Table 1

SQL Data Types Mapped to Java Types   Table 2

SQL Data Type	Java Type
CHAR	String
VARCHAR	String
LONGVARCHAR	String
NUMERIC	java.lang.Bignum
DECIMAL	java.lang.Bignum
BIT	boolean
TINYINT	integer
SMALLINT	integer
INTEGER	integer
BIGINT	long
REAL	float
FLOAT	double
DOUBLE	double
BINARY	byte[]
VARBINARY	byte[]
LONGVARBINARY	byte[]
DATE	java.sql.Date
TIME	java.sql.Time
TIMESTAMP	java.sql.Timestamp

Java Object Types Mapped to SQL Data Types   Table 3

Java Type	SQL Data Type
Boolean	BIT
byte[]	VARBINARY or LONGVARBINARY
Double	DOUBLE
Float	REAL
Integer	INTEGER
java.lang.Bignum	NUMERIC
java.sql.Date	DATE
java.sql.Time	TIME
java.sql.Timestamp	TIMESTAMP
Long	BIGINT
String	VARCHAR or LONGVARCHAR

SQL Data Types Mapped to Java Object Types

Table 4

SQL Data Type	Java Type
CHAR	String
VARCHAR	String
LONGVARCHAR	String
NUMERIC	java.lang.Bignum
DECIMAL	java.lang.Bignum
BIT	Boolean
TINYINT	Integer
SMALLINT	Integer
INTEGER	Integer
BIGINT	Long
REAL	Float
FLOAT	Double
DOUBLE	Double
BINARY	byte[]
VARBINARY	byte[]
LONGVARBINARY	byte[]
DATE	java.sql.Date
TIME	java.sql.Time
TIMESTAMP	java.sql.Timestamp

ResultSet "get" Methods

Table 5

	Numeric	Decimal	Tinyint	Binary	Varbinary	Bit	Date	Double	Float	Real	Integer	Bigint	Smallint	Char	Varchar	Time	Timestamp	Longvarchar	Longvarbinary
getBigDecimal	●	●	◆			◆		◆	◆	◆	◆	◆	◆	◆	◆			◆	
getByte	◆	◆	●			◆		◆	◆	◆	◆	◆	◆	◆	◆			◆	
getBytes				●	●														◆
getBoolean	◆	◆	◆			●		◆	◆	◆	◆	◆	◆	◆	◆			◆	
getDate							●							◆	◆		◆	◆	
getDouble	◆	◆	◆			◆		●	●	◆	◆	◆	◆	◆	◆			◆	
getFloat	◆	◆	◆			◆		◆	●	●	◆	◆	◆	◆	◆			◆	
getInt	◆	◆	◆			◆		◆	◆	◆	●	◆	◆	◆	◆			◆	
getLong	◆	◆	◆			◆		◆	◆	◆	◆	●	◆	◆	◆			◆	
getObject	◆	◆	◆	◆	◆	◆	◆	◆	◆	◆	◆	◆	◆	◆	◆	◆	◆	◆	◆
getShort	◆	◆	◆			◆		◆	◆	◆	◆	◆	●	◆	◆			◆	
getString	◆	◆	◆			◆		◆	◆	◆	◆	◆	◆	●	●	◆		◆	
getTime														◆	◆	●	◆	◆	
getTimeStamp							◆							◆	◆		●	◆	
getAsciiStream				◆	◆									◆	◆			●	◆
getBinaryStream				◆	◆									◆	◆			◆	●
getUnicodeStream				◆	◆									●					●

◆ = Method is capable of retrieving this SQL data type.
● = Preferred "get" method for this SQL data type.

Prepared and Callable Statement setObject Mappings   Table 6

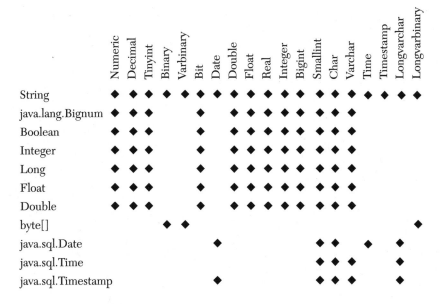

	Numeric	Decimal	Tinyint	Binary	Varbinary	Bit	Date	Double	Float	Real	Integer	Bigint	Smallint	Char	Varchar	Time	Timestamp	Longvarchar	Longvarbinary
String	◆	◆	◆	◆	◆	◆	◆	◆	◆	◆	◆	◆	◆	◆	◆	◆	◆	◆	◆
java.lang.Bignum	◆	◆	◆			◆		◆	◆	◆	◆	◆	◆	◆	◆				
Boolean	◆	◆	◆			◆		◆	◆	◆	◆	◆	◆	◆	◆				
Integer	◆	◆	◆			◆		◆	◆	◆	◆	◆	◆	◆	◆				
Long	◆	◆	◆			◆		◆	◆	◆	◆	◆	◆	◆	◆				
Float	◆	◆	◆			◆		◆	◆	◆	◆	◆	◆	◆	◆				
Double	◆	◆	◆			◆		◆	◆	◆	◆	◆	◆	◆	◆				
byte[]				◆	◆														◆
java.sql.Date							◆							◆	◆		◆	◆	
java.sql.Time														◆	◆	◆		◆	
java.sql.Timestamp							◆							◆	◆	◆		◆	

◆ = setObject can be set to the SQL data type and then be passed the Java data

APPENDIX **C**

java.sql Package Class Reference

The Date Class Methods

toString

Function:	Returns a String containing the date in the format "yyy-mm-dd."
Syntax:	public String toString();
Arguments:	none
Return Values:	String: The date value.
Example:	String myDate = date.toString()
See also:	Chapter 11: The Date Class

valueOf

Function:	Converts a String in the format "yyyy-mm-dd" to a Date object.
Syntax:	public static Date valueOf (String date);
Arguments:	date: The string to be converted to a Date object. Must be "yyyy-mm-dd" format.
Return Values:	Date: The Date object.
Example:	Date myDate = valueOf("1997-07-07");
See also:	Chapter 11, The Date Class

The DriverManager Class Methods

deregisterDriver

Function:	Removes a Driver from the list of avaliable drivers.
Syntax:	public static void deregisterDriver (Driver driver) throws SQLException
Arguments:	driver: The driver object to remove from the list.
Return Values:	none
Example:	deregisterDriver(foobar.foo.Driver);
See also:	Chapter 4: More Driver Manager Interface Methods

getConnection

Function:	Attempts to establish a connection to the referenced database.
Syntax:	public static syncronized Connection getConnection (String url, Properties loginProps) throws SQLException
Arguments:	url: The URL of the database to connect to. props: The Properties object containing login information.
Return Values:	Connection: A Connection object is returned if successful, null if connection fails.
Example:	Connection conn = driverManager.getConnection("jdbc:foobar:foo:db1", "jdbcuser","jdbcisfun");
Syntax:	public static syncronized Connection getConnection (String url, String user, String passwd) throws SQLException
Arguments:	url: The URL of the database to connect to. user: The user name. passwd: The user password.
Syntax:	public static syncronized Connection getConnection (String url) throws SQLException

Arguments:	url: The URL of the database to connect to.
Return Values:	Connection: A Connection object is returned if successful, null if connection fails.

Example:	Properties props = new Properties ();
	    props.put ("user", "jdbcuser");
	    props.put ("passwd", "jdbcisfun");
	    Connection conn = driverManager.getConnection("jdbc:foobar:foo:db1");

Return Values:	Connection: A Connection object is returned if successful, null if connection fails.

Example:	Properties props = new Properties ();
	    props.put ("user", "jdbcuser");
	    props.put ("passwd", "jdbcisfun");
	    Connection conn =
	driverManager.getConnection("jdbc:foobar:foo:db1",props);

See also:	Chapter 4, Establishing a Connection

getDriver

Function:	Locates an appropriate driver for the referenced URL from the list of available drivers.
Syntax:	public static Driver getDriver (String url) throws SQLException
Arguments:	url: The URL of the database to locate the driver for.
Return Values:	Driver: A Driver object is returned if an appropiate driver is found, otherwise null is returned.
Example:	Driver driver = driverManager.getDriver("jdbc:foobar:foo:db1");
See also:	Chapter 4, More DriverManager Methods

getDrivers

Function:	Gets a list of all drivers currently loaded and available.
Syntax:	public static Enumeration getDrivers getDrivers();
Arguments:	none
Return Values:	Enumeration: An enumerated of drivers currently loaded.
Example:	Enumeration enum = driverManager.getDrivers();
See also:	Chapter 4, More DriverManager Methods

getLoginTimeout

Function:	Gets the maximum time (in seconds) a driver will wait for a connection.
Syntax:	public static void getLoginTimeout ();
Arguments:	none
Return Values:	none

Example: int maxTimeout = DriverManager.getLoginTimeout ();
See also: Chapter 4, More DriverManager Interface Methods

getLogStream

Function: Gets the current PrintStream being used by the DriverManager.
Syntax: public static PrintStream getLogStream();
Arguments: none
Return Values: PrintStream: The current log output stream.
Example: PrintStream ps = DriveManager.getLogStream();
See also: Chapter 4, More DriverManager Interface Methods

println

Function: Prints a message to the current LogStream.
Syntax: public static void println (String message);
Arguments: message: The message to be output to the log stream.
Return Values: none
Example: driveManager.println ("Logging is turned on!");
See also: Chapter 4, More DriverManager Interface Methods

registerDriver

Function: Adds the driver to the list of available drivers. This is normally done automat-
                  ically when the Driver is insantiated.
Syntax: public static syncronized void registerDriver (Driver driver) throws SQLEx-
                  ception
Arguments: Driver: The Driver object to be added to the list.
Return Values: none
Example: driverManager.registerDriver(driver);
See also: Chapter 4, Loading and Registering the JDBC Driver

setLoginTimeout

Function: Sets the maximum time (in seconds) that a driver should wait when attempt-
                  ing to connect to a database before giving up.
Syntax: public static void setLoginTimout (int seconds)
Arguments: seconds: The number of seconds to wait.
Return Values: none
Example: driverManager.setLoginTimeout (60);
See also: Chapter 4, More DriverManager Interface Methods

setLogStream

Function:	Sets the PrintStream to direct logging messages to.
Syntax:	public static void setLogStream (PrintStream output)
Arguments:	output: The PrintStream to used for logging output.
Return Values:	none
Example:	driverManager.setLogStream(output);
See also:	Chapter 4, More DriverManger Interface Methods

The DriverPropertyInfo Class Variables

name

Usage:	Contains the name of the property. (i.e. user, password etc.)
Example:	String loginProp = DriverProperyInfo.name;
See also:	Chapter 4, The getPropertiesInfo Method
	Chapter 11, The DriverPropertiesInfor Class

description

Usage:	Contains the property description.
Example:	String loginPropDesc = DriverProperyInfo.description;
See also:	Chapter 4, The getPropertiesInfo Method
	Chapter 11, The DriverPropertiesInfor Class

required

Usage:	This variable is set to true if the login property is required.
Example:	boolean mustUse = DriverProperyInfo.required;
See also:	Chapter 4, The getPropertiesInfo Method
	Chapter 11, The DriverPropertiesInfor Class

value

Usage:	Contains the value of the property.
Example:	String propValue = DriverProperyInfo.value;
See also:	Chapter 4, The getPropertiesInfo Method
	Chapter 11, The DriverPropertiesInfor Class

choices

Usage:	Contains a list of values supplied by the database that are available for the property.
Example:	String[] myChoices = DriverProperyInfo.choices;
See also:	Chapter 4, The getPropertiesInfo Method
	Chapter 11, The DriverPropertiesInfor Class

The Time Class Methods

toString

Function:	Returns a String containing the time in the format "hh:mm:ss".
Syntax:	public String toString ();
Arguments:	none
Return Values:	String: The time value.
Example:	String whatTime = Time.toString();
See also:	Chapter 4, The getPropertiesInfo Method
	Chapter 11, The DriverPropertiesInfor Class

valueOf

Function:	Converts a String of the format "hh:mm:ss" to a Time object.
Syntax:	public static Time valueOf(String time);
Arguments:	time: The time to be converted to a Time object. Must be "hh:mm:ss" format.
Return Values:	Time: The Time object.
Example:	Time myTime = valueOf ("23:30:00");
See also:	Chapter 4, The getPropertiesInfo Method
	Chapter 11, The DriverPropertiesInfor Class

The Timestamp Class Methods

toString

Function:	Returns a String containing the timestamp in the format "yyyy-mm-dd hh:mm:ss.f...".
Syntax:	public String toString ();
Arguments:	none

Return Values:	String: The timestamp value.
Example:	String whatTime = Timestamp.toString();
See also:	Chapter 11, The TimeStamp Class

valueOf

Function:	Converts a String of the format "yyyy-mm-dd hh:mm:ss.f" to a Timestamp object.
Syntax:	public static Timestamp valueOf(String timestamp);
Arguments:	timestamp: The time to be converted to a Time object. Must be "hh:mm:ss" format.
Return Values:	Time: The Timestamp object.
Example:	Time myTime = valueOf ("1997-07-30 23:30:00");
See also:	Chapter 11, The TimeStamp Class

The Types Class Variables

The types class contains variables used to identify SQL types. Each variable is an integer value. Not all databases support all defined types.

- BIGINT
- BINARY
- BIT
- CHAR
- DATE
- DECIMAL
- DOUBLE
- FLOAT
- INTEGER
- LONGVARCHAR
- NULL
- NUMERIC
- OTHER
- REAL
- SMALLINT
- TIME
- TIMESTAMP
- TINYINT
- VARBINARY
- VARCHAR

java.sql Package Interface Reference

The CallableStatement Interface Methods

getBigDecimal

Function:	Returns the value of parameter specified by the paramater index number as a BigDecimal.
Syntax:	public abstract BigDecimal getBigDecimal (int index, int scale) throws SQLException
Arguments:	index: The parameter index number. (Relative position within the statement.)
	scale: The number of digits to the right of the decimal point to include in the value.
Return Values:	BigDecimal: The value of the parameter.
Example:	BigDecimal bd = callStatement.getBig-Decimal(1);
See also:	Chapter 6, Getting Out Parameters

getBoolean

Function:	Returns the value of parameter specified by the paramater index number as a boolean.
Syntax:	public abstract boolean getBoolean (int index) throws SQLException
Arguments:	index: The parameter index number. (Relative position within the statement.)
Return Values:	true or false: The value of the parameter.
Example:	boolean yes = callStatement.getBoolean(1);
See also:	Chapter 6, Getting Out Parameters

getByte

Function:	Returns the value of the parameter specified by the parameter index number as a byte.
Syntax:	public abstract byte getByte (int index) throws SQLException
Arguments:	index: The parameter index number. (Relative position within the statement.)
Return Values:	byte: The value of the parameter.
Example:	byte myByte = callStatement.getByte(1);
See also:	Chapter 6, Getting Out Parameters

getBytes

Function:	Returns the value of the parameter specified by the parameter index number as an array of bytes.
Syntax:	public abstract byte[] getBytes (int index) throws SQLException
Arguments:	index: The parameter index number. (Relative position within the statement.)
Return Values:	bytes[]: The value of the parameter.
Example:	bytes[] myBytes = callStatement.getBytes(1);
See also:	Chapter 6, Getting Out Parameters

getDate

Function:	Returns the value of the parameter specified by the parameter index number as a Date object.
Syntax:	public abstract Date getDate (int index) throws SQLException
Arguments:	index: The parameter index number. (Relative position within the statement.)
Return Values:	Date: The value of the parameter.
Example:	Date today = callStatement.getDate(1);
See also:	Chapter 6, Getting Out Parameters

getDouble

Function:	Returns the value of the parameter specified by the parameter index number as a double.
Syntax:	public abstract double getDouble (int index) throws SQLException
Arguments:	index: The parameter index number. (Relative position within the statement.)
Return Values:	double: The value of the parameter.
Example:	double myDouble = callStatement.getDouble(1);
See also:	Chapter 6, Getting Out Parameters

getFloat

Function:	Returns the value of the parameter specified by the parameter index number as a floating point number.
Syntax:	public abstract float getFloat(int index) throws SQLException
Arguments:	index: The parameter index number. (Relative position within the statement.)
Return Values:	float: The value of the parameter.
Example:	float myFloat = callStatement.getFloat(1);
See also:	Chapter 6, Getting Out Parameters

getInt

Function:	Returns the value of the parameter specified by the parameter index number as an integer.
Syntax:	public abstract int getInt (int index) throws SQLException
Arguments:	index: index: The parameter index number. (Relative position within the statement.)
Return Values:	int: The value of the parameter.
Example:	int myInt = callStatement.getInt(1);
See also:	Chapter 6, Getting Out Parameters

getLong

Function:	Returns the value of the parameter specified by the parameter index number as a long integer.
Syntax:	public abstract long getLong(int index) throws SQLException
Arguments:	index: The parameter index number. (Relative position within the statement.)
Return Values:	long: The value of the parameter.
Example:	long myLong = callStatement.getLong(1);
See also:	Chapter 6, Getting Out Parameters

getObject

Function:	Returns the value of the parameter specified by the parameter index number as an Object object. The objects type is determined by the default mapping of the SQL data type to Java data type.
Syntax:	public abstract Object getObject (int index) throws SQLException
Arguments:	index: The parameter index number. (Relative position within the statement.)
Return Values:	Object: The value of the parameter.
Example:	Object myObject = callStatement.getObject(1);
See also:	Chapter 6, The getObject Method

getShort

Function:	Returns the value of the parameter specified by the parameter index number as a short integer.
Syntax:	public abstract short getShort int index) throws SQLException
Arguments:	index: The parameter index number. (Relative position within the statement.)
Return Values:	short: The value of the parameter.
Example:	short myShort = callStatement.getShort(1);
See also:	Chapter 6, Getting Out Parameters

getString

Function:	Returns the value of the parameter specified by the parameter index number as a String object.
Syntax:	public abstract String getString (int index) throws SQLException
Arguments:	index: The parameter index number. (Relative position within the statement.)
Return Values:	String: The value of the parameter.
Example:	String mySting = callStatment.getString(1);
See also:	Chapter 6, Getting Out Parameters

getTime

Function:	Returns the value of the parameter specified by the parameter index number as a Time object.
Syntax:	public abstract Time getTime (int index) throws SQLException
Arguments:	index: The parameter index number. (Relative position within the statement.)
Return Values:	Time: The value of the parameter.
Example:	Time myTime = callStatement.getTime(1);
See also:	Chapter 6, Getting Out Parameters

getTimeStamp

Function:	Returns the value of the parameter specified by the parameter index number as a TimeStamp object.
Syntax:	public abstract TimeStamp (int index) throws SQLException
Arguments:	index: The parameter index number. (Relative position within the statement.)
Return Values:	TimeStamp: The value of the parameter.
Example:	java.sql.TimeStamp myTimeStamp = callStatement.getTimeStamp(1);
See also:	Chapter 6, Getting Out Parameters

registerOutParameter

Function:	Registers the specified output parameter to receive the SQL data type indicated by the argument passed. If the output is registered as either DECIMAL or NUMERIC the scale of the value may also be specified.
Syntax:	public abstract void registerOutParameter (int index, int sqlType) throws SQLException
	public abstract void registerOutParameter(int index, int sqlType, int scale) throws SQLException
Arguments:	index: The parameter index number. (Relative position within the statement.) sqlType: One of the data types contained in the java.sql.Types class.
Return Values:	none
Example:	callStatement.registerOutParameter(1,java.sql.Types.VARCHAR); callStatement.registerOutParameter(1,java.sql.Types.NUMERIC,3);
See also:	Chapter 6, The registerOutParameter Method

wasNull

Function:	Determines if the last value read by a "get" method was a SQL null value.
Syntax:	public abstract boolean wasNull() throws SQLException
Arguments:	none
Return Values:	true or false: True is returned if the last value read contained a null value.
Example:	java.sql.TimeStamp myTimeStamp = callStatement.getTimeStamp(1); boolean wasItNull = callStatement.wasNull(1);
See also:	Chapter 6, The wasNull Method

The Connection Interface Variables

All of the following variables are normally used in conjunction with the `set-TransactionIsolation()` method. Refer to Chapter 5: Transaction Isolation for more information.

TRANSACTION_NONE

Usage: Isolation level 0; Database does not support transactions.

TRANSACTION_ READ_COMMITTED

Usage: Isolation level 2; Sets the isolation level to prevent dirty reads. Non-repeate-
                    able and phantom reads are not prevented at this level.

TRANSACTION_ READ_UNCOMMITTED

Usage: Isolation level 1; Sets the isolation level to the lowest level. Dirty reads, non-
                    repeatable and phantom reads are allowed.

TRANSACTION_REPEATABLE_READ

Usage: Isolation level 4; Sets the isolation level to prevent dirty reads and non-
                    repeatable reads. Phantom reads are allowed.

TRANSACTION_SERIALIZABLE

Usage: Isolation level 8; Sets the isolation level so that dirty reads, non-repeatable
                    and phanom reads are prevented.

The Connection Interface Method Index

clearWarnings

Function: Deletes all warning messages in the SQLWarning chain.
Syntax: public abstract void clearWarnings() throws SQLException
Arguments: none
Return Values: none
Example: connection.clearWarnings();
See also: Chapter 5, Session Management

close

Function: Closes the connection to the database. All resources associated with the
                    Connection are released.
Syntax: public abstract close() throws SQLException
Arguments: none

Return Values:	none
Example:	connection.close();
See also:	Chapter 5, Session Management

commit

Function:	Immediately commits all transactions to the database. All updates and chages are made permanent.
Syntax:	public abstract void commit() throws SQLExcption
Arguments:	none
Return Values:	none
Example:	connection.commit();
See also:	Chapter 5, Getting Committed

createStatement

Function:	Creates a Statement object for the execution of static SQL statements.
Syntax:	public abstract Statement createStatment () throws SQLException.
Arguments:	none
Return Values:	Statement: The Statement object.
Example:	Statement stmt = connection.createStatement();
See also:	Chapter 5, Making a Statement

getAutoCommit

Function:	Determines if the AutoCommit feature is currently on. (Default is on.)
Syntax:	public abstract boolean getAutoCommit() throws SQLException
Arguments:	none
Return Values:	true or false: True is returned if all transactions are commit at the completion of the transaction.
Example:	boolean isAutoCommit = connection.getAutoCommit();
See also:	Chapter 5, Getting Committed

getCatalog

Function:	Determines which, if any, catalog is currently active.
Syntax:	public abstract String getCatalog() throws SQLException
Arguments:	none
Return Values:	String: The name of the current catalog.
Example:	String catalog = connection.getCatalog();
See also:	Chapter 5, The getCatalog/setCatalog Method

getMetaData

Function:	Creates a DatabaseMetaData object for the current connection.
Syntax:	public abstract DatabaseMetaData getMetaData () throws SQLException;
Arguments:	none
Return Values:	DatabaseMetaData: The DatabaseMetaData object containing information about the database currently connected to.
Example:	DatabaseMetaData dbmd = connection.getMetaData();
See also:	Chapter 5, The getMetaData Method

getTransactionIsolation

Function:	Determines the current transaction isolation level.
Syntax:	public abstract int getTransactionIsolation () throws SQLException
Arguments:	none
Return Values:	int: An integer representing the current transaction isolation level.

Example:	int transactLevel = connection.getTransactionIsolation();
	   if (transactLevel = TRANSACTION_NONE)
	      System.out.println("Database does not support transactions");

See also:	Chapter 5, Transaction Isolation

getWarnings

Function:	Retrieves the current SQLWarnings associated with the current connection.
Syntax:	public abstract SQLWarning getWarnings() throws SQLException
Arguments:	none
Return Values:	SQLWarning: The SQLWarning object containing all warning messages sent by the database.
Example:	SQLWarning dbWarnings = connection.getWarnings();
See also:	Chapter 5, Session Management

isClosed

Function:	Determines if the referenced Connection has been closed.
Syntax:	public abstract boolean isClosed() throws SQLException
Arguments:	none
Return Values:	true or false: True if the Connection has been closed.
Example:	boolean isConnClosed = connection.isClosed();
See also:	Chapter 5, Session Management

isReadOnly

Function:	Determines if the connection is in read-only mode.
Syntax:	public abstract boolean isReadOnly() throws SQLException
Arguments:	none
Return Values:	true or false: True if the connection only permits data reads form the database.
Example:	boolean readOnly = connection.isReadOnly();
See also:	Chapter 5, Session Management

nativeSQL

Function:	Returns the native form of the refernced SQL statement.
Syntax:	public abstract String nativeSQL (String sqlString) throws SQLException
Arguments:	sqlString: A valid SQL statement that may contain JDBC specific grammar.
Return Values:	String: The native SQL statement translation of the sqlString.
Example:	String sqlString = "SELECT * from emp whre hire_date = {d '1995-01-30'}" String nativeString = connection.nativeSQL(sqlString);
See also:	Chapter 5, The nativeSQL Method

prepareCall

Function:	Creates a CallableStatement object for use with SQL statements requiring IN and Out parameters.
Syntax:	public abstract CallableStatement prepareCall (String sqlString) throws SQLException
Arguments:	sqlString: The SQL statement to be executed. Normally it will contain at least one place holder (?) for an IN or OUT parameter.
Return Values:	CallableStatement: The CallableStatement object containing the SQL statement.
Example:	CallableStatement cs = connection.prepareCall();
See also:	Chapter 5, The CallableStatement Object

prepareStatement

Function:	Creates a PreparedStatement object for use with SQL statements requiring IN parameters.
Syntax:	public abstract PreparedStatement prepareStatement (String sqlString) throws SQLException
Arguments:	sqlString: An SQL statement to be executed. Normally it will contain at least one placeholder (?) for an IN parameter.
Return Values:	PreparedStatement: The PreparedStatement object containing the SQL statement.
Example:	PreparedStatement pstmt = connection.prepareStatement (sqlstring);
See also:	Chapter 5

rollback

Function:	Immediately performs a transaction rollback on the database, cancelling all pending transactions.
Syntax:	public abstract void rollback() throws SQLException
Arguments:	none
Return Values:	none
Example:	connection.rollback();
See also:	Chapter 5, Getting Committed

setAutoCommit

Function:	Toggles the automatic commit feature on or off. (Default is on.)
Syntax:	public abstract void setAutoCommit (boolean autoCommit) throws SQLException
Arguments:	autoCommit: True is used to turn the auto commit feature on, false to turn it off.
Return Values:	none
Example:	connection.setAutoCommit(false);
See also:	Chapter 5, Getting Committed

setCatalog

Function:	Selects which catalog within the database is to be used. If the database does not support catalogs the setCatalog command is ignored.
Syntax:	public abstract void setCatalog(String catalog) throws SQLException
Arguments:	catalog: Name of the catalog to make active.
Return Values:	none
Example:	connection.setCatalog("myCatalog");
See also:	Chapter 5, The getCatalog/setCatalog Method

setReadOnly

Function:	Sets the current connection to read-only mode.
Syntax:	public abstract void setReadOnly(boolean readOnly)
Arguments:	readOnly: A boolean of true is used to set the connection in read-only mode.
Return Values:	none
Example:	connection.setReadOnly(true);
See also:	Chapter 5, Session Management

setTranactionIsolation

Function:	Sets the transaction isolation level for all subsequent transactions.
Syntax:	public abstract void setTransactionIsolation(int level) throws SQLException
Arguments:	level: The level is normally set using one of the following variables defined in the interface:

TRANSACTION_NONE
TRANSACTION_ READ_COMMITTED
TRANSACTION_ READ_UNCOMMITTED
TRANSACTION_REPEATABLE_READ
TRANSACTION_SERIALIZABLE

Return Values:	none
Example:	connection.setTransactionIsolation(TRANSACTION_REPEATABLE_READ);
See also:	Chapter 5, Transaction Isolation

The DatabaseMetaData Interface Methods

Many of the methods in the `DatabaseMetaData` interface are used to simply probe the database for a single piece of information. The information the method seeks is very evident from the method name. As a result of this, the syntax and description for each of these methods would be extremely redundant. To simplify things, each of the methods in the `DatabaseMetaData` class is grouped into three catagories. The first category is those methods that return a boolean operator. The second is those that return an integer value representing some maximum value. The third group is those methods that do not fit in either catagory and require explanation.

Category I – Methods that Return a Boolean

Function:	Returns true if the "statement" made by the method name is true. For example: allProceduresAreCallable() will return true if all procedures are callable.
Syntax:	public boolean <method name> () throws SQLException.
Arguments:	none
Return Values:	true or false: Returns true if the "statement" is true.
Example:	boolean isTrue = rsmd.allProceduresAreCallable();
See also:	

allProceduresAreCallable
allTablesAreSelectable

dataDefinitionCauseTransactionCommit
dataDefinitionIgnoredInTransactions
doesMaxRowSizeIncludeBlobs
isCatalogAtStart
isReadOnly
nullAreSortedAtEnd
nullPlusNonNullsIsNull
nullsAreSorted
nullsAreSortedAtStart
nullsAreSortedLow
storesLowerCaseIdentifiers
storesLowerCaseQuotedIdentifiers
storesMixedCaseIdentifiers
storesMixedCaseQuotedIdentifiers
storesUpperCaseIdentifiers
storesUpperCaseQuotedIdentfiers
suportsMixedCaseQuotedIdentifiers
supportsAlterTableWithAddColumn
supportsAlterTableWithDropColumn
supportsCatalogsInDataMinipulations
supportsCatalogsInIndexDefintions
supportsCatalogsInPrivilegeDefinitions
supportsCatalogsInProcedures
supportsCatalogsInTableDefinitions
supportsColumnAliasing
supportsConvert
supportsCoreSQLGrammar
supportsCorrelatedSubqueries
supportsDataDefinitionAndDataManipulationTransactions
supportsDataManipulationTranactionsOnly
supportsDifferentTableCorrelationNames
supportsExpressionsInOrderBy
supportsExtendedSQLGrammar
supportsFullOuterJoins
supportsGroupBy
supportsGroupByBeyondSelect
supportsGroupByUnrelated
supportsLikeEscapeClause
supportsLimitedOuterJoins
supportsMinimumSQLGrammar
supportsMixedCaseIdentifiers

supportsMultipleResultSets
supportsMultipleTransactions
supportsNonNullableColumns
supportsOpenCursorAcrossCommit
supportsOpenCursorsAcrossRollback
supportsOrderByUnrelated
supportsOuterJoins
supportsPositionedDelete
supportsPositionedUpdate
supportsSchemasInDataManipulation
supportsSchemasInProcedureCalls
supportsSchemasInTableDefinitions
supportsSchemasInIndexDefinitions
supportsSchemasInPrivilegeDefinitions
supportsSelectForUpdate
supportsStoredProcedures
supportsSubqueriesInComparisons
supportsSubqueriesInQuantifieds
supportsSubqueriesInIns
supportsTableCorrelationNames
supportsTransactionIsolationLevel
supportsTransactions
supportsUnion
supportsUnionAll
usesLocalFilePerTable
usesLocalFiles

Catagory II - Methods that Return a Integer Representing a Maximum Value

Function: Returns the maximum value for the item refered to by the method name.
Syntax: public boolean <method name> () throws SQLException.
Arguments: none
Return Values: int: The maximum value.
Example: int maxNumberOfColumns = rsmd.getMaxColumnsInTable();
See also:
getMaxBinaryLiteralLength
getMaxCatalogNameLength
getMaxCharLiteralLength
getMaxColumnNameLength

getMaxColumnsInGroupBy
getMaxColumnsInIndex
getMaxColumnsInOrderBy
getMaxColumnsInSelect
getMaxColumnsInTable
getMaxConnections
getMaxCursorNameLength
getMaxIndexLength
getMaxProcedureNameLength
getMaxRowSize
getMaxSchemaNameLenth
getMaxStatementLength
getMaxStatements
getMaxTableNameLength
getMaxTablesInSelect
getMaxUserNameLength

Catagory III – DatabaseMetaData Methods not Returning a Boolean or Maximum Integer Value

getBestRowIdentifier

Function: Returns a ResultSet containing information describing the optimal set of columns that uniquely identifies each row. Each row in the ResultSet describes a column and its properties.

Syntax: public abstract ResultSet getBestRowIdentifier (String catalog,
                                     String Schema
                                     String Table,
                                     int scope,
                                     boolean nullable) throws
     SQLException

Arguments: catalog: The database catalog that contains the table to be queried. For databases that do not support catalogs the value can be null.
schema: The schema within the catalog containing the table. May also be null.
table: The table to be return information for.
scope: One of three integer variables describing what the scope of the results should be. The following are valid values:
           bestRowTemporary
           bestRowTransaction

	bestRowSession
Return Values:	ResultSet: The Result set contains the following columns:
	SCOPE: An integer representing the scope for which the column is valid. The value should match that of the scope input argument.
	COLUMN_NAME: The name of the column.
	DATA_TYPE: The SQL data type of the column as defined in java.sql.Types.
	TYPE_NAME: The database specific data type.
	COLUMN_SIZE: The precision of the column.
	BUFFER_LENGTH: <empty>
	DECIMAL_DIGITS: The scale of the column.
	PSEUDO_COLUMN: Determines if the column is a psuedo value.
Example:	ResultSet rs = dbmd.getBestRowIdentifier ("","myschema","mytable", java.sql.DatabaseMetaData.bestRowSession);

```
System.out.println("The optimal column set is :);
while (rs.next())
{
  System.out.println(rs.getString(COLUMN_NAME));
}
```

See also:	

getCatalogs

Function:	Returns a ResultSet containing a list of all catalogs available in the database. Null is returned if the database does not support catalogs.
Syntax:	public abstract ResultSet getCatalogs() throws SQLException
Arguments:	none
Return Values:	ResultSet: The ResultSet contains a single column containing the names of the avaliable catalogs: TABLE_CAT.
Example:	ResultSet rs = dbmd.getCatalogs();
See also:	Chapter 10, The getCatalog Method

getCatalogSeparator

Function:	Determines what character(s) is used to separate the catalog name from the schema or table name.
Syntax:	public abstract String getCatalogSeparator () throws SQLException
Arguments:	none
Return Values:	String: The character(s) that are used to separate catalog names from schema/tables.
Example:	String separator = dbmd.getCatalogSeparator();
See also:	Chapter 10, The getCatalogSeparator and isCatalogAtStart Methods

getCatalogTerm

Function:	Determines what the database specific name for "Catalog" is.
Syntax:	public abstract String getCatalogTerm () throws SQLException
Arguments:	none
Return Values:	String: The term.
Example:	String cTerm = dbmd.getCatalogTerm();
See also:	Chapter 10, The getCatalogTerm Method

getColumnPrivileges

Function:	Returns a ResultSet containing a information describing the access rights for a table's columns.
Syntax:	public abstract ResultSet getColumnPrivileges (String catalog, String schema String table, String pattern) throws SQLException
Arguments:	catalog: The database catalog that contains the table to be queried. For databases that do not support catalogs the value can be null.
	schema: The schema within the catalog containing the table. May also be null.
	table: The table to be return information for.
	pattern: A name pattern to be matched. May include wild card: "%".
Return Values:	ResultSet: The ResultSet contains the following columns describing the privileges for this table:
	TABLE_CAT: The catalog containing the table.
	TABLE_SCHEM: The schema name containg the table.
	TABLE_NAME:The name of the table.
	GRANTOR: The name of the grantor.
	GRANTEE: Name of who the privilege is granted to.
	PRIVILEGE: What privilege was granted.
	IS_GRANTABLE: Can the person grant this privilege to others?
Example:	ResultSet rs = dbmd.getColumnPrivileges("","myschema","mytable","%");
See also:	

getColumns

Function:	Returns a ResultSet containing information describing each column of a table.
Syntax:	public abstract ResultSet getColumns(String catalog, String schema String table, String pattern) throws SQLException

Arguments: catalog: The database catalog that contains the table to be queried. For databases that do not support catalogs the value can be null.

    schema: The schema within the catalog containing the table. May also be null.

    table: The table to be return information for.

    pattern: A name pattern to be matched. May include wild card: "%".

Return Values: ResultSet: The ResultSet contains the following columns describing the columns:

    TABLE_CAT: The catalog containing the table.

    TABLE_SCHEM: The schema name containg the table.

    TABLE_NAME: The name of the table.

    COLUMN_NAME: The name of the column.

    DATA_TYPE: The SQL data type of the column as defined in java.sql.Types.

    TYPE_NAME: The database specific data type.

    COLUMN_SIZE: The maximum of the column.

    BUFFER_LENGTH: <empty>

    DECIMAL_DIGITS: The scale of the column.

    NUM_PREC_RADIX: The radix (normally 10 or 2).

    NULLABLE: Are nulls allowed ?

    REMARKS: Comments about the column from the database.

    COLUMN_DEF: Default value if any.

    SQL_DATA_TYPE: <empty>

    SQL_DATETIME_SUB: <empty>

    CHAR_OCTET_LENGTH: If the column contains characters, this is the maximum numbe of bytes in the column.

    ORDINAL_POSTION: The ordinal postion of the column within the database. The first row is index number 1.

    IS_NULLABLE: Indicates if the column is nullable.

Example:

```
ResultSet rs = dbmd.getColumns(("","myschema","mytable","%");
System.out.println(rs.getString(COLUMN_NAME));
while (rs.next())
{
System.out.println("Column Name: " + rs.getString(COLUMN_NAME));
System.out.println("Column Type: " + rs.getString(DATA_TYPE));
System.out.println("Is Nullable: " + rs.getString(IS_NULLABLE));
}
```

getCrossReference

Function: Returns a ResultSet describing the primary/foreign key relationship between two tables.

Syntax: public abstract ResultSet getCrossReference (String primaryCatalog,
                                                String primarySchema,
                                                String primary Table,
                                                String foreignCatalog,
                                                String foreignSchema,
                                                String foreignTable,
) throws SQLException

Arguments: primaryCatalog: The database catalog that contains the primary table to be queried.

                primarySchema: The schema within the catalog containing the primary table.

                primary Table: The primary table to be return information for.

                foreignCatalog: The database catalog that contains the foreign table to be queried

                foreignSchema: The schema within the catalog containing the foreign table.

                foreignTable: The foreign table to be return information for.

Return Values: ResultSet: The ResultSet contains the following columns describing the primary/foreign key relationships between the two tables:

                PKTABLE_CAT: The database catalog that contains the primary table.

                PKTABLE_SCHEM: The schema within the catalog containing the primary table.

                PKTABLE_NAME: The primary table to be return information for.

                PKCOLUMN_NAME: The primary key column name.

                FKTABLE_CAT: The database catalog that contains the foreign table.

                FKTABLE_SCHEM: The schema within the catalog containing the foreign table.

                FKTABLE_NAME: The foreign table to be return information for.

                FKCOLUMN_NAME: The foreign key column name.

                KEY_SEQ: The sequence number with the foreign key.

                UPDATE_RULE: What happens when the primary key is updated?

                DELETE_RULE: What happens when the primary key is deleted?

                FK_NAME: What is the foreign keys name?

                PK_NAME: What is the primary keys name ?

                DEFERRABILITY: Can the evaluation of the foreign key be deferred until commit.

Example: ResultSet rs = dbmd.getImportedKeys("","myPschema","myPtable",
                                            "","myFschema","myFtable");

getDatabaseProductName

Function:	Returns the name of the database product.
Syntax:	public abstract String getDatabaseProductName () throws SQLException
Arguments:	none
Return Values:	String: The name of the product.
Example:	String myDBName = dbmd.getDatabaseProductName();
See also:	Chapter 10, Product Identification

getDriverName

Function:	Returns the name of the driver.
Syntax:	public abstract String getDriver () throws SQLException
Arguments:	none
Return Values:	String: The name of the driver.
Example:	String myDriverName = dbmd.getDriverName();
See also:	Chapter 10, Product Identification

getDatabaseProductVersion

Function:	Returns the database revision number.
Syntax:	public abstract String getDatabaseProductVersion () throws SQLException
Arguments:	none
Return Values:	String: The version number including all decimal points. (i.e. 7.1.3.1);
Example:	String dbVersion = dbmd.getDatabaseProductVersion();
See also:	Chapter 10, Product Identification

getDefaultTransactionIsolation

Function:	Determines the default transaction isolation level for the database.
Syntax:	public abstract int getDefaultTransactionIsolation() throws SQLException
Arguments:	none
Return Values:	int: The default transaction isolation level as defined in java.sql.Connection.

Example:	int transactLevel = rsmd.getDefaultTransactionIsolation();
	if (transactLevel = java.sql.Connection.TRANSACTION_NONE)
	System.out.println("Database does not support transactions");

getDriverVersion

Function:	Returns the driver full revision number.
Syntax:	public abstract String getDriverVersion() throws SQLException
Arguments:	none
Return Values:	String: The version number including all decimal points. (i.e. 7.1.3.1);
Example:	String driverVersion = dbmd.getDriverVersion ();
See also:	Chapter 10, Product Identification

getDriverMajorVersion

Function:	Determines the major revision number of the driver.
Syntax:	public abstract int getMajorVersion()
Arguments:	none
Return Values:	int: The major revision number of the driver.
Example:	int driverMajorRev = dbmd.getMajorVersion();
See also:	Chapter 4: More Driver methods
	Chapter 10, Product Identification

getDriverMinorVersion

Function:	Determines the minor revision number of the driver.
Syntax:	public abstract int getMinorVersion()
Arguments:	none
Return Values:	int: The minor revision number of the driver.
Example:	int driverMinorRev = dbmd.getMinorVersion();
See also:	Chapter 4: More Driver methods
	Chapter 10, Product Identification

getExportedKeys

Function: Returns a ResultSet describing all of the keys that are exported by a table.

Syntax: public abstract ResultSet getCrossReference (String catalog,
String schema,
String table) throws
SQLException

Arguments: catalog: The database catalog that contains the table to be queried. For databases that do not support catalogs the value can be null.
schema: The schema within the catalog containing the table. May also be null.
table: The table to be return information for.

Return Values: ResultSet: The ResultSet contains the following columns describing the keys exported by the table:
PKTABLE_CAT: The database catalog that contains the primary table.

PKTABLE_SCHEM: The schema within the catalog containing the primary table.

PKTABLE_NAME: The primary table to be return information for.

PKCOLUMN_NAME: The primary key column name.

FKTABLE_CAT: The database catalog that contains the foreign table.

FKTABLE_SCHEM: The foreign table schema being exported.

FKTABLE_NAME: The foreign table name being exported.

FKCOLUMN_NAME: The exported foreign key column name.

KEY_SEQ: The sequence number with the foreign key.

UPDATE_RULE: What happens when the primary key is updated?

DELETE_RULE: What happens when the primary key is deleted?

FK_NAME: What is the foreign keys name?

PK_NAME: What is the primary keys name ?

DEFERRABILITY: Can the evaluation of the foreign key be deferred until commit.

Example: ResultSet rs = dbmd.getExportedKeys();

See also:

getExtraNameCharacters

Function: Returns a list of any characters beyond standard alphanumeric characters and the underbar "_" that can be used within table names. (i.e. hyphens "-", plus "+" etc.);

Syntax: public abstract getExtraNameCharacters () throws SQLException

Arguments: none

Return Values: String: A list of all "extra" characters allowed.

Example: String extras = rsmd.getExtraNameCharacters();

See also:

getIdentifierQuoteString

Function: Determines what charcter, if any, is used to quote SQL identifiers.

Syntax: public abstract String getIdentifierQuoteString () throws SQLException

Arguments: none

Return Values: String: The string that is used to quote SQL identifiers.

Example: String theQouteString = dbmd.getIdentifierQuoteString()

See also:

getImportedKeys

Function: Returns a ResultSet describing all of the keys that are imported by the table.

Syntax: public abstract ResultSet getCrossReference (String catalog,
                         String schema,

| | String table) throws |
| | SQLException |

Arguments: catalog: The database catalog that contains the table to be queried. For databases that do not support catalogs the value can be null.

schema: The schema within the catalog containing the table. May also be null.

table: The table to be return information for.

Return Values: ResultSet: The ResultSet contains the following columns describing the keys imported by the table:

PKTABLE_CAT: The database catalog that contains the primary key's table.

PKTABLE_SCHEM: The schema within the catalog containing the primary key's table.

PKTABLE_NAME: The table containing the primary key .

PKCOLUMN_NAME: The primary key column name.

FKTABLE_CAT: The database catalog that contains the foreign table.

FKTABLE_SCHEM: The foreign table schema being exported.

FKTABLE_NAME: The foreign table name being exported.

FKCOLUMN_NAME: The exported foreign key column name.

KEY_SEQ: The sequence number with the foreign key.

UPDATE_RULE: What happens when the primary key is updated?

DELETE_RULE: What happens when the primary key is deleted?

FK_NAME: What is the foreign keys name?

PK_NAME: What is the primary keys name?

DEFERRABILITY: Can the evaluation of the foreign key be deferred until commit.

Example: ResultSet rs = dbmd.getImportedKeys();

getNumericFunctions

Function: Returns a comma separated list containing all numeric functions supported by the database. (i.e. abs, sin, cos etc..)

Syntax: public abstract String getNumericFunctions() throws SQLException

Arguments: none

Return Values: String: A comma seperated list of functions.

Example:

See also:

getPrimaryKeys

Function: Returns a ResultSet describing all of the primay keys within a table.

Syntax: public abstract ResultSet getPrimaryKeys (String catalog,
                                                           String schema, String table)

	throws SQLException
Arguments:	catalog: The database catalog that contains the table to be queried. For databases that do not support catalogs the value can be null.
	schema: The schema within the catalog containing the table. May also be null.
	table: The table to be return information for.
	pattern: A name pattern to be matched. May include wild card: "%".
Return Values:	ResultSet: The ResultSet contains the following columns describing the primary keys for this table:
	TABLE_CAT: The catalog containing the table.
	TABLE_SCHEM: The schema name containg the table.
	TABLE_NAME: The name of the table.
	COLUMN_NAME: The name of the primary key column.
	KEY_SEQ: The sequence number for the key.
	PK_NAME: The name of the primary key.
Example:	ResultSet rs = dbmd.getPrimaryKeys();

getProcedures

Function:	Returns a ResultSet describing all stored procedures available in the catalog.
Syntax:	public abstract ResultSet getProcedures (String catalog,
	String schemaPattern,
	String procedurePattern)
	throws SQLException
Arguments:	catalog: The database catalog that contains the procedure to be queried for. For databases that do not support catalogs the value can be null.
	schemaPattern: A schema name pattern to be matched. May include wild card: "%".
	procedurePattern: A procedure name pattern to be matched. May include wild card: "%".
Return Values:	ResultSet: The ResultSet contains the following columns describing the stored procedures in the catalog.
	PROCEDURE_CAT: The catalog containing the procedure.
	PROCEDURE_SCHEM: The schema within the catalog containing the procedure.
	PROCEDURE_NAME: The name of the procedure.
	REMARKS: Expanatory comments for the procedure.
	PROCEDURE_TYPE: The type of procedure as determined by what type of results it returns.
Example:	RestultSet rs = dbmd.getProcedures();
See also:	Chapter 10, Stored Procedures

getProcedureTerm

Function:	Determines the database specific term for "procedure."
Syntax:	public abstract String getProcedureTerm () throws SQLException
Arguments:	none
Return Values:	String: The database specific term for "procedure".
Example:	String dbProcName = dbmd.getProcedureTerm();
See also:	Chapter 10, Stored Procedures

getSchemas

Function:	Returns a ResultSet containing a list of all schemas available in the database.
Syntax:	public abstract ResultSet geSchemas () throws SQLException
Arguments:	none
Return Values:	ResultSet: The ResultSet contains a single column that contains the name of all schemas available.
	TABLE_SCHEM: The name of the schema.
Example:	ResultSet rs = dbmd.geSchemas();
See also:	Chapter 10, Working with Schema Objects

getSchemaTerm

Function:	Determines the database specific term for "schema."
Syntax:	public abstract String getSchemaTerm () throws SQLException
Arguments:	none
Return Values:	String: The term used by the database for "schema".
Example:	String schemaTerm = dbmd.getSchemaTerm();
See also:	Chapter 10, Working with Schema Objects

getSearchStringEscape

Function:	Determines what string is used to as the escape charcter for wile cards.
Syntax:	public abstract String getSearchStringEscape () throws SQLException
Arguments:	none
Return Values:	String: The escape character used to ensure literal translation of special characters.
Example:	String theEscape = dbmd.getSearchStringEscape();

getSQLKeywords

Function:	Returns a comma seperated list of SQL keywords used by the database.
Syntax:	public abstract String getSQLKeywords () throws SQLException
Arguments:	none
Return Values:	String: A comma seperated list of keywords.
Example:	String keyWords = dbmd.getKeywords();

getStringFunctions

Function:	Returns a comma seperated list of all string functions supported by the database.
Syntax:	public abstract String getStringFunctions () throws SQLException
Arguments:	none
Return Values:	String: A comma seperated list of all string functions.
Example:	String stringFunctions = dbmd.getStringFunctions();

getSystemFunctions

Function:	Returns a comma seperated list of all system functions supported by the database.
Syntax:	public abstract String getSystemFunctions () throws SQLException
Arguments:	none
Return Values:	String: A comma seperated list of all system functions.
Example:	String stringFunctions = dbmd.getSystemFunctions();

getTablePrivileges

Function:	Return a ResultSet describing the access rights to a table(s).

Syntax:	public abstract ResultSet getTablePrivileges (String catalog,
	                                            String schemaPattern
	                                            String tablePattern
	                                            ) throws SQLException

Arguments:	catalog: The database catalog that contains the table to be queried. For databases that do not support catalogs the value can be null. schema: The schema pattern to use as the schema selection criteria. May include wild card: "%". table: The table pattern to user as the table selction criteria. May include wild card: "%".
Return Values:	ResultSet: The ResultSet contains the following columns describing the privileges for this table: TABLE_CAT: The catalog containing the table.

TABLE_SCHEM: The schema name containg the table.

TABLE_NAME:The name of the table.

GRANTOR: The name of the grantor.

GRANTEE: Name of who the privilege is granted to.

PRIVILEGE: What privilege was granted.

IS_GRANTABLE: Can the person grant this privilege to others ?

Example: ResultSet rs = dbmd.getTablePrivileges("","myschema","mytable","%");

See also: Chapter 10, Getting Table Privileges

getTables

Function: Returns a ResultSet containing a list of all tables available matching the catalog, schema and table type selection critiria.

Syntax: public abstract ResultSet getTables (String catalog,
                                                     String schemaPattern
                                                     String tablePattern
                                                     String[] types) throws SQLException

Arguments: catalog: The database catalog that contains the table to be queried. For databases that do not support catalogs the value can be null.

schema: The schema pattern to use as the schema selection criteria. May include wild card: "%".

table: The table pattern to user as the table selction criteria. May include wild card: "%".

types[]: An array containing a list of all table types to be returned.

Return Values: ResultSet: The ResultSet contains the following columns describing the privileges for this table:

TABLE_CAT: The catalog containing the table.

TABLE_SCHEM: The schema name containg the table.

TABLE_NAME: The name of the table.

TABLE_TYPE: The type of table. (i.e. TABLE, VIEW etc).

REMARKS: Expanatory notes for the table.

Example: String[] tabTypes = {"View","TABLE","SYS"};

ResultSet rs = dbmd.getTables("", "%","%", tabTypes);

See also: Chapter 10, Getting a List of Tables

getTableTypes

Function:	Returns a ResultSet listing the table types available.
Syntax:	public abstract ResultSet geTableTypes () throws SQLException
Arguments:	none
Return Values:	ResultSet: The ResultSet contains a single column that contains the nams of all the table types available:
	TABLE_TYPE: The catalog containing the table.
Example:	ResultSet rs = dbmd.getTableTypes();
See also:	Chapter 10, Getting a List of Table Types

getTimeDateFunctions

Function:	Returns a comma separated list of all time and date functions supported by the database.
Syntax:	public abstract String getTimeDateFunctions () throws SQLException
Arguments:	none
Return Values:	String: A comma seperated list of all time and date functions.
Example:	String stringFunctions = dbmd.getTimeDateFunctions();

getTypeInfo

Function:	Returns a ResultSet describing all of the standard SQL types supported by the database.
Syntax:	public abstract ResultSet getTypeInfo () throws SQLException
Arguments:	none
Return Values:	ResultSet: The ResultSet contains the following columns describing the SQL types:
	TYPE_NAME: The type name.
	DATA_TYPE: The SQL data type as defined in java.sql.Types.
	PRECISION: The maximum precision.
	LITERAL_PREFIX: The prefix used to qoute literals.
	LITERAL_SUFFIX: The suffix used to qoute literals.
	CREATE_PARAMS: Parameters used to create the type.
	NULLABLE: Can you use null's with this type?
	CASE_SENSITIVE: Is the type case sensitive?
	SEARCHABLE: Can the type be used in a "WHERE" clause?
	UNSIGNED_ATRIBUTE: Is this type a signed number?
	FIXED_PREC_SCALE: Can this type be a currency ?
	AUTO_INCREMENT: Can the type be used for auto-incrementing a value?
	LOCAL_TYPE_NAME: What is the database SQL type name?
Example:	ResultSet typeInfo = dbmd.betTypeInfo();

getURL

Function:	Determines the current URL for the database is.
Syntax:	public abstract String getURL() throws SQLException
Arguments:	none
Return Values:	String: The URL.
Example:	String loggedInto = dbmd.getURL();

getUserName

Function:	Determines what the current database user name is.
Syntax:	public abstract String getUserName () throws SQLException
Arguments:	none
Return Values:	String: The name of the user.
Example:	String user = dbmc.getUserName();

getVersionColumns

Function:	Returns a ResultSet describing all columns within a table that are automatically updated when the a value in the table is updated.
Syntax:	public abstract ResultSet getVersionColumns (String catalog, String schema, String table) throws SQLException
Arguments:	catalog: The database catalog that contains the table to be queried. For databases that do not support catalogs the value can be null.
	schema: The schema within the catalog containing the table. May also be null.
	table: The table to be return information for.
	pattern: A name pattern to be matched. May include wild card: "%".
	ResultSet: The Result set contains the following columns:
	SCOPE: An integer representing the scope for which the column is valid. The value should match that of the scope input argument.
	COLUMN_NAME: The name of the column.
	DATA_TYPE: The SQL data type of the column as defined in java.sql.Types.
	TYPE_NAME: The database specific data type.
	COLUMN_SIZE: The precision of the column.
	BUFFER_LENGTH: <empty>
	DECIMAL_DIGITS: The scale of the column.
	PSEUDO_COLUMN: Determines if the column is a psuedo value.
Example:	ResultSet rs = dbmd.getVersionColumns();

The Driver Interface Method Index

acceptsURL

Function:	Returns true if the driver is able to open a connection to the database given by the URL.
Syntax:	public abstract boolean acceptsURL (String url) thows SQLException
Arguments:	url: The URL of the database to be connected to.
Return Values:	true or false: True if the driver is able to open a connection to the database, otherwise returns false.
Example:	boolean urlIsOk = acceptsURL(jdbc:foobar:foo)
See also:	Chapter 4: Establishing a Connection

connect

Function:	Attempts to make a database connection to the given URL.
Syntax:	public abstract Connection connect(String url, Properties loginProps) throws SQLException
Arguments:	url: The URL of the database to connect to.
	loginProps: The login properties needed by the database to complete the connection.
	Most often the user name and password.
Return Values:	Connection: Connection object returned if successful, null if connection fails.
Example:	Driver drv1 = new foobar.foo.Driver

```
    Properties props = new Properties ();
    props.put ("user", "jdbcuser");
    props.put ("passwd", "jdbcisfun");
    Connection conn1 = drv1.connect("jdbc:foobar:foo:db1",props);
```

See also:	Chapter 4: Establishing a Connection

getMajorVersion

Function:	Determines the major revision number of the driver.
Syntax:	public abstract int getMajorVersion()
Arguments:	none
Return Values:	int: The major revision number of the driver.
Example:	int driverMajorRev = drv1.getMajorVersion();
See also:	Chapter 4: More Driver methods

getMinorVersion

Function:	Determines the minor revision number of the driver.
Syntax:	public abstract int getMinorVersion()
Arguments:	none
Return Values:	int: The minor revision number of the driver.
Example:	int driverMinorRev = drv1.getMinorVersion();
See also:	Chapter 4: More Driver methods

getPropertyInfo

Function:	Returns an array of DriverPropertyInfo objects describing login properties accepted by the database.
Syntax:	public abstract DriverPropertiesInfo[] getPropertyInfo (String url, Properties loginProps) throws SQLException
Arguments:	url: The URL of the database to connect to. loginProps: The known login properties needed by the database to complete the connection.
Return Values:	DriverPropertiesInfo[]: A list of properties the database accepts.
Example:	Driver drv1 = new foobar.foo.Driver Properties props = new Properties (); props.put ("user", "jdbcuser"); props.put ("passwd", "jdbcisfun"); DriverPropertiesInfo[] dpInfo = drv1.getPropertyInfo(jdbc:foobar:foo:db1, props);
See also:	Chapter 4: More Driver methods, Chapter 11: The DriverPropertiesInfo class

jdbcCompliant

Function:	Determines if the driver is JDBC COMPLIANT.
Syntax:	public abstract boolean jdbcCompliant()
Arguments:	none
Return Values:	true or false: True if the driver has passed all compliance testing, false if not.
Example:	boolean isCompliant = drv1.jdbcCompliant();
See also:	Chapter 4: More Driver methods

The PreparedStatement Interface Method Index

clearParameters

Function:	Clears all parameters associated with a PreparedStatement. After execution of this method all parameters have the value null.
Syntax:	public abstract void clearParameters () throws SQLException
Arguments:	none
Return Values:	none
Example:	prepStatement.clearParameters();
See also:	

execute

Function:	Executes the associated SQLStatement when the number of results returned are unkown.
Syntax:	public abstract boolean execute ( ) throws SQLException
Arguments:	none
Return Values:	true or false: True if the execution of the SQL statement resulted in any returned results.
Example:	boolean isResults = prepStatement.execute(s);
See also:	Chapter 6, The Execution Methods

executeQuery

Function:	Executes an SQL query statement.
Syntax:	public abstract ResultSet executeQuery () throws SQLException
Arguments:	none
Return Values:	ResultSet: The ResultSet object containing the data returned by the database.
Example:	ResultSet rs = prepStatement.executeQuery();
See also:	Chapter 6, The Execution Methods

executeUpdate

Function:	Excecutes an SQL update, insert or delete statement.
Syntax:	public abstract int executeUpdate() throws SQLException
Arguments:	none
Return Values:	int: The number of rows effected by the update, insert of delete.
Example:	int rowsChanged = prepStatement.executeUpdate();
See also:	Chapter 6, The Execution Methods

setAsciiStream

Function:	Binds an ASCII stream value to an input parameter.
Syntax:	public abstract void setAsciiStream (int index, InputStream in, int length)
Arguments:	index: The parameter index number. (Relative position within the statement.)
	in: The InputStream to read the value from.
	length: The number of bytes in the stream.
Return Values:	none
Example:	FileReader textFile = new FileReader(fileName);
	prepStatement.setAsciiStream(1,textFile,256);
See also:	Chapter 6, Setting In Parameters

setBigDecimal

Function:	Binds a BigDecimal value t an input parameter.
Syntax:	pubic abstract void setBigDecimal(int index,
	BigDecimal number) throws SQLException
Arguments:	index: The parameter index number. (Relative position within the statement.)
	number: The BigDecimal object to be bound.
Return Values:	none
Example:	BigDecimal bd = (1000*1000*1000*1000);
	prepStatement.setBigDecimal(1,bd);
See also:	Chapter 6, Setting In Parameters

setBinaryStream

Function:	Binds a binary stream value to an input parameter.
Syntax:	public abstract void setBinaryStream (int index, InputStream in, int length)
Arguments:	index: The parameter index number. (Relative position within the statement.)
	in: The InputStream to read the value from.
	length: The number of bytes in the stream.
Return Values:	none
Example:	FileInputStream binFile = new FileInputStream(fileName);
	prepStatement.setBinaryStream(1,binFile,256);
See also:	Chapter 6, Setting In Parameters

setBoolean

Function:	Binds a boolean value to an input parmeter.
Syntax:	public abstract void setBoolean (int index, boolean value) throws SQLExeption
Arguments:	index: The parameter index number. (Relative position within the statement.)
Return Values:	none
Example:	prepStatement.setBoolean(1,(boolean)false);
See also:	Chapter 6, Setting In Parameters

setByte

Function:	Binds a byte value to an input parameter.
Syntax:	public abstract void setByte (int index, byte value) throws SQLExeption
Arguments:	index: The parameter index number. (Relative position within the statement.) value: The byte value to be bound.
Return Values:	none
Example:	prepStatement.setByte(1,myByte);
See also:	Chapter 6, Setting In Parameters

setBytes

Function:	Binds multiple byte values to an input parameter.
Syntax:	public abstract void setBytes (int index, Byte value[]) throws SQLExeption
Arguments:	index: The parameter index number. (Relative position within the statement.) value[]: An array of bytes to be bound.
Return Values:	none
Example:	prepStatement.setBytes(1,myBytes[]);
See also:	Chapter 6, Setting In Parameters

setDate

Function:	Binds a Date object value to an input parameter.
Syntax:	public abstract void setDate (int index, Date value) throws SQLExeption
Arguments:	index: The parameter index number. (Relative position within the statement.) value: The Date object to be bound.
Return Values:	none
Example:	Date today = new Date (97, 07,23,23,00); prepStatement.setDate(1,today);
See also:	Chapter 6, Setting In Parameters

setDouble

Function:	Binds a double value to an input parameter.
Syntax:	public abstract void setDouble (int index, double value) throws SQLExeption
Arguments:	index: The parameter index number. (Relative position within the statement.) value: The Double object to be bound.
Return Values:	none
Example:	prepStatement.setDouble(1,(Double)12323);
See also:	Chapter 6, Setting In Parameters

setFloat

Function:	Binds a floating point value to an input parameter.
Syntax:	public abstract void setFloat (int index,float value) throws SQLExeption
Arguments:	index: The parameter index number. (Relative position within the statement.) value: The floating point value to be bound.
Return Values:	none
Example:	prepStatement.setFloat(1,(float)3.1473);
See also:	Chapter 6, Setting In Parameters

setInt

Function:	Binds a integer value to an input parameter.
Syntax:	public abstract void setInteger (int index, int value) throws SQLExeption
Arguments:	index: The parameter index number. (Relative position within the statement.) value: The value of the integer to be bound.
Return Values:	none
Example:	prepStatement.setInt(1,34);
See also:	Chapter 6, Setting In Parameters

setLong

Function:	Binds a long value to an input parameter.
Syntax:	public abstract void setLong (int index, long value) throws SQLExeption
Arguments:	index: The parameter index number. (Relative position within the statement.) value: The value of the long to be bound.
Return Values:	none
Example:	prepStatement.setLong(1,(long)232522323253986);
See also:	Chapter 6, Setting In Parameters

setNull

Function:	Binds a null value to an input parameter.
Syntax:	public abstract void setNull (int index, int sqlType) throws SQLExeption
Arguments:	index: The parameter index number. (Relative position within the statement.) sqlType: The SQL data type of the recieving column. See java.sql.Types for list of accepted values.
Return Values:	none
Example:	prepStatement.setNull(1,java.sql.Types.VARCHAR);
See also:	Chapter 6, Setting In Parameters

setObject

Function:	Binds an Object to an input parameter. The object will be converted to an SQL data type before being sent to the database. In the first instance, the SQL data type is determined by the default mapping specified by JDBC. In the second and third version, you can specify the SQL data type as an argument.
Syntax:	public abstract void setObject (int index, Object obj) throws SQLExeption 　　public abstract void setObject (int index, Object obj, 　　　　　　　　　　　　　　int targetType) throws SQLExeption 　　public abstract void setObject (int index, Object obj 　　　　　　　　　　　　int targetType 　　　　　　　　　　　　int scale) throws SQLExeption
Arguments:	index: The parameter index number. (Relative position within the statement.) targetType: The SQL data type that the object will be converted to. scale: The scale to be used for the object if the object is to be converted to SQL data types NUMERIC or DECIMAL.
Return Values:	none
Example:	float myNumber = 3.14; prepStatement.setObject(1, myNumber,java.sql.Types.NUMERIC,2);
See also:	Chapter 6, The setObject Method

setShort

Function:	Binds a short value to an input parameter.
Syntax:	public abstract void setShort (int index, short value) throws SQLExeption
Arguments:	index: The parameter index number. (Relative position within the statement.) value: The value of the short to be bound.
Return Values:	none
Example:	prepStatement.setShort(1,(short)3);
See also:	Chapter 6, Setting In Parameters

setString

Function:	Binds a String value to an input parameter.
Syntax:	public abstract void setString (int index, String value) throws SQLExeption
Arguments:	index: The parameter index number. (Relative position within the statement.) value: The String value to be bound.
Return Values:	none
Example:	String myString = "The test string"; prepStatement.setString(1,myString);
See also:	Chapter 6, Setting In Parameters

setTime

Function:	Binds a Time value to an input parameter.
Syntax:	public abstract void setTime (int index, Time value) throws SQLExeption
Arguments:	index: The parameter index number. (Relative position within the statement.)
	value: The Time object to be bound.
Return Values:	none
Example:	java.sql.Time now = new java.sql.Time (01,20,00);
	prepStatement.setTime(1,now);
See also:	Chapter 6, Setting In Parameters

setTimeStamp

Function:	Binds a TimeStamp value to an input parameter
Syntax:	public abstract void setTimeStamp (int index,
	TimeStamp value) throws
	SQLExeption
Arguments:	index: The parameter index number. (Relative position within the statement.)
Return Values:	none
Example:	java.sql.TimeStamp ts = new java.sqlTimeStamp(97,07,23,01,30,00,00);
	prepStatement.setTimeStamp(1,ts);
See also:	Chapter 6, Setting In Parameters

setUnicodeStream

Function:	Binds a Unicode input stream to an input parameter
Syntax:	public abstract void setUnicodeStream (int index, InputStream in,
	int length) throws SQLExeption
Arguments:	index: The parameter index number. (Relative position within the statement.)
	in: The input stream to read the Unicode from.
	length: The number of bytes in the input stream.
Return Values:	none
Example:	FileReader textFile = new FileReader(fileName);
	prepStatement.setUnicodeStream(1,textFile,256);
See also:	Chapter 6, Setting In Parameters

The ResultSet Interface Methods

clearWarnings

Function:	Deletes all warning messages in the SQLWarning chain.
Syntax:	public abstract void clearWarnings() throws SQLException
Arguments:	none
Return Values:	none
Example:	resultSet.clearWarnings();
See also:	Chapter 8, ResultSet Management

close

Function:	Closes the ResultSet and realease all resources associated with it.
Syntax:	public abstract void close () throws SQLException
Arguments:	none
Return Values:	none
Example:	statement.close();
See also:	Chapter 8, ResultSet Management

findColumn

Function:	Returns the column index number corresponding to the column name argument.
Syntax:	public abstract int findColumn (String columnName) throws SQLException
Arguments:	columnName: The name of the column to retrieve the index for. Case sensitivity is dependent on the database.
Return Values:	index: The name of column to be retrieved.
Example:	int colNumber = resultSet.findColumn("USER_TABLE"):
See also:	Chapter 8, Determining the Column

getAsciiStream

Function:	Retrieves the value of the specified column from the current row as an ASCII stream. The column can be represented by either the column index or the column name.
Syntax:	public abstract InputStream getAsciiStrem (int index) throws SQLException public abstract InputStream getAsciiStrem (String columnName) throws SQLException
Arguments:	index: The index number of the column to be retrieved. columnName: The name of the column to be retrieved.

Return Values: InputStream: The input stream used to retrieve the data.
Example: FileReader textFile = new FileReader(fileName);
                 testFile = resultSett.getAsciiStream(1);
                 FileReader textFile = new FileReader(fileName);
                 testFile = resultSett.getAsciiStream("BIG_COLUMN");
See also: Chapter 8, Using the "set" Methods

getBigDecimal

Function: Returns the value of the referenced column from the current row as a
                 BigDecimal object.
Syntax: public abstract BigDecimal getBigDecimal (int index) throws SQLException
                 public abstract get (String columnName) throws SQLException
Arguments: index: The column index number to retrieve data from.
                 columnName: The column name to retrieve data from.
Return Values: BigDecimal: The value of the column.
Example: BigDecimal myBigDec = restultSet.getBigDecimal(1);
                 BigDecimal myBigDec = restultSet.getBigDecimal("COLUMN1");
See also: Chapter 8, Using the "set" Methods

getBinaryStream

Function: Retrieves the value of the specified column from the current row as an binary
                 data stream. The column can be represented by either the column index or
                 the column name.
Syntax: public abstract InputStream getBinaryStream(int index) throws SQLException
                 public abstract InputStream getBinaryStream
                                             (String columnName) throws SQLException
Arguments: index: The index number of the column to be retrieved.
                 columnName: The name of the column to be retrieved.
Return Values: InputStream: The input stream used to retrieve the data.
Example: FileInputStream binFile = new FileInputStream(fileName);
                 binFile = resultSet.getBinaryStream(1);
                 FileInputStream binFile = new FileInputStream(fileName);
                 binFile = resultSet.getBinaryStream("BINARY_COLUMN");
See also: Chapter 8, Using the "set" Methods

getBoolean

Function: Returns the value of the referenced column from the current row as a
                 boolean.

Syntax:	public abstract (int index) throws SQLException
	public abstract get (String columnName) throws SQLException
Arguments:	index: The column index number to retrieve data from.
	columnName: The column name to retrieve data from.
Return Values:	true or false: The value of the column.
Example:	
See also:	Chapter 8, Using the "set" Methods

getByte

Function:	Returns the value of the referenced column from the current row as a byte.
Syntax:	public abstract byte getByte(int index) throws SQLException
	public abstract byte getByte (String columnName) throws SQLException
Arguments:	index: The column index number to retrieve data from.
	columnName: The column name to retrieve data from.
Return Values:	byte:The value of the column.
Example:	byte myByte = resultSet.getByte(2);
	byte myByte = resultSet.getByte("COLUMN1");
See also:	Chapter 8, Using the "set" Methods

getBytes

Function:	Returns the value of the referenced column from the current row as an array of bytes.
Syntax:	public abstract byte[] getBytes(int index) throws SQLException
	public abstract byte[] getBytes (String columnName) throws SQLException
Arguments:	index: The column index number to retrieve data from.
	columnName: The column name to retrieve data from.
Return Values:	byte[]: The value of the column.
Example:	byte[] myBytes = resultSet.getBytes(1);
	byte[] myBytes = resultSEt.getBytes("COUMN1");
See also:	Chapter 8, Using the "set" Methods

getCursorName

Function:	Returns the name of the current cursor.
Syntax:	public abstract String getCursor () throws SQLException
Arguments:	none
Return Values:	String: The name of the current cursor.
Example:	String cursorName = resultSet.getCursorName();
See also:	Chapter 8, Using the "set" Methods

getDate

Function:	Returns the value of the referenced column from the current row as a Date object.
Syntax:	public abstract Date getDate (int index) throws SQLException
	public abstract Date getDate (String columnName) throws SQLException
Arguments:	index: The column index number to retrieve data from.
	columnName: The column name to retrieve data from.
Return Values:	Date:The value of the column.
Example:	java.sql.Date myDate = resultSet.getDate(1);
	java.sql.Date myDate = resultSet.getDate("A_DATE");
See also:	Chapter 8, Using the "set" Methods

getDouble

Function:	Returns the value of the referenced column from the current row as a double precision number.
Syntax:	public abstract double getDouble (int index) throws SQLException
	public abstract double getDouble (String columnName) throws SQLException
Arguments:	index: The column index number to retrieve data from.
	columnName: The column name to retrieve data from.
Return Values:	double:The value of the column.
Example:	double myDouble = resultSet.getDouble(1);
	double myDouble = resultSet.getDouble("COLUMN1");
See also:	Chapter 8, Using the "set" Methods

getFloat

Function:	Returns the value of the referenced column from the current row as a floating point number.
Syntax:	public abstract float getFloat (int index) throws SQLException
	public abstract float getFloat (String columnName) throws SQLException
Arguments:	index: The column index number to retrieve data from.
	columnName: The column name to retrieve data from.
Return Values:	float: The value of the column.
Example:	float myFloat = resultSet.getFloat(1);
	float myFloat = resultSet.getFloat("COLUMN1");
See also:	Chapter 8, Using the "set" Methods

getInt

Function:	Returns the value of the referenced column from the current row as a integer.
Syntax:	public abstract int getInt (int index) throws SQLException
	public abstract int getInt (String columnName) throws SQLException
Arguments:	index: The column index number to retrieve data from.
	columnName: The column name to retrieve data from.
Return Values:	integer: The value of the column.
Example:	int myInt = resultSet.getInt(1);
	int myInt = resultSet.getInt("COLUMN1");
See also:	Chapter 8, Using the "set" Methods

getLong

Function:	Returns the value of the referenced column from the current row as a long integer.
Syntax:	public abstract (int index) throws SQLException
	public abstract get (String columnName) throws SQLException
Arguments:	index: The column index number to retrieve data from.
	columnName: The column name to retrieve data from.
Return Values:	long: The value of the column.
Example:	long myLong = resultSet.getLong(1);
	long myLong = resultSet.getLong("COLUMN1");
See also:	Chapter 8, Using the "set" Methods

getMetaData

Function:	Returns a meta data object for the ResultSet.
Syntax:	public abstract ResultSetMetaData getMetaData () throws SQLException
Arguments:	none
Return Values:	ResultSetMetaData: The ResultSetMetaData object for the ResultSet.
Example:	ResultSetMetaData rsmd = resultSet.getMetaData();
See also:	Chapter 8, Using the "set" Methods

getObject

Function:	Returns the value of the referenced column from the current row as an Object. The data type of the object will be determined by the default mapping for the SQL data type.
Syntax:	public abstract Object getObject (int index) throws SQLException
	public abstract Object getObject (String columnName) throws SQLException
Arguments:	index: The column index number to retrieve data from.

columnName: The column name to retrieve data from.

Return Values: Object: The value of the column.

Example: Object myObject = resultSet.getObject(1);

                 Object myObject = resultSet.getObject("COLUMN1");

See also: Chapter 8, Data Conversion

getShort

Function: Returns the value of the referenced column from the current row as a short integer.

Syntax: public abstract short getShort (int index) throws SQLException

                 public abstract short getShort (String columnName) throws SQLException

Arguments: index: The column index number to retrieve data from.

                 columnName: The column name to retrieve data from.

Return Values: short: The value of the column.

Example: short myShort = resultSet.getShort(1);

                 short myShort = resultSet.getShort("COLUMN1");

See also: Chapter 8, Using the "set" Methods

getString

Function: Returns the value of the referenced column from the current row as a String object.

Syntax: public abstract String getString (int index) throws SQLException

                 public abstract String getString (String columnName) throws SQLException

Arguments: index: The column index number to retrieve data from.

                 columnName: The column name to retrieve data from.

Return Values: String:The value of the column.

Example: String myString = resultSet.getString(1);

                 String myString = resultSet.getString(1);

                 String myString = resultSet.getString ("COLUMN1");

See also: Chapter 8, Using the "set" Methods

getTime

Function: Returns the value of the referenced column from the current row as a java.sql.Time object.

Syntax: public abstract Time getTime (int index) throws SQLException

                 public abstract Time getTime (String columnName) throws SQLException

Arguments: index: The column index number to retrieve data from.

                 columnName: The column name to retrieve data from.

Return Values: Time: The value of the column.

Example:	Time myTime = resultSet.getTime (1);
	Time myTime = resultSet.getTime ("COLUMN1");
See also:	Chapter 8, Using the "set" Methods

getTimestamp

Function:	Returns the value of the referenced column from the current row as a java.sql.TimeStamp object.
Syntax:	public abstract (int index) throws SQLException
	public abstract get (String columnName) throws SQLException
Arguments:	index: The column index number to retrieve data from.
	columnName: The column name to retrieve data from.
Return Values:	Timestamp: The value of the column.
Example:	Timestamp ts = resultSet.getTimestamp (1);
	Timestamp ts = resultSet.getTimestamp ("COLUMN1");
See also:	Chapter 8, Using the "set" Methods

getUnicodeStream

Function:	Returns the value of the referenced column from the current row as an InputStream containing Unicode.
Syntax:	public abstract InputStream getUnicodeStream (int index) throws SQLException
	public abstract InputStream getUnicodeStream (String columnName) throws SQLException
Arguments:	index: The column index number to retrieve data from.
	columnName: The column name to retrieve data from.
Return Values:	InputStream: The value of the column.
Example:	FileReader textFile = new FileReader(fileName);
	textFile = resultSet.getUnicodeStream(1);
	FileReader textFile = new FileReader(fileName);
	textFile = resultSet.getUnicodeStream("COLUMN1");
See also:	Chapter 8, Using the "set" Methods

getWarnings

Function:	Retrieves the current SQLWarnings associated with the current ResultSet.
Syntax:	public abstract SQLWarning getWarnings() throws SQLException
Arguments:	none
Return Values:	SQLWarning: The SQLWarning object containing all warning messages sent by the database.
Example:	SQLWarning rsWarnings = connection.getWarnings();
See also:	Chapter 8, Using the "set" Methods

next

Function:	Advances the ResultSet row cursor to the next row.
Syntax:	public abstract boolean next () throws SQLException
Arguments:	none
Return Values:	true or false: The next method will return true until there are no more results left in the ResultSet.
Example:	while (rs.next()) ....
See also:	Chapter 8, Determining the Row

wasNull

Function:	Determines if the last value read by a "get" method was a SQL null value.
Syntax:	public abstract boolean wasNull() throws SQLException
Arguments:	none
Return Values:	true or false: True is returned if the last value read contained a null value.
Example:	java.sql.TimeStamp myTimeStamp = callStatement.getTimeStamp(1); boolean wasItNull = resultSet.wasNull();
See also:	

ResultSetMetaData Interface Variables

Each of the following variables are used in conjunction with the `is-Nullable()` method.

columnNoNulls

Usage:	column does not allow null values.

columnNullable

Usage:	column does allow null values.

columnNullableUnkown

Usage:	It can not be determined if the column accepts nulls.

ResultSetMetaData Interface Methods

getCatalogName

Function:	Determines the name of the catalog that contains the referenced column.
Syntax:	public abstract String getCatalogName (int index) throws SQLException
Arguments:	index: The column index number to determine the catalog for.
Return Values:	String: The name of the catalog. If the database does not support catalogs, null is returned.
Example:	String currentCat = rsmd.getCatalogName(2);
See also:	Chapter 9, Determining a Columns Source

getColumnCount

Function:	Determines the number of columns contained in the ResultSet.
Syntax:	public abstract int getColumnCount () throws SQLException
Arguments:	none
Return Values:	int: The number of columns in the ResultSet.
Example:	int colCount = rsmd.getColumnCount();
See also:	Chapter 9, The getColumnCount Method

getColumnDisplaySize

Function:	Determines the maximum display width for the column.
Syntax:	public abstract int getColumnDisplaySize (int index) throws SQLException
Arguments:	index: The column index number to retrieve the size for.
Return Values:	int: The maximum column display width.
Example:	int colSize = rsmd.getColumnDisplaySize(1);
See also:	Chapter 9, Columns with Text Values

getColumnLabel

Function:	Determines the preferred display name for the column.
Syntax:	public abstract String getColumnLabel (int index) throws SQLException
Arguments:	index: The column index number to retrieve the label of.
Return Values:	String: The preferred name.
Example:	String colLabel = rsmd.getColumnLabel(1);
See also:	Chapter 9, Determining Column Titles

getColumnName

Function:	Determines the name of the column as it is known to the database.
Syntax:	public abstract String getColumnName (int index) throws SQLException
Arguments:	index: The column index number to retrieve the name of.
Return Values:	String: The database name for the column.
Example:	String colName = rsmd.getColumnName(1);
See also:	Chapter 9, Determining Column Titles

getColumnType

Function:	Determines the SQL data type for the column.
Syntax:	public abstract int getColumnType (int index) throws SQLException
Arguments:	index: The column index number to retrieve the data type of.
Return Values:	int: An integer representing the SQL data type from java.sql.Types.
Example:	int myType = rsmd.getColumnType(1);

```
switch (myType)
{

  case java.sql.Types.BINARY:

  case java.sql.Types.VARCHAR:
}
```

See also:	Chapter 9, Discovering SQL Data Types

getColumnTypeName

Function:	Determines the SQL data type for the column as it is known to the database. (Not all database data types are in java.sql.Types)
Syntax:	public abstract String getColumnTypeName (int index) throws SQLException
Arguments:	index: The column index number to retrieve the data type name for.
Return Values:	String: The database specific name for the column data type.
Example:	String dbTypeName = rsmd.getColumnTypeName(1);
See also:	Chapter 9, Discovering SQL Data Types

getPrecision

Function:	Determines what precision is used for the column. (Decimals to the left of the decimal point.)
Syntax:	public abstract int getPrecision (int index) throws SQLException
Arguments:	index: The column index number to determine the precision for.
Return Values:	int: The precision of the column.
Example:	int colPrecision = rsmd.getPrecision(1);
See also:	Chapter 9, Columns with Numeric Values

getScale

Function:	Determines what scale is used for the column. (Decimals to the right of the decimal point.)
Syntax:	public abstract (int index) throws SQLException
Arguments:	index: The column index number to determine the scale for.
Return Values:	int: The scale of the column.
Example:	int colScale = rsmd.getScale91);
See also:	Chapter 9, Columns with Numeric Value

getSchemaName

Function:	Determines the name of the schema that contains the column.
Syntax:	public abstract String getSchemaName (int index) throws SQLException
Arguments:	index: The column index number to determine the schema for.
Return Values:	String: The schema name.
Example:	String schema = rsmd.getSchemaName(1);
See also:	Chapter 9, Determing a Columns Source

getTableName

Function:	Determines the name of the table that contains the column.
Syntax:	public abstract String getTableName (int index) throws SQLException
Arguments:	index: The column index number to determine the schema for.
Return Values:	String: The name of the table.
Example:	String table = rsmd.getTableName(1);
See also:	Chapter 9, Determing a Columns Source

isAutoIncrement

Function:	Determines if the column is automatically numberd by the database. (A sequence number.) If it is, the column will also be read-only.
Syntax:	public abstract boolean isAutoIncrement (int index) throws SQLException
Arguments:	index: The column to test.
Return Values:	true or false: Returns true if the column is auto incremented.
Example:	boolean isAutoInc = rsmd.isAutoIncrement(1);
See also:	Chapter 9, The isAutoIncrement Method

isCaseSensitive

Function:	Determines if the database is case sensitive when referencing the columns name.
Syntax:	public abstract boolean isCaseSensitive (int index) throws SQLException
Arguments:	index: The column to test.
Return Values:	true or false: Returns true if the column name must match exactly when referenced.
Example:	boolean isSensitive = rsmd.isCaseSensitive(1);
See also:	Chapter 9, Column Properties

isCurrency

Function:	Determines if the column represents currency.
Syntax:	public abstract boolean isCurrency (int index) throws SQLException
Arguments:	index: The column to test.
Return Values:	true or false: Returns true if the column represents currency.
Example:	boolean isMoney = rsmd.isCurrency(1);
See also:	Chapter 9, Column Properties

isDefinitelyWritable

Function:	Determines if the column will be written to by a write operation. (A column could be writable by the user, but be locked. In this case isReadOnly will return false, yet the.write will fail.)
Syntax:	public abstract boolean isDefinitelyWritable (int index) throws SQLException
Arguments:	index: The column to test.
Return Values:	true or false: Returns true if a write operation will succeed on the column.
Example:	boolean isReallyWritable = rsmd.isDefinitelyWritable(1);
See also:	Chapter 9, Column Properties

isNullable

Function:	Determines if the column is able to accept null values.
Syntax:	public abstract int isNullable (int index) throws SQLException
Arguments:	index: The column to test.
Return Values:	int: Returns an integer representing the status of null handling. The values can be determined by refering to
Example:	boolean isNullOk = rsmd.isNullable(1).
See also:	Chapter 9, Column Properties

isReadOnly

Function:	Determines if the column is read-only.
Syntax:	public abstract boolean isReadOnly (int index) throws SQLException
Arguments:	index: The column to determine is read-only.
Return Values:	boolean: Returns true if the column is read-only
Example:	boolean canOnlyRead = rsmd.isReadOnly(1);
See also:	Chapter 9, Column Properties

isSearchable

Function:	Determines if the column can be used in a WHERE clause.
Syntax:	public abstract boolean isSearchable (int index) throws SQLException
Arguments:	index: The column to test.
Return Values:	true or false: Returns true if the column can be used in WHERE clauses.
Example:	boolean isWhereOK = rsmd.isSearchable(1);
See also:	Chapter 9, Column Properties

isSigned

Function:	Determines if the column contains signed numbers.
Syntax:	public abstract boolean isSigned (int index) throws SQLException
Arguments:	index: The column to test.
Return Values:	true or false: Returns true if the column contains signed numbers.
Example:	boolean isSignedNums = rsmd.isSigned(1);
See also:	Chapter 9, Column Properties

isWritable

Function:	Determines if the column is writable by the user. (Does not guarantee that a write will succeed.)
Syntax:	public abstract boolean isWritable (int index) throws SQLException
Arguments:	index: The column to test.
Return Values:	true or false: Returns true if the column is writable by the user.
Example:	boolean maybeWrite = rsmd.isWritable(1);
See also:	Chapter 9, Column Properties

The *Statement* Interface Method Index

cancel

Function:	Cancels the execution of a statement (Statement, PreparedStatement or CallableStatment) thread.
Syntax:	public abstract void cancel () throws SQLExecution
Arguments:	none
Return Values:	none
Example:	statement.cancel();
See also:	Chapter 6, Managing Statemnt Objects

clearWarnings

Function:	Deletes all warning messages in the SQLWarning chain.
Syntax:	public abstract void clearWarnings() throws SQLException
Arguments:	none
Return Values:	none
Example:	statement.clearWarnings();
See also:	

close

Function:	Closes the Statement and releases all resources including the ResultSet associated with it.
Syntax:	public abstract void close () throws SQLException
Arguments:	none
Return Values:	none
Example:	statement.close();
See also:	

execute

Function:	Executes an SQL statement that may have an unkown number of results.
Syntax:	public abstract boolean execute (String sqlString) throws SQLException
Arguments:	sqlString: The SQL statement to be executed.
Return Values:	true or false: True is returned if the the first set of results from the sqlString execution are a ResultSet. If the execution resulted in either no results or an upate count, then false is returned.
Example:	boolean isResultSet = statement.execute(sqlString);
See also:	Chapter 6, The Execution Methods

executeQuery

Function:	Executes an SQL "select" statement.
Syntax:	public abstract ResultSet executeQuery(String sqlString) throws SQLException
Arguments:	sqlString: The SQL statement to be executed.
Return Values:	ResultSet: The ResultSet object containing the data returned by the database.
Example:	ResultSet rs = statement.executeQuery("SELECT * FROM emp");
See also:	Chapter 6, The Execution Methods

executeUpdate

Function:	Excecutes an SQL update, insert or delete statement.
Syntax:	public abstract int executeUpdate(String sqlString) throws SQLException
Arguments:	sqlString: The SQL statement to be executed.
Return Values:	int: The number of rows effected by the update, insert of delete.
Example:	int rowsChanged = statement.executeUpdate("INSERT INTO emp VALUES \"a\"");
See also:	Chapter 6, The Execution Methods

getMaxFieldSize

Function:	Determines the maximum number of bytes that can be returned for any given column. Only valid for SQL types BINARY, VARBINAIRY, LONG-VARBINAIRY, CHAR, VARCHAR or LONGVARCHAR.
Syntax:	public abstract int getMaxFieldSize () throws SQLException
Arguments:	none
Return Values:	int: The maximun number of bytes.
Example:	int maxWidth = statement.getMaxFieldSize();
See also:	Chapter 6, Managing Statement Objects

getMaxRows

Function:	Determines the maximum number of rows that can be returned in a Result-Set.
Syntax:	public abstract int getMaxRows () throws SQLException
Arguments:	none
Return Values:	int: The maximum number of rows.
Example:	int maxRows = statement.getMaxRows
See also:	Chapter 6, Managing Statement Objects

getMoreResults

Function: Moves to the Statements next result. Only used in conjunction with the execute statement and where multiple results are returned by the SQL statement.

Syntax: public abstract boolean getMoreResults () throws SQLException

Arguments: none

Return Values: true or false: True is returned when the next result in the result chain is a ResultSet. False is returned if the the next result is either null (no results left) or the results are an update count.

Example:
```
boolean moreResults = statement.getMoreResults();
    if (!moreResults)
      {
        int updateCount = statment.getUpdateCount();
        if (updateCount == -1)
          {
            System.out.println ("No more results");
          }
      }
    else
      {
        ResultSet rs = statement.getResultSet();
      }
```

See also: Chapter 6, Handling Multiple Results

getQueryTimeout

Function: Determines the maximum number of seconds the driver will wait for the execution of a Statement. Default value is zero; unlimited.

Syntax: public abstract int getQueryTimeout () throws SQLException

Arguments: none

Return Values: int: The number of seconds the driver will wait.

Example: int longestWait = statement.getQueryTimeout();

See also: Chapter 6, Managing Statement Objects

getResultSet

Function: Returns the current result set for the Statement. Only used in conjunction with execute methods.

Syntax: public abstract ResultSet getResultSet () throws SQLException

Arguments: none

Return Values:	ResultSet: The current ResultSet for the Statement. Will be null if the result is an update count.
Example:	ResultSet rs = statement.execute("Select * from user_tables");
See also:	Chapter 6, The execute Method

getUpdateCount

Function:	Determines the number of rows affected by the last SQL statement. Is only meaningful for INSERT, UPDATE or INSERT statements.
Syntax:	public abstract int getUpdateCount () throws SQLException
Arguments:	none
Return Values:	int: The number of rows effected by the statement execution. Will be -1 if the result is a ResultSet or if there no more results.
Example:	int updateCount = statement.getUpdatecount();
See also:	Chapter 6, The execute Method

getWarnings

Function:	Retrieves the current SQLWarnings associated with the current Statement.
Syntax:	public abstract SQLWarning getWarnings() throws SQLException
Arguments:	none
Return Values:	SQLWarning: The SQLWarning object containing all warning messages sent by the database.
Example:	SQLWarning stmtWarnings = statement.getWarnings();
See also:	

setCursorName

Function:	Sets the cursor name to be used by the Statement. Only useful for databases that support positional updates and deletes.
Syntax:	public abstract void setCursorName(String name) throws SQLException
Arguments:	name: The name of the cursor.
Return Values:	none
Example:	statement.setCursorName("jdbcCursor");
See also:	Chapter 6, Managing Statement Objects

setEscapeProcessing

Function: Toggles the escape syntax processing on or off. Escape prossessing is enabled by default. For applications that do not use any escape syntax, this feature can be turned off to speed up SQL statement processing.

Syntax: public abstract void setEscapeProcessing (boolean enable) throws SQLException

Arguments: true or false: True enables escape syntax processing, false disables it.

Return Values: none

Example: statement.setEscapeProcessing(false);

See also: Chapter 6, Managing Statement Objects

setMaxFieldSize

Function: Sets the maximum number of bytes that can be returned for any given column. Only valid for SQL types BINARY, VARBINAIRY, LONGVARBINAIRY, CHAR, VARCHAR or LONGVARCHAR.

Syntax: public abstract void setMaxFieldSize (int bytes) throws SQLException

Arguments: bytes: The maximum number of bytes to allow.

Return Values: none

Example: statement.setMaxFielSize(256);

See also: Chapter 6, Managing Statement Objects

setMaxRows

Function: Sets the maximum number of rows that can be returned in a ResultSet. If more results are returned by the query they are truncated.

Syntax: public abstract void setMaxRow(int rows) throws SQLException

Arguments: rows: The maximum number of rows to allow.

Return Values: none

Example: statement.setMaxRows(1000);

See also: Chapter 6, Managing Statement Objects

setQueryTimeout

Function: Sets the maximum number of seconds the driver will wait for the execution of a Statement. Default value is zero; unlimited.

Syntax: public abstract void setQueryTimeout (int seconds) throws SQLException

Arguments: seconds: The maximum number of seconds to wait.

Return Values: none

Example: statement.setQueryTimeout(120);

See also: Chapter 6, Managing Statement Objects

java.sql Package Exception Reference

The DataTruncation Class Methods

getDataSize

Function:	Gets the number of bytes that should have been transferred to/from the database
Syntax:	public int getDataSize();
Arguments:	none
Return Values:	int: The number of bytes that should have been transferred.
Example:	int originalSize = DataTruncation.getDataSize();

getIndex

Function:	Returns the index number of the column that was truncated.
Syntax:	public int getIndex();
Arguments:	none
Return Values:	int: The column index number.
Example:	int truncatedColumn = DataTruncation.getIndex();

getParameter

Function:	Determines if the truncated value was a column or an OUT/IN parameter.
Syntax:	public boolean getParameter();
Arguments:	none
Return Values:	true or false: Returns true if the truncated value was an OUT or IN parameter.
Example:	boolean wasParameter = DataTruncation.getParameter();

getRead

Function:	Determines if the value was truncated when written to or read from the database.
Syntax:	public boolean getRead();
Arguments:	none
Return Values:	true or false: Returns true if the the error occured when reading from the database.
Example:	boolean readError = DataTruncation.getRead();

getTransferSize

Function:	Returns the number of bytes that were transferred before the error occured.
Syntax:	public int getTransferSize();
Arguments:	none
Return Values:	int: The number of bytes transferred.
Example:	int goodBytes = DataTrunction.getTransferSize()

The SQLException Class Methods

getErrorCode

Function:	Returns the vendor error code number.
Syntax:	public int getErrorCode();
Arguments:	none
Return Values:	int: The vendor error code number.
Example:	int errorCode = SQLException.getErrorCode();

getNextException

Function:	Returns the next SQLException object in the chain. Returns null if no more exist.
Syntax:	public SQLException getNextException();
Arguments:	none
Return Values:	SQLException: The next SQLException object in the chain.
Example:	SQLException mySQLException = sqlException.getNextException();

getSQLState

Function:	Returns the SQL state information.
Syntax:	public String getSQLState();
Arguments:	none
Return Values:	String: The value of the state at the time of the exception.
Example:	String sqlState = sqlException.getSQLState();

setNextException

Function:	Adds a new SQLxception object to the chain.
Syntax:	public synchronized void setNextException(SQLException sqlException);
Arguments:	sqlException: The SQLException object to add to the chain.
Return Values:	none
Example:	sqlException.setNextException(mySQLException);

The SQLWarnings Class Methods

getNextWarning

Function:	Returns the next SQLWarning object in the chain.
Syntax:	public SQLWarning getNextWarning();
Arguments:	none
Return Values:	SQLWarning: The next SQLWarning object in the chain.
Example:	SQLWarning sqlWarn = sqlWarning.getNextWarning();

setNextWarning

Function:	Adds a new SQLWarning object to the chain.
Syntax:	public void setNextWarning(SQLWarning sqlWarning);
Arguments:	sqlWarning: The SQLWarning object to be added to the tree.
Return Values:	none
Example:	sqlWarning.setNextWarning(mySQLWarning);

Index

%, 111, 157
/, 111
?, 72, 88. *See* place holder
_, 111, 157
~, 112

A

acceptURL(), 49, 50
Access Protocol, 55
ANSI SQL90
    Entry Level, 6
    Full, 7
    Intermediate Level, 7
API
    JavaBeans, 178
    JDBC, 1, 3, 4
appendErrorMessage(), 184
applets, 2, 5, 8
application, 2
    multi-threaded, 100
    single-threaded, 100
    trusted, 8
    untrusted, 8
AutoCommit, 73
    status, 74

C

call level interface, 18. *See* CLI
CallableStatement interface, 9, 36, 87
CallableStatement Object, 72
cancel(), 100
Cartesian product, 100
catalog, 83, 143, 149
chain, 171
Class.forName(), 35, 46
clearErrorMessage(), 185
clearParameters(), 105
clearWarnings(), 81, 131
CLI, 18, 23
Client/Server, 8
    Three-Tier, 25, 213
    Two-Tier, 22
Client/Server models, 15
close(), 37, 82, 131
code signing, 8
column
    count, 134
    heading, 135
    index, 126

name, 127
properties, 143
read only, 144
search criteria, 144
size, 103
size, 136
source, 143
title, 135
writable, 145
commit, 73
commit(), 75
connect(), 46, 51
Connecting to a Database, 51, 53
Connection
    close(), 37
Connection interface, 10, 35, 49, 69
Connection Object, 69
convert, 119
create, 110
createStatement(), 36, 70
currency, 139

D

data conversion, 129
data corruption, 76
Data Definition Language. *See* DDL
data integrity, 76
Data Manipulation Language.
    See DML
data misinterpretation, 76
data truncation, 89, 137, 172
database state, 147
DatabaseMetaData interface, 10, 38, 147
DataTable class, 179, 199
DataTable(), 200
DataTruncation class, 11, 172
Date class, 10
date literals, 115
DBAccess class, 179, 184
DBClient class, 228
DDL, 70
    create statement, 110
DDL statements, 110
debug, 180
DECIMAL, 89
deregisterDriver(), 63
Design Considerations, 15
dirty reads, 76, 78

DML, 7, 110, 177
Documentation, 12
Driver interface, 10, 45
DriverListManager class, 179
DriverManager
    initialize, 48
DriverManager class, 10, 35, 45, 46
DriverPropertyInfo class, 12, 169
DriverPropertyInfo object, 60
Drivers, 4, 168
    JDBC-Net-All-Java, 19
    JDBC-ODBC Bridge ODC, 16
    list, 46
    loading, 35, 47
    Native-API-Partly-Java, 18
    Native-Protocol-All-Java, 21
    registering, 34
    tracking, 46
    Type I, 16
    Type II, 18
    Type III, 19
    Type IV, 21
    version number, 59
dynamic applications, 63
dynamic SQL, 70, 72
dynamic SQL statements, 88

E

Equals(), 168
error handling, 170
escape, 112
    character, 111, 114
    sequence, 105
    sequence processing, 105
    syntax, 84, 113
escape syntax, 113, 114
    convert, 118
    database functions, 114
    date format, 115
    keywords, 113
    outer join, 118
    scalar functions, 116
    stored procedures, 114
    time format, 116
Exception
    handeling, 37
    SQLException, 38
    throws clause, 38

execute(), 36, 93, 94, 95
executeQuery(), 36, 93, 94, 108
executeSQL(), 187
executeUpdate(), 36, 93, 94

F

findColumn(), 127
functions, 114

G

getAsciiStream(), 129
getAutoCommit(), 74
getBigDecimal(), 129
getBinaryStream(), 129
getBoolean(), 93, 129
getByte(), 93, 129
getBytes(), 93, 129
getCatalog(), 83, 151, 184
getCatalogName(), 143
getCatalogNames(), 186
getCatalogSeperator(), 150
getCatalogTerm(), 83, 150
getColumn(), 201
getColumnCaseSensitive(), 203
getColumnCount(), 41, 134
getColumnIsCurrency(), 203
getColumnLabel(), 135
getColumnName(), 41, 135
getColumnPrecision(), 202
getColumnScale(), 202
getColumnScales(), 202
getColumnSize(), 41, 202
getColumnSizes(), 202
getColumnTitle(), 201
getColumnTitles(), 201
getColumnType, 41
getColumnType(), 140, 202
getColumnTypeName(), 142
getColumnTypes(), 202
getConnection(), 35, 49
getDataSize(), 172
getDate(), 93, 129
getDBInfo(), 185
getDouble(), 93, 129
getDriver(), 63
getDriverInfo(), 185
getDriverMajorVersion(), 148
getDriverMinorVersion(), 148
getDriverName(), 148
getDriverProperties(), 169
getDrivers(), 64
getDriverVersion(), 148
getErrorCode(), 170
getErrorMessage(), 185
getFloat(), 93, 129

getIndex(), 173
getInt(), 37, 129
getList(), 179
getLoginProperties(), 185
getLoginTimeout(), 65
getLogStream(), 66
getLong(), 93, 129
getMajorVersion(), 59
getMaxFieldSize(), 102
getMaxRows(), 103
getMessage(), 38
getMetaData (), 40
getMetaData(), 41, 84, 131
getMinorVersion(), 59
getMoreResults(), 96, 97
getNanos(), 168
getNextException(), 171
getNull(), 129
getNumberOfColumns(), 203
getNumberOfRows(), 203
getObject(), 93, 129
getObjectAt(), 201
getParameter(), 173
getPrecision(), 137
getPropertiesInfo(), 60
getPropertyInfo(), 61
getQueryTimeout(), 104
getRead(), 173
getResultSet(), 96, 97
getRow(), 201
getScale(), 137
getSchema(), 184
getSchemaName(), 143, 155
getSchemaNames(), 186
getSchemas(), 153
getSchemaTerm(), 153
getSesssion(), 186
getShort(), 93, 129
getSQLLevelInfo(), 186
getSQLState(), 170
getString(), 37, 93, 126, 129
getTableName(), 143
getTableNames, 186
getTablePrivileges(), 157
getTables(), 156, 184
getTableTypes(), 156, 186
getTime(), 93, 129
getTimeStamp(), 93, 129
getTransactionIsolation(), 77
getTransferSize(), 172
getUnicodeStream(), 129
getUpdateCount(), 96, 97
getWarnings(), 81, 131
group by, 109

H

Host Information, 55

I

import, 34
IN, 70, 71
IN parameters
    setting, 88
InputStream, 90
insert, 109
Interfaces, 9
Internet, 15
Intranets, 15
isAutoIncrement(), 144
isCatalogAtStart(), 150
isClosed(), 82
isDefinitelyWritable(), 145
isNullable(), 143
isolation level, 77
isReadOnly(), 83, 144
isSearchable(), 144
isSigned(), 137
isWritable(), 145

J

Java Development Toolkit. *See* JDK
Java Fondation Class. *See* JFC
java.sql package, 9
java.sql Package, 9
    Classes, 10
    Exceptions, 11
    import, 34
    Interfaces, 9
JavaBeans, 178
JDBC, 1
    goal, 3
    origin, 3
    products, 9
    specifications, 1
    URL, 54, 56
JDBC COMPLIANT, 9
jdbcCompliant(), 62
JDBC-ODBC bridge, 9, 11
JDK, 12, 13, 229
JFC, 2, 228, 229

L

like, 111, 115
listener, 26, 28
loading drivers, 47
Loading Multiple Drivers, 48
log stream, 66
mapping, 89

M

Meta Data, 38

Database, 38, 40
ResultSet, 38, 41
msg(), 184, 200
multiple results, 95, 96
multi-threaded, 100
multi-tiered, 15

N

native protocol, 4
nativeSQL(), 84
next(), 37, 125
non-repeatable reads, 76, 79
NUMERIC, 89

O

ODBC, 3, 11, 113
openTable(), 187
order by, 109
OUT, 70
registering parameters, 90
return value, 91, 92
outer join, 118
full, 119
left, 119
right, 119

P

Path to the Resource, 56
pattern matching, 111
phantom read, 80
phantom reads, 76
place holder, 71
precision, 137
pre-compile, 71
pre-compiled statements, 71
prepareCall(), 70
PreparedStatement interface, 10, 36, 87
PreparedStatement Object, 70, 71
prepareStatement(), 70, 71
println(), 66
printWarnings(), 82
privileges
granting, 157
table, 157
Products, 9
Properties object, 53
property list, 62
proxy, 25, 27

Q

queries
simple, 108

R

RDBMS, 6
read only, 83

read-only, 144
registerDriver(), 35, 47, 63
registerOutParameter(), 72, 91
registry, 215
Relational Database Management System. *See* RDBMS
remote implementation, 214
remote interface, 214, 216
remote method invocation, 26. *See* RMI
RemoteException, 220
results, 36
multiple, 95, 96
properties, 133
unknown, 95
ResultSet interface, 10, 36, 123
ResultSet object, 123, 124
ResultSetMetaData interface, 10, 38, 133
ResultSetMetaData object, 133
RMI, 26, 28, 213
rmic, 214
rmiregistry, 215
rollback(), 76
row count, 94
row cursor, 125

S

saveList(), 179
scalar functions, 116
scale, 90, 137
schema, 143, 149, 153
current, 153
list, 153
search criteria, 144
Security, 8
applets, 8
application, 8
sequence number, 144
server
proxy, 25, 27
server process, 26
session, 81
setAutoClearErrorMessage(), 185
setAutoCommit, 74
setBignum(), 89
setBinaryStream(), 90
setBoolean(), 89
setByte(), 89
setBytes(), 89
setCatalog(), 83
setCursorName(), 104
setDate(), 89
setDouble(), 89
setErrorMessage(), 184

setEscapeProcessing(), 105
setFloat(), 89
setInt(), 89
setLoginProperties(), 185
setLoginTimeout(), 65
setLogStream(), 66
setLong(), 89
setMaxFieldSize(), 102
setMaxRows(), 103
setNanos(), 168
setNextException(), 171
setNull(), 89
setObject, 89
setObject(), 89
setQueryTimeout(), 104
setReadOnly(), 83
setShort(), 89
setString, 89
setTime, 89
setTimeStamp, 89
setTransactionIsolation(), 76, 77
signed numbers, 137
single threaded, 100
skeletons, 214
SQL, 4, 5, 6
complex statements, 110
create statement. *See* DDL
data type conversion, 93
data types, 139
DDL statements, 110
dynamic, 70
escape, 112
group by clause, 109
insert statement, 95, 109
insert values, 109
like operator, 111, 115
order by clause, 109
select, 94
select statement, 108
statement formatting, 107
static, 70
time, 165
update, 95
where clause, 108
SQL grammar, 113
SQL89, 7
SQL92. *See* ANSI SQL92
SQLException, 170
SQLException class, 11, 170
SQLWarning, 170
SQLWarning class, 11, 171
stack, 219
Statement
close(), 37

Statement interface, 10, 36, 87
Statement object, 70
static SQL, 70
stored procedures, 72, 114
   IN/OUT parameters, 72
stubs, 214
supportsCatalogsInDataManipulation(),
   152
supportsCatalogsInProcedureCalls(), 152
supportsCatalogsInTableDefinitions(),
   148, 152, 153
supportsPositionedDelete(), 104
supportsSchemasInDataManipulation(),
   155
supportsSchemasInProcedureCalls(),
   155
supportsSchemasInTableDefinitions(),
   155

T
table, 155
   list, 156
   privileges, 157
table types, 156
Test Suite, 9, 11
thread, 100
Three-Tier Client/Server Model, 25
throws clause, 38
Time class, 11, 165
time literals, 115
time-out, 66
TimeStamp class, 11, 166
toString(), 166, 168
transaction, 73, 74
   commit, 74
   dirty reads, 78
   getTransactionIsolation(), 77
   isolation, 76
   isolation mode, 76
   management, 74
   non-repeatable reads, 76, 79
   phantom read, 80
   phantom reads, 76
   rollback, 74
   setTransactionIsolation(), 77
   TRANSACTION_READ_
      COMMITTED, 79
   TRANSACTION_REPEATABLE_
      READ, 79
   TRANSACTION_SERIALIZABLE,
      81
transaction level, 77
TRANSACTION_READ_
   COMMITTED, 79

TRANSACTION_READ_
   UNCOMMITED, 76
TRANSACTION_REPEATABLE_
   READ, 79
TRANSACTION_SERIALIZABLE, 77,
   81
trusted, 8
Two-Tier Client/Server Model, 22
Type class, 11
Types class, 169

U
Uniform Resource Locator. *See* URL
unknown Result, 95
unsigned numbers, 137
untrusted, 8
updates
   simple, 109
URL, 59
   access protocol, 55
   host information, 55
   Internet, 54
   JDBC, 54, 57
   path to resource, 56
   protocol name, 56, 57
   subname, 56, 57
   sub-protocol, 57
User credentials, 9

V
validateURL class, 50
valueOf(), 166, 167
variable, 36
vendor extensions, 7
vendor neutral, 7

W
Warnings
   SQLWarnings, 81
writable, 145

X
X/OPEN, 170

**Java Development Kit
Version 1.1.4
Binary Code License**

This binary code license ("License") contains rights and restrictions associated with use of the accompanying software and documentation ("Software"). Read the License carefully before installing the Software. By installing the Software you agree to the terms and conditions of this License.

1. **Limited License Grant.** Sun grants to you ("Licensee") a non-exclusive, non-transferable limited license to use the Software without fee for evaluation of the Software and for development of Java(compatible applets and applications. Licensee may make one archival copy of the Software. Licensee may not re-distribute the Software in whole or in part, either separately or included with a product. Refer to the Java Runtime Environment Version 1.1.4 binary code license (http://www.javasoft.com/products/JDK/1.1.4/index.html) for the availability of runtime code which may be distributed with Java compatible applets and applications.

2. **Java Platform Interface.** Licensee may not modify the Java Platform Interface ("JPI", identified as classes contained within the "java" package or any subpackages of the "java" package), by creating additional classes within the JPI or otherwise causing the addition to or modification of the classes in the JPI. In the event that Licensee creates any Java-related API and distributes such API to others for applet or application development, Licensee must promptly publish an accurate specification for such API for free use by all developers of Java-based software.

3. **Restrictions.** Software is confidential copyrighted information of Sun and title to all copies is retained by Sun and/or its licensors. Licensee shall not modify, decompile, disassemble, decrypt, extract, or otherwise reverse engineer Software. Software may not be leased, assigned, or sublicensed, in whole or in part. Software is not designed or intended for use in on-line control of aircraft, air traffic, aircraft navigation or aircraft communications; or in the design, construc-

tion, operation or maintenance of any nuclear facility. Licensee warrants that it will not use or redistribute the Software for such purposes.

4. **Trademarks and Logos.** This License does not authorize Licensee to use any Sun name, trademark or logo. Licensee acknowledges that Sun owns the Java trademark and all Java-related trademarks, logos and icons including the Coffee Cup and Duke ("Java Marks") and agrees to: (i) to comply with the Java Trademark Guidelines at http://java.com/trademarks.html; (ii) not do anything harmful to or inconsistent with Sun's rights in the Java Marks; and (iii) assist Sun in protecting those rights, including assigning to Sun any rights acquired by Licensee in any Java Mark.

5. **Disclaimer of Warranty.** Software is provided "AS IS," without a warranty of any kind. ALL EXPRESS OR IMPLIED REPRESENTATIONS AND WARRANTIES, INCLUDING ANY IMPLIED WARRANTY OF MERCHANTABILITY, FITNESS FOR A PARTICULAR PURPOSE OR NON-INFRINGEMENT, ARE HEREBY EXCLUDED.

6. **Limitation of Liability.** SUN AND ITS LICENSORS SHALL NOT BE LIABLE FOR ANY DAMAGES SUFFERED BY LICENSEE OR ANY THIRD PARTY AS A RESULT OF USING OR DISTRIBUTING SOFTWARE. IN NO EVENT WILL SUN OR ITS LICENSORS BE LIABLE FOR ANY LOST REVENUE, PROFIT OR DATA, OR FOR DIRECT, INDIRECT, SPECIAL, CONSEQUENTIAL, INCIDENTAL OR PUNITIVE DAMAGES, HOWEVER CAUSED AND REGARDLESS OF THE THEORY OF LIABILITY, ARISING OUT OF THE USE OF OR INABILITY TO USE SOFTWARE, EVEN IF SUN HAS BEEN ADVISED OF THE POSSIBILITY OF SUCH DAMAGES.

7. **Termination.** Licensee may terminate this License at any time by destroying all copies of Software. This License will terminate immediately without notice from Sun if Licensee fails to comply with any provision of this License. Upon such

termination, Licensee must destroy all copies of Software.

8. **Export Regulation.** Software, including technical data, is subject to U.S. export control laws, including the U.S. Export Administration Act and its associated regulations, and may be subject to export or import regulations in other countries. Licensee agrees to comply strictly with all such regulations and acknowledges that it has the responsibility to obtain licenses to export, re-export, or import Software. Software may not be downloaded, or otherwise exported or re-exported (i) into, or to a national or resident of, Cuba, Iraq, Iran, North Korea, Libya, Sudan, Syria or any country to which the U.S. has embargoed goods; or (ii) to anyone on the U.S. Treasury Department's list of Specially Designated Nations or the U.S. Commerce Department's Table of Denial Orders.

9. **Restricted Rights.** Use, duplication or disclosure by the United States government is subject to the restrictions as set forth in the Rights in Technical Data and Computer Software Clauses in DFARS 252.227-7013(c)(1)(ii) and FAR 52.227-19(c)(2) as applicable.

10. **Governing Law.** Any action related to this License will be governed by California law and controlling U.S. federal law. No choice of law rules of any jurisdiction will apply.

11. **Severability.** If any of the above provisions are held to be in violation of applicable law, void, or unenforceable in any jurisdiction, then such provisions are herewith waived to the extent necessary for the License to be otherwise enforceable in such jurisdiction. However, if in Sun's opinion deletion of any provisions of the License by operation of this paragraph unreasonably compromises the rights or increase the liabilities of Sun or its licensors, Sun reserves the right to terminate the License and refund the fee paid by Licensee, if any, as Licensee's sole and exclusive remedy.